Conscious Moving

AN EMBODIED GUIDE FOR HEALING, LEARNING, CONTEMPLATING, AND CREATING

CHRISTINE CALDWELL
PhD, LPC, BC-DMT

North Atlantic Books
Huichin, unceded Ohlone land
Berkeley, California

Published by
North Atlantic Books
Huichin, unceded Ohlone land
Berkeley, California

Printed in Canada

Cover art © deomis via Shutterstock
Cover design by Howie Severson
Interior illustrations by Page Zekonis
Book design by Happenstance Type-O-Rama

Conscious Moving: An Embodied Guide for Healing, Learning, Contemplating, and Creating is sponsored and published by North Atlantic Books, an educational nonprofit based in the unceded Ohlone land Huichin (Berkeley, CA) that collaborates with partners to develop cross-cultural perspectives; nurture holistic views of art, science, the humanities, and healing; and seed personal and global transformation by publishing work on the relationship of body, spirit, and nature.

North Atlantic Books's publications are distributed to the US trade and internationally by Penguin Random House Publisher Services. For further information, visit our website at www.northatlantic books.com.

Lyrics from "Aren't You Meant to Fly?" by The Wanderer are used with permission.

Aston Kinetics is a trademark of Judith Aston-Linderoth.

Library of Congress Cataloging-in-Publication Data

Names: Caldwell, Christine, 1952- author.
Title: Conscious moving : an embodied guide for healing, learning, contemplating, and creating / Christine Caldwell, PhD, LPC, BC-DMT.
Description: Berkeley, CA : North Atlantic Books, [2024] | Includes bibliographical references and index. | Summary: "An exploration of somatic awareness and embodied intuition and a guide to how conscious movement practices can help us be more present, be more grounded and intentional, and claim bodily autonomy"-- Provided by publisher.
Identifiers: LCCN 2023054367 (print) | LCCN 2023054368 (ebook) | ISBN 9798889840275 (trade paperback) | ISBN 9798889840282 (ebook)
Subjects: LCSH: Self-consciousness (Awareness) | Mind and body.
Classification: LCC BF311 .C149 2024 (print) | LCC BF311 (ebook) | DDC 153--dc23/eng/20240126
LC record available at https://lccn.loc.gov/2023054367
LC ebook record available at https://lccn.loc.gov/2023054368

1 2 3 4 5 6 7 8 9 MARQUIS 28 27 26 25 24

This book includes recycled material and material from well-managed forests. North Atlantic Books is committed to the protection of our environment. We print on recycled paper whenever possible and partner with printers who strive to use environmentally responsible practices.

To all artists out there,
To all healers out there,
To all teachers out there,
To all contemplatives out there,
This covers just about everyone.
Thank you, thank you, thank you!

Contents

Introduction. 1

PART I
The Fundamentals of Conscious Moving

1 The Fundamental Principles of Conscious Moving . . . 12

2 The Awareness Phase of Conscious Moving. 31

3 The Owning Phase of Conscious Moving 55

4 The Appreciation Phase of Conscious Moving 83

5 The Action Phase of Conscious Moving 99

PART II
Applying Conscious Moving to Healing,
the Arts, Contemplative Practice, and Education

Introduction. 116

6 Amber Gray—Working with Trauma and Oppression
in Multicultural Contexts. 117

7 Laia Jorba Galdos—Moving the Self in Dialogue:
A Contextual and Fluid Process to Identity
Exploration 133

8 Rachelle Janssen—Revisioning Addiction through
Conscious Moving 150

9 Joana Debelt—Conscious Moving in the Service
of Learning 161

10 Melissa Walker—Conscious Moving as a Means
of Working with Desire Differences in Intimate
Partnership 172

11 Gretl Bauer—Conscious Moving: Support for
Art-Based Expeditions into the Realm of
Grief Work 185

12 Antje Scherholz—Conscious Moving with Groups:
    The Application of the Moving Cycle in the
    Context of Group Psychotherapy 207

13 Thomas von Stuckrad—Sharing Beauty:
    How Conscious Moving Can Guide a Moving
    Cycle Session 223

PART III
Moving Forward

14 Integrating the Living Wisdom of Others
    in These Fields 235

15 Conscious Moving Specifics in Healing, Art-Making,
    Learning, and Contemplative Practice 251

16 Accompanying a Conscious Moving Session
    for Others 265

    Epilogue: Our Storied Bodies 275

    Acknowledgments 278

Appendices

Appendix A: The Movement Continuum
(or Mobility Gradient) 280

Appendix B: Resources for Conscious Moving 281

Index 282

About the Author 289

Introduction

Body I am through and through, and nothing more.

—F. NIETZSCHE, *THUS SPAKE ZARATHUSTRA*

The word and the act of *moving* permeates our world. It suffuses our bodies, it gets us from place to place, it serves as a signal, and it holds social forces. Physicists tell us that everything moves, from subatomic particles to galaxies. Biologists use it to define life, and geologists tell us that our Earth constantly stretches, shivers, and creeps. Engineering understands that for something to work, it needs to move, whether it is a piston or an electron. When we say, "I am moved" by something, we mean that our emotional selves have been routed in another direction. Tiny movements in the face of a friend tell us something is upsetting them, and unwittingly our face changes in response. When we talk about protest movements, images of marches and sign waving emerge; the protestors call for change, and change can be a synonym for movement. Movement is everywhere. Everything moves.

Perhaps, by seeing movement as a kind of unifying principle, one that stitches together myriad places and peoples and actions, we can delve into our lives in a more engaged way. If we start out assuming that movement is everywhere and that everything moves, we might use this notion as a way to gracefully take part in more purposeful projects.

This book is one such project. While saluting many different areas of movement inquiry, and working to thread them in wherever possible, this book homes in on the disciplines where I have more lived experience and years of study. Broadly speaking, this book examines and celebrates conscious human movement in the fields of healing, the arts, contemplative practice, and education.

The main location of my work has been in the disciplines of psychotherapy, counseling, and healing, but I never managed to stay put in these areas. My degrees are in anthropology (BA), dance therapy (MA), and somatic psychology (PhD). From the onset, I felt it was all related—my choreography spoke of my psyche, and my body felt mine as well as the body of my cultural and ancestral peoples. My jobs consistently landed me in schools and universities. For several years, I was a senior student of Thich Nhat Hanh, a Zen Buddhist teacher and activist. Really, my work specializes in the human body as it moves deliberately, and what that means for learning, art-making, contemplative practice, and healing.

Even in the 1970s, it felt absurd to me to separate physical from emotional, mental, and social health. Although the idea of these human conditions being interrelated used to be a fringe notion, these days, most of us deeply appreciate how our emotions affect our physical health, how physical activity influences mental and emotional well-being, how thought patterns can impel our bodies to function differently, and how the well-being or illness of others connects us. This book asserts that this interrelatedness occurs because movement inhabits all these experiences, and movement in any system reverberates into others. Whether it involves the sizzling of neurons in our brain, the gurgling of a tense stomach, or the clenching of a fist, movement stitches together the whole of us. This movement does not stay inside of us either. Just like sound waves, light waves, and gravitational waves, movement emerges from our localized bodies and continues out into the rest of the world. We are all reverberating to the movements produced around us, at times in a clashing bump and in others a graceful dance. Art, learning, and healing are simply different applications of the same root movements within and around us. Again, although these ideas seemed odd at the time, now they are enjoying a high level of support in the creative arts therapies, behavioral medicine, embodiment practices, and experiential learning. Movement underlies it all. While this book examines art, contemplative disciplines, education, and therapy, it acknowledges that movement does not confine itself to these disciplines. It simply radiates out from its origins, through space and time, in waves of ever-more-subtle influence.

If we take it as a given that these fields, and many others, are sharing movement processes, and that this interrelatedness occurs because human movement exposes the networking between them, we can explore the idea that working directly with movement can help us to learn, heal, and create within a more unified experience. Yes, there are separate fields, but they are perceived as such only because we choose to look at and express our experiences from specific vantage points. All vantage points are valid. Yet we might define distress, bias, and illness as limiting vantage points that stifle our ability to see other perspectives. We can use movement to develop skills of shifting and holding different perspectives. We can dance with different viewpoints, be moved and enriched by them, and learn to turn away from viewpoints that no longer fit, that harm ourselves or others, or that don't give us a more complete picture of ourselves and the world.

I hold a view that movement is about life; that aliveness is the movement of our breath, our heart, our muscle fibers, our brain waves; and that death is when those movements cease. Certainly that is true on a cellular level, but when scientists examine the world as it gets smaller, down below the level of cells (the basic unit of life), they will point out that molecules move, that atoms move, that subatomic particles move so crazily that we can't keep track of where they are; they zing around up to the speed of light and exist in multiple places at once. Those little buggers tunnel, orbit, and jump around all over the place. On the other end of the scale, these same folks remind us that not only do we move around the sun on Earth, but the solar system moves within the spiral arm of our galaxy, and that our galaxy is just one of the billions that are all wheeling around each other as well as expanding away from each other. Movement is everywhere, at every level.

Taking on that viewpoint humbled me and led me to try to study physics, geology, chemistry, and biology. Further humbled, I came to see that all disciplines were studying movement in one form or another, whether it was quantum mechanics, tectonic plates, tropisms in plants, or chemical reactions. Still, I kept coming back to my body. How can I study and learn from my own movement experiences? Can studying my own localized body help me navigate from understanding how to take care of myself, all the way to the grander project of working to understand and act in the world in a clearer and more helpful way? These musings and movings gave rise to this book.

This book celebrates and explores our ability to nimbly dance among interrelated personal experiences and scientific findings while touching on landscapes that are rarely visited outside spiritual traditions. It directly explores movements that underlie and nourish our experiences. It investigates moving for moving's sake before we know how those movements will land in the world. It may be akin to what physics strives for—a unified field theory—a quest to understand the forces of nature as all stemming from one unity. It's not that we should strive to achieve some kind of movement nirvana while here on Earth. It's that we likely will feel more human, more ourselves, when we can see ourselves reflected in all that surrounds us. It will help us find that place within us that simply moves. We are a localized part of all that movement. This is what I call *Conscious Moving (CM)*, or the *Moving Cycle (MC)* in a psychotherapy context.

The Moving Cycle: The Therapeutic Specialization of Conscious Moving

Back in the day, I chose to become a body-centered psychotherapist because this felt like a discipline that could best hold my broad interests. During an anthropology class in college (UCLA), we watched a film on trance dancing in Indigenous cultures. The film spoke of using movement, community, and altered states of consciousness as a means of healing. The healing was generalized—there was no strong distinction between physical, emotional, mental, or social healing. The healing was shared as well, as the trance dancer was moving not just for themselves but also for their whole community, and in some cases, the whole world. Movement was necessary, community was necessary, and altered consciousness was necessary. Even though the field of anthropology was rife with patronizing, patriarchal, and racist attitudes in the late 1970s, the dances I witnessed in the film moved me deeply. Rather than choosing to become an anthropologist, I chose movement. I walked across campus to the Dance department.

In the Dance department, I was enveloped in movement as art-making, as well as movement as healing. I was supported in both by my mentors, dance therapist Alma Hawkins and dance ethnographer Allegra Fuller Snyder. I supplemented my studies with private training in Gestalt therapy and Aston-Patterning, a movement education system developed by Judith Aston-Linderoth, now called Aston Kinetics™. I felt mostly at home. The last ingredient in my career recipe did not fall into place until a year after I graduated when I began teaching at universities. A few years after that, I landed at Naropa University, where I spent the next thirty-five years as a professor. It was in academic settings, where scholarship was expected and teaching and writing and research were the expression of one's scholarship, that I truly thrived.

The Moving Cycle was gestated and born under circumstances of multiple privileges and hard work. The Moving Cycle was sheltered as it grew in the cauldron of students, colleagues, and cross-disciplinarity. Because I was the founder of the Somatic Psychology department, itself a branch in Naropa's Counseling Psychology programs, and because I was both a registered dance therapist and body psychologist, my work tended to specialize in the healing component of movement. I kept my art-making and my studying of learning and education going on my own. Most of my previous writings are about the healing power of movement. This book breaks that tradition and returns to a broader understanding of movement, one that shelters all manner of change agents. This book explores movement's root and follows it to the various branches that grow from it. The book uses the term *conscious movement* because the term expresses this root before it branches off into more specific disciplines, such as the healing practices of the Moving Cycle.

The Movement Continuum

Why would we want to use the term *conscious movement*? Broadly, through all the disciplines mentioned earlier, movement can be seen as occurring along a continuum, but let's zoom in on the human movement continuum (see

Figure 1).* On one end of the continuum, movement is automatic and free of deliberation, will, or conscious attention. It is often quite simple. Think of our reflexes, like blinking or knee jerks. Also, imagine blood moving around our body, cells dividing, or breathing during sleep. Lots of automatic movements thrum within us, movements that we sometimes can track, while others are too subtle for us to ever be aware of. Evolution has set up these movements to be automatic for the sake of our continuity and well-being. Having to consciously will and manage all these movements would be impossible and would prevent us from doing anything else. Life on Earth began this way, almost four billion years ago, with single cells replicating, adapting, and developing automatically.

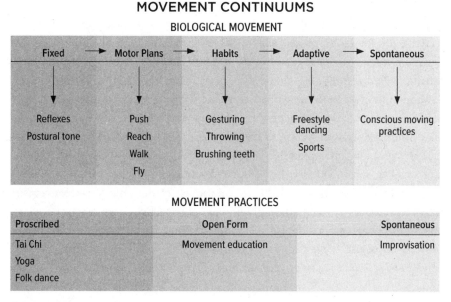

Figure 1: Movement Continuums

A little bit farther along the human movement continuum is what biology calls *motor plans*. These are movements based on muscle contractions, often involving the coordination of several muscle groups at a time. Think pushing, reaching, grasping, walking, twisting. These movements begin to develop in babies through the support of reflexes. They need to be practiced in order to be accomplished; babies' arms reflexively flail around for a bit before they gradually, with repetition, coordinate muscle contractions toward the goal of reaching for and landing on their parent's nose. Once they can do this, the motor plan of

_____

* For an expanded image of the movement continuum or mobility gradient, see Appendix A.

reaching and grasping is set down in their body and can be done semiautomatically for the rest of their lives. You can pay attention to it, but it doesn't require much conscious management. We could think of it as a movement habit, and these habits are crucial for our well-being.* Like any habit, they can be efficient or inefficient and can be hard to change.

As we travel further along the movement continuum, our actions become more conscious and deliberate, and we have to pay attention to initiate them, sustain them, and bring them to a close. At this point along the line, we dance, play, sing, have conversations, have sex, and in general, occupy the present moment by paying attention to what we are doing as we do it and adapting it on the fly. This spontaneity is just as critical to our well-being as our more automatic movements. Increasingly, these conscious movements have been correlated with healthy aging, the prevention of various illnesses, and overall happiness (Cuignet et al. 2020). Research has also shown that in situations of stress and trauma, we have a tendency to retreat to more automatic, simple, and comforting movements (called *dissolutions*) in an attempt at safety and survival (Porges 2011). Although sensible in the short run, retreating consistently to a more habituated and stereotyped way of moving through the world tends to make us depressed, less healthy, and more prone to addictive processes and substances (Caldwell 2019). Conscious movement is where change comes from. We need both ongoing stability and the ability to spontaneously change when necessary. Because art, education, reflection, and therapy all require change, conscious movement can become our natural method of undoing, of letting go of what does not work and finding new options. It also celebrates moving the same ways we have been moving for decades, even across generations.

A Continuum of Conscious Movement Practices

We can also play with a different movement continuum that maps the ideas just discussed onto various movement practices. If we take this idea of Conscious Moving as being the basis of change in lots of different disciplines, we can also see that lots of existing methods for moving consciously work well within their sphere of expertise. On one end of the continuum lie the practices that tend to

---

* For an excellent discussion of reflexes supporting more complex movement, please see the work of Bonnie Bainbridge Cohen, called *Body-Mind Centering*. Linda Hartley's book *The Wisdom of the Body Moving* is also a good guide (see References).

be highly proscribed and handed down over time, practices where you are asked to move consciously in a very specific way and where getting the movement just right (for your body) is part of the conscious work. Think learning to play a particular chord on the piano, or a particular tennis swing. Think yoga, tai chi, or any number of contemplative movement disciplines. These practices have accumulated wisdom over the years about certain specific movements that can be used for healing, learning, performance, or contemplation.

Then, more in the middle of the continuum, are disciplines that ask you to observe and "be with" a particular motor plan as a way not only to study it but to potentially change how you habitually do it. Think of various movement awareness and education disciplines, such as the Feldenkrais Method, Alexander Technique, Sensory Awareness, some types of physical therapy, and some types of yoga. For instance, you might be asked to turn your head slowly to the right, noticing the small details of the motion so that you might gain more control of the tension in your neck. There is less emphasis on doing the movement a certain way; there is more emphasis on carefully playing with the way that a movement is done.

At the far end of the movement practice continuum we find disciplines that encourage spontaneous movement to emerge, rising up from present-moment experiences and evolving through their own momentum with the least amount of cognitive control possible. Here is where the Moving Cycle lives as a body-centered psychotherapy form, and for those of you familiar with dance therapy, where the practice of Authentic Movement resides. In contemplative practice, the form originally called Contemplative Dance, developed by Barbara Dilley at Naropa University (Dilley is interviewed in Chapter 14), is a good example of resting into the ongoingness of movement that occurs when we pay high-quality attention to the process. In music and dance, improvisation lives here.

The common denominator is high-quality attention to ongoing movement, whether it's exacting or more spontaneous. The addition of nonjudgmental and focused attention is a consistent thread in this book and is the reason we use the word *Conscious* when we talk about Moving. As philosopher Elizabeth Behnke once said, we "inhabit the movement from within" via our sustained and open attention to it (Behnke 2018). This book sees movement as a unifying principle, but other embodied disciplines could also see other elements as crucial, such as conscious breathing, conscious sensing, and conscious relating. Just about any human endeavor can benefit from conscious attention. We will argue that movement underlies all these endeavors, but let's not hold that vantage point too tightly.

How the Body Works
Is How the Book Works

 From the outset, the root of conscious movement dictates certain values that are acknowledged and explored in this book. One of these values contributed to how this book is organized. Yes, I am the founder of the Moving Cycle and Conscious Moving (CM), but the founder is no more or less important than any other component of the system, just as a leaf is no more or less important than a branch or trunk of a tree. For this reason, the ability to explore Conscious Moving needs many voices and different vantage points to help it flourish.

As a way to expand these vantage points, I created a website that is a companion to the book; please feel free to use it as you progress through the book. It houses interviews, videos, and resources that will enrich your reading experience. In some chapters, following along on the website by watching videos or reading interviews will greatly enhance your understanding of the material. Visit the website, www.consciousmoving.com, and navigate to the Book Resources tab. You can also access the website via the QR code on this page.

I have written Part I of the book to set the ground in place. This first portion lays out the fundamental principles and practices of Conscious Moving. Fundamentally, Conscious Moving involves the deliberate use of attention as well as conscious participation with natural movement oscillations. It also recognizes that movement tends to cycle, and we need to trust in our emerging and evolving bodily motion. In terms of practice, Conscious Moving involves four stages, each of which accesses resources that enable conscious movement experiences and our deliberate holding of and caring for them. Chapters 2 through 5 detail the stages that Conscious Moving cycles through, both before and during an elaboration into specific realms like education, art, or healing.

Part II is written by my current and former students living around the globe who are all a part of the CM tree. Their voices illuminate how the work is living in the world and how it is being applied in the arts, in education, and in healing. These folks understand Conscious Moving in their own ways, and they express their own knowing, which may differ from mine. Although most Conscious Moving practitioners have an extensive background in healing, most also come to the work with strong art-making, contemplative practice, and teaching experience. In Chapter 13, written by Thomas von Stuckrad, you will be able to watch videos of the work as it is expressed in a training environment for Moving Cycle practitioners. You will need to access these videos on the website in order to follow the chapter.

In Part III—Chapter 14—I write about a series of interviews I did with various movement specialists, using their wisdom as a means of surfacing common theories and practices alive in the world today. Transcripts of the edited interviews are on the book's website, under the Book Resources tab. Please access them when you read this chapter so that you can get a feel for their work and their ideas. These professionals embody the widespread nature of Conscious Moving, and our ability to apply it broadly using open attention, immersion in direct experiences, and disciplined inquiry as a means to create art, to learn and change, to heal, and to live a contemplative life. Also in this section, the book dives more deeply into the specific disciplines of art, education, contemplative practice, and healing, weaving in specific viewpoints and applications of CM to these disciplines.

Part III also brings us back to the root and asks you, the reader, about yourself and how you want to move. How do you tap into the movement that permeates and surrounds you? How do you make use of it in the world? How do you recognize and support the various conscious movements that are ongoing in and around you? This book wants to move you. It hopes to speak to all of us in the language of small shivers, grand gestures, dance floors, and city streets. It hopes to set our feet on a path and give us the power to change directions. It strives to open our awareness to the presence of movement everywhere, in everything, and at every level of existence. On a practical level, an immersion in that immensity isn't sustainable as we get the kids ready for school. How does it make itself felt in the act of putting on shoes and strapping on seat belts? How does it inform our political activism? Our sexuality? How can it support both the small and big things that we do?

These questions are neither unique nor special to Conscious Moving; many of them echo in other modern and ancient ways of knowing, which can be reassuring. When we see our work expressed in many different systems and disciplines, that's a strong hint that we're on the right track. The work works (scientists would say that it has explanatory or predictive power). Perhaps any uniqueness that Conscious Moving holds lies in how it is assembled as a system, and how it is lived by its practitioners.

Everything and everyone moves. It all begins with movement, and movement sustains it all. Conscious Moving attempts to acknowledge this gargantuan unified field while concentrating most of its efforts on shaping that unity into different specific applications in the everyday world. For readers, it may be fascinating to contemplate movement as a force that underlies everything, but again, we need to wash the dishes as well; this book addresses how we can consciously participate with movements that arise within us and around us so that we can shape ourselves toward the practicalities of our creative life, our well-being, our activism, and our learning. The book does not prescribe certain movement practices but encourages you to find existing movement practices that work for you, and to know when you are in the midst of creating your own practices as they coalesce from your unique present-moment experiences. It assumes that becoming more conscious of your own movement, and moving more deliberately at times, will allow you to access knowledge and understanding that no book can offer. You are the mover and the one being moved. Trust that, and Conscious Moving has begun.

References

Behnke, Elizabeth. 2018. "On the Transformation of the Time-Drenched Body: Kinaesthetic Capability-Consciousness and Recalcitrant Holding Patterns." *Journal of Consciousness Studies* 25 (7–8): 89–111.

Caldwell, Christine. 2019. "Micromovements: Filling Out the Movement Continuum in Clinical Practice." In *The Routledge International Handbook of Embodied Perspectives in Psychotherapy: Approaches from Dance Movement and Body Psychotherapies*, edited by Helen Payne, Sabine Koch, Jennifer Tantia, and Thomas Fuchs. New York: Routledge.

Cuignet, Timothée, Camille Perchoux, Geoffrey Caruso, Olivier Klein, Sylvain Klein, Basile Chaix, Yan Kestens, and Philippe Gerber. 2020. "Mobility among Older Adults: Deconstructing the Effects of Motility and Movement on Wellbeing." *Urban Studies* 57(2): 383–401. https://doi.org/10.1177/0042098019852033.

Hartley, Linda. 1995. *The Wisdom of the Body Moving: An Introduction to Body-Mind Centering*. Berkeley; North Atlantic Books.

Nietzsche, Freidrich. 2022. *Thus Spake Zarathustra: A Book for All or None*. London: Notting Hill.

Porges, Stephen. 2011. *The Polyvagal Theory: Neurophysiological Foundations of Emotions, Attachment, Communication, Self-Regulation*. New York: W. W. Norton.

PART I

The Fundamentals of Conscious Moving

1

The Fundamental Principles of Conscious Moving

Since everything is moving throughout time and space, it's hard to know where to begin. Somewhat arbitrarily, we can start by examining the way humans move. By studying various features of human movement, we can apply them to fundamental principles that inform our own Conscious Moving practices and apply them to learning things, being creative, and maximizing our well-being. But before we begin, a caveat. Knowledge is not something we get from "out there." It also lives within us in sociocultural, political, and personal contexts. Our locations in time and space and society generate viewpoints that allow us to see some things clearly while others are more obscured. Our available resources enable or disempower us to inquire freely. Given this, *Conscious Moving is not a "truth" out there, but a process of inhabiting movement so that emerging and evolving viewpoints can organize us, allow us to live as robustly as possible, and then move us on.* Conscious Moving in this sense is designed to shake up viewpoints in order to access resources. It should look operationally different in a Brazilian favela and an Inuit village, as well as how it emerges from a transgender rather than a cisgender body. We tap into a unified, universal presence and then specify it in our bodies for a period of time. Then we can let that specific movement go. That is Conscious Moving.

Conscious Moving can be seen from six perspectives on what movement is and how it operates. By understanding these six principles and then later mapping them onto the four phases of CM, we can create practices that might look like a therapy session, a classroom project, or an afternoon with some paint cans and a concrete wall.

Principle 1: Movement Oscillates and Cycles and Spirals

If we start by contemplating our body's interior, over and over we see movements that go back and forth. The term we use for this is *oscillation*, defined as movement back and forth at a regular speed, like the beating of the heart, the inhale and exhale of the lungs, the contraction and release of muscle fibers, the rapid alternation of electrical and chemical stimulation in a neuron, and the squeeze and release of the gut (peristalsis). Although these oscillations are not as locked in as the ticking of a clock, they occur everywhere in the body and support more passive movements like the circulation of body fluids. Our body lives in a constant oscillatory symphony of movement, with different parts moving back and forth at different speeds, and these speeds altering with changing circumstances. All that oscillating creates a kind of hovering around certain metabolic set points, such as our body temperature and our oxygen levels, often called *homeostasis*. For us, this is life. Even non-life oscillates, as we can see when physicists talk about pulsars and electromagnetic waves and when they measure things with oscilloscopes. But the gorgeous thing is that we can feel our body oscillations quite directly as we tune in to our sensations and movements.

If, while standing, you alternate your weight back and forth between your left and right foot, you are moving, but not really going anywhere. This moving in place is actually important for our stability and our sense of ongoingness. When we go from one place to another (called *locomotion*), we take advantage of some of our oscillations (like flexing and extending muscles) to change where we are. From a biological perspective, bodily change usually involves some kind of growth, repair, or development. We get taller. We increase the number of neurons in our brains. We close up a wound. We need change as well as stability. Stability ensues when we oscillate in place. Mobility, or movement for change, begins to be possible when we cycle.

A *cycle* can be defined as a series of events that repeat regularly, in the same order. We will see later that this ordering of events gives us the four phases of Conscious Moving. But at this point we can play with the idea that cycles arise as complex oscillations, pulling in and coordinating movements from different parts of the body. Think of menstrual cycles or our sleep/wake cycles. These complex processes require a coordination of different body structures—hormone production, gland secretions, and so on—that are often distributed throughout the body. Because of this our movement complexifies and is able to respond to more sophisticated challenges.

These movement cycles in turn support our next level of complexity, one where change becomes more of an immediate option. When we open up a cycle three-dimensionally, we get a spiral. A spiral curves around on itself, but as it comes around to where it began, it arcs slightly above or below or to the side of its starting point, creating a progression into a third dimension. We end up in a slightly different place on the next go-round. By complexifying oscillations we get cycles, and by complexifying cycles we get spirals. Spirals help us to move our body three-dimensionally in gravity in more effective ways. Try the difference between getting up off the floor by pushing straight up, which tends to involve fighting with gravity in order to overcome it, and getting up by rocking and rolling your weight and turning a bit as you rise. Done well, a spiral off the floor is less effortful, more graceful, and more satisfying.* Spirals transition us from two-dimensional motion to three-dimensional motion and can craft more complex actions (up and left and forward, for instance). We still use the support of oscillations and cycles, but now we can really go places.

One of the most elemental oscillations in life is the alternation between work and rest; between effort and the release of effort. A muscle fiber in the heart or the arm contracts, then it lets go. A quiet inhale involves muscle contraction, and its exhale involves letting go into gravity. Peristalsis grips the intestinal tube, and then the tube relaxes and expands. This squeeze-release alternation sequences food through the digestive tract. Neurons always pause (called a *refractory period*) before they can fire again. We wake and we sleep. This type of oscillation is so profound that we will talk about it several times, but to start, we can appreciate that at the level of our bodies, effort and the release of effort are both necessary to get just about anything done. Without this fundamental oscillation, we can't digest, breathe, pump blood, process sensorimotor information, or walk across the room.

As we go along in the book, we will also tie this to our relationship with gravity. Briefly, there are two ways to produce most movements: by efforting into gravity (like raising your arm by contracting a muscle) and by letting go into gravity (releasing the muscle contraction in that arm and it falls with gravity). We will also see this on larger levels—to wake up in the morning we gear up, and to go to sleep we let go. Both not being able to work and not being able to let go of work interfere with our well-being. Later we will expand this cyclic notion to a spiral of work—play-rest—with the word *play* being equivalent to the word *inquiry*.

So what has all this got to do with things like therapeutic change, learning, art-making, and getting the kids to school? Art, learning, and therapy all involve

---

* For an excellent explanation of three-dimensional movement and spirals, please see the work of Judith Aston-Linderoth—Aston Kinetics™—and her book *Aston Postural Assessment*. Her work involves careful and deliberate basic actions like arcing and spiraling as a way to liberate support so that persistent holding patterns in the body can release.

some kind of change. Art is famous for taking one thing and helping you see it differently. Learning opens you up to a new experience, and as a result, you know something new. Therapy involves letting go of old habits of being and doing, and finding new ways of being and doing in the world. This concept of change is applied to art-making by Gretl Bauer in Chapter 11, where she uses a specific Conscious Moving practice called *Pressure, Pleasure, and Inquiry* to process different kinds of grief.

To accomplish change, as Gretl notes, we need to know how to change with deliberateness and care, and as we have seen, complex movement can show us how that can happen—we can use the skilled actions of our bodies. These movements have evolved over billions of years from a myriad of oscillations, cycles, and spirals in the natural world as a template for engaging in deliberate change.

Principle 2: Movement Continuums Abound

Likely because of movement's oscillatory home base, the distance traveled across any space generates a continuum. Movements range from small to large, from simple to complex, from highly constrained to mostly free, from flexed to extended. Health can be defined as adaptively moving all along the breadth of a movement continuum. From this idea we might think that a healthy person can get big and small. They can curl up into a little ball or extend their arms and legs out to their limit. This idea, however, is reductionistic and fraught with the potential for bias. Any time we look at movement and assign value to it, before we ever look at a particular moving person and their physical and sociocultural embeddedness, we are setting ourselves up for prejudging, which is antithetical to well-being and equity. Unconsciously, we can begin to make some movements more or less healthy, more aesthetic or less aesthetic, or more or less sophisticated. We create judgments about those binaries where there once was a simple oscillation of life. Our work will be about deliberateness in motion rather than maximizing a range of motion. We don't strive for "more is better." We work to consciously move with what we are already doing as a means of supporting what we want to do going forward.

To expand on this "more is not necessarily better" notion, we can see all human bodies as oscillating within a restricted range of movement. Humans can only see a certain range in the spectrum of light (the visible spectrum). Our knee joints can only move in a flexing or extending manner. When we *confine* movement within certain limits, we *define* who or what that thing is. Defining a human by how it does and doesn't move helps us understand identity, and how we can both celebrate and challenge our identities (Caldwell 2016). By working consciously with movement continuums and the limits they hold, Conscious Moving allows us to both take ourselves seriously and not too seriously.

Principle 2 of Conscious Moving also speaks to a continuum involving the amount of energy we need to move ourselves. One of the first things to note is that the more complex a movement is, the more energy it tends to use. Our brains, for instance, use way more calories per gram of weight than any other part of our body. The brain does some simple operations, but it is most famous for its biggest energy hog—consciousness. Consciousness is so metabolically expensive that we regularly have to turn it off to conserve energy (sleep) so we can do other things like repair cell damage. Looked at from a different viewpoint, evolution holds that organisms try to conserve energy wherever possible because you never know when you will need that energy for something more important. For this reason, we form habits. To put it a bit too simply, our body is programmed to pick up on any action it is doing repeatedly and make it a habit (a motor plan). Habits take much less energy to perform than conscious tracking and organizing. Remember when you were first learning a new skill, like throwing and catching a ball? At first, it was clumsy and fraught with mistakes and took a lot of energy, but as you practiced it got easier. Now, you barely have to think about it; your body just knows the moves. Our bodies love to form habits, and this is good. It frees us up to do other things, like grow and learn and play and heal.

Returning to the issue of movement continuums and adding in the notion of effort, we can play with the idea that deliberately investigating our movement continuums, through both efforting and releasing effort, can expose the restricted ranges that form our identities. We are not everybody and everything (though we are related to everyone and everything). But playing around the edges of our range allows us to play with the limits of our capacities, which can be a healing, educational, or aesthetic process. Our identities live in the constraints and freedoms of our moving bodies.

Principle 3: The Movement of Attention Structures and Determines Experiences

The term *conscious* holds within it the idea of paying attention. We can define attention in a few ways: as a tuning toward something (Csordas 1993), as an ability to focus selectively on a stimulus or task (Williamson, Anzalone, and Hanft 2000), or as a selection and tracking of an event (Pollak and Tolley-Scholl

2004). Paying attention occurs when the nervous system begins to sort through incoming sensations and decides which are important enough to be dealt with unconsciously/automatically and which need to rise to consciousness so we can work with them in a complex way, using thoughts and feelings. Conscious attention is quite metabolically demanding. We have to pay attention to a task until it becomes automatic, yet even then it takes some attention in the background until the task is done (Woollacott and Shumway-Cook 2002). We actually pay attention subconsciously to lots of different actions we do ongoingly, such as maintaining our posture or being minimally alert to potential dangers.

Attention holds a special status in Conscious Moving because it sits at the beginning of so many types of movement and influences them so deeply. Attention also interests other disciplines, notably biology, psychology, education, and especially contemplative practices. One of the features of attention is that it is selective. We unconsciously and consciously select what to pay attention to and what not. What we make important enough to attend to strongly influences how we see the world and how we construct our sense of self. Many psychologists see this process as fundamental to mental health and mental illness (Kabat-Zinn 2005). Psychologist and creativity researcher Mihaly Csikszentmihalyi puts forth the idea that the names we use to describe personality traits—such as extrovert, high achiever, or paranoid—refer to the specific patterns people have used to structure their attention (1990). Educators see children as able to attend well, or not, in learning situations, and this basic skill underlies their ability to learn (Ruff and Klevjord Rothbart 1996). Artists specialize in attending to the world in different ways, enabling us to play with how we see a vase of sunflowers. Let's unpack those last few sentences in more detail, starting with psychology. Many psychologists focus their work on what a client is aware of, thinking about, obsessed with, feeling frequently, or repressing, seeing these actions as indicators of well-being or illness. These actions result from how attention is allocated and ordered. Early childhood experiences of parental attunement, neglect, or abuse are seen as structuring the child's attentional resources. Because attention is a limited resource, an abused child who needs to constantly monitor how drunk their mother is as a way to stay relatively safe doesn't have leftover energy to pay attention to states like curiosity, play, feelings and wants, or learning. All their attention goes to what is most important—staying safe in an unsafe world. This child can grow up emotionally stunted, educationally challenged, and isolated from others (Frank and La Barre 2011). Psychotherapy and contemplative practices such as meditation work to help people get more control of their attentional systems. They attempt to give people strategies for turning attention away from dissociative states, for instance, and putting their attention on a stabilizing resource, such as being able to stay in eye contact with a loving friend.

In education, professionals investigate how attention relates to learning, often through the mechanism of sensory processing (Williamson, Anzalone, and Hanft 2000). Kids with learning difficulties are often assessed for conditions such as attention deficit disorder (ADD) and attention deficit and hyperactive disorder (ADHD). What experts have uncovered is that when a child's nervous system screens out too many stimuli so that important information never gets processed, or it doesn't screen out enough so that sensations flood consciousness and overwhelm it, the child's ability to pay attention and manage their behavior erodes. Learning falls away because new information cannot get accessed. Mental and emotional illness have more opportunity to take root (Pollak and Tolley-Schell 2004).

In art-making and creativity studies, attention becomes a powerful plaything. Normal ways of seeing are upended. Normal ways of moving fly out the window as a dancer rolls and leaps. Everyday perceptions of color, shape, and identity get challenged in a painting. Artists will oscillate between strict practice (one thousand plies in ballet, scales on a piano) and more open freedoms that come under the rubric of improvisation. The value here lies in acknowledging that attention becomes habitual due to the need to conserve energy and create a stable sense of self, and that attention must also be routinely upended in order to update attentional habits in the service of creativity (Nachmanovitch 1990). We will see this in practice in Gretl Bauer's chapter (Chapter 11), where she works with found objects, and by seeing them differently, she creates new objects—a sock becomes a bird, or a fanciful coronavirus.

Perhaps more than any other discipline, the practices of meditation and contemplation can be seen as training attention. Many Eastern philosophies (and a few Western ones) see the ability to achieve bare or evenly hovering attention as the pinnacle of practice (Ray 2018). What gets interesting is that bare attention focuses on the act of attending in itself and not on the contents of what we are paying attention to. Having good control over where attention goes and doesn't go, how long it stays there, and how easily it can disengage from a stimulus sits at the intersection of art, education, and therapy, and it has largely been articulated and taught through meditative practices thousands of years old. My Buddhist teacher Thich Nhat Hanh was fond of saying that attention is like sunlight and water to a plant. What you pay attention to will grow. And what you withdraw your attention from will wither (2017). We can grow and become better people when we consciously pay attention to what benefits ourselves and others, and we can withhold attention from characteristics inside of us that hurt ourselves or others. Good attentional practices generate increased awareness and the ability to be "awake" more consistently.

Using a different metaphor, attention can be seen as being like a telescope or a microscope. By focusing the lens of attention, we can become aware of bigger and smaller things that are there but that we couldn't see before. The world becomes bigger, richer, and more wondrous. In psychotherapy, common wisdom states that we have easy access to all the stuff of consciousness but that we also possess an unconscious that stores images, emotions, memories, sensations, and attitudes that we operate from but are largely unaware of. These stored elements, usually laid down in childhood, can be partially accessed by using attention as a lens, as a way to focus on something currently not in view. Sigmund Freud used the practices of hypnosis, dream analysis, and free association to work with the unconscious directly. *Free association* involved talking in a kind of improvisational manner, gradually relaxing conscious defenses that obscure the unconscious. It also involved, according to Freud, the therapist suspending their "critical faculty," or the tendency to critically evaluate the patient's experiences.

All this points us to the observation that attention is thoroughly embodied, inextricably linked into sensorimotor processes. Psychiatrist Allan Schore has noted that our senses are active constructors of our experiences (1994). Psychologist Alan Fogel talks about the term *embodied self-awareness*, which he defines as our ability to pay attention to ourselves, to feel the textures and depths of our sensations, to explore the nuances and depths of our emotions, and to perceive our movements in relation to others and our surroundings in the present moment, without judgment (2009). Fogel also includes the idea of *body schema*, stating that "It is actually impossible to have smoothly coordinated social action without body schema self-awareness, the sense of where 'my' body leaves off and 'yours' begins" (2009, 13). In more medical circles, physician Edmund Jacobson, back in the mid-twentieth century, found that when we relax our muscles, attention tends to wane, and we tend to get sleepy (1967). When we tense up, we initially get more alert, but if the tension becomes chronic, we habituate to it and stop paying attention to it. When we visually attend to something, we must use small muscles around our eyeballs to focus on it and see it clearly. When we meditate, we are often instructed to sit on a cushion with a relaxed but upright posture. This posture relaxes our large movement muscles but engages our small spinal postural muscles, which in turn creates optimal circumstances for our ability to attend to attention (Johnson 1996). Because attention is a process of turning toward something and therefore turning away from something else, this act of turning requires an engaged body. Yes, the brain is working to generate attention, and the brain is certainly part of the body, but in addition to the brain, the rest of our body structures and determines our attention just as actively.

Interestingly, in education, attention deficits are addressed in children largely through movement and sensory practices. Some children are given earphones that screen out sounds that could overwhelm auditory processing, and gloves to minimize tactile stimuli. Physical and occupational therapies involve lots of movement because sensory processing disorders are linked to deficits in a child's *proprioception*—their ability to sense where they are in space, their body position, their balance, their locomotor movements, and their postural tone. In these sessions, kids are helped to swing, roll, somersault, leap, and make other movements that change their relationship to gravity and help them wake up proprioceptive skills, which in turn helps develop functional sensory processing and by extension, attentional skills (Hannaford 2005). Public playgrounds are proprioceptive laboratories. Educator Joana Debelt, in Chapter 9, will speak to this when she talks about learning as a result of attending to small movements and "body voices."

In Conscious Moving (CM) we train attention directly through the moving body, calling it *physical free association*. Attention naturally oscillates. It constantly moves, detaching from one thing and moving on to another, changing what is attended to. We oscillate our attention in and out; we notice something inside our bodies (hunger, tension, pleasure), and then we point our attention outward into the world, noticing the sky, the dog, and the teacher in our classroom. If we stay too long in one place, we dissociate from the other.

CM works with the in-and-out oscillatory process deliberately, and this is done for personal exploration as well as training for facilitators of CM. Other practices work with other attentional oscillations, such as the ability to oscillate between a focus on some small detail, like the tiny muscle at the corner of your mouth, back out to a panoramic awareness of the entire atmosphere you occupy. Having control of this oscillation helps us to pick up information from a myriad of sources, large and small. Oscillating attention is also seen as a practice of getting unstuck when our attention is fixated.

In Chapter 13, Thomas von Stuckrad uses videos of Moving Cycle sessions to illustrate this physical free association that arises from careful, calm, and open attention. The high-quality attention that the "witness" in a CM session gives to the "mover" acts as sunlight and water to the focus of attention in the mover.

This shared attention to what spontaneously arises becomes quite visible in these videos.

Another way CM works with attention is to specifically study attentional patterns and wounds. We have seen previously that a normal part of development involves turning repeated attentional foci into habits as a way to become skilled at something and conserve energy. We deem certain stimuli as unimportant or unsavory, so we learn to ignore them. We develop fascinations with certain things or people or events and have trouble not attending to them. Attentional habits are normal and ubiquitous, and they can also get quite dysfunctional. We have to find ways to alter the old patterns of attention when they no longer serve. Conscious Moving works to illuminate our attentional patterns through various movement practices and to help them change where needed.

One way to look at the development of dysfunctional attentional patterns is to inquire into how we were paid attention to in our early years and to acknowledge how we might have been attentionally wounded. We can be wounded by attentional neglect—we were invisible in our family. Or, certain things about us were attended to while others were neglected. We might have been attended to when we were fulfilling expectations and neglected when we did things that were deemed unimportant or wrong. Another attentional wound arises from critical attention, where we learned to fear being attended to because it meant being constantly evaluated and judged. Still, another attentional wound can form in an atmosphere of constant attention, where we were always being monitored and never left alone to relax and be with ourselves.

These attentional wounds structure our adult relationships so that we experience others through their distorting lenses, often creating a series of self-fulfilling prophecies about who others are and how they feel about us. Several of the movers in Thomas's videos report getting in touch with these early grooves in their attention, and how they were able to move differently in this current context. CM goes to the root of attention via conscious movement practices so that these wounds can be healed.

Principle 4: Movement Is Phenomenological

The nexus for learning, healing, and creativity lies in the lived experience of our body; the *phenomena* of the body if you will. This means that while it can be interesting and useful to think about experiences, living them in the present moment locates us in the territory of creative, educational, and healing resources. As Elizabeth Behnke said, when we *inhabit an experience from within*, without making it right or wrong, something about that quality of attentional inhabiting makes things possible that aren't available when we step back and abstract ourselves from an experience in order to think or talk about it (Behnke 1997). Basically, we are able to move with it, move through it, and move on from it. These three movings awaken learning, healing, and creativity.

To put a fancy word on it, CM is a phenomenological enterprise. The work occurs within movement experiments that use high-quality attention and physical free association, which in turn support emerging movement sequences, which then support actively holding what has emerged in an atmosphere of caring and reflecting, and then ending with adapting these movements for use in daily life. Those are the four phases of Conscious Moving. There is no ideal way to move, and no magic movements that address all ills. We simply allow our unfolding experiences to be our guide.

This can be harder than you think. Similar to Anna Freud's (1963) observation that we can endlessly defend ourselves against how we really feel or what we really think, we can also get stuck in movements that are familiar and distracting. We can hide out in stereotyped gestures and well-worn paths of action (Caldwell 1996). There's nothing wrong with these movements; they can be a great comfort and guide in many circumstances. But in the special time and space of a CM session, we find ways to sink down underneath these familiarities to more poignant places. Conscious Moving employs a few specific strategies to support this temporary dropping of normal consciousness. First, we can suspend any interpretation, judgment, analysis, or explanation about our moving. We enter a kind of movement meditation, where attention is evenly suspended and we simply occupy the moving experience. We don't try to control or solve. We often call this *staying in description*, where we are noticing movement and cooperating with it rather than trying to accomplish something with it. *Description* implies finding words for something, yet in CM we are supported to temporarily suspend any kind of "wording" at all. We also call it *postponing meaning-making*. By postponing meaning-making, we allow movement narratives to become more clear as they are, without the distortion of our typical explanations of them, explanations that often come from habits of interpretation (called *appraisal* by neuroscientists) and old attentional wounds.

When we can tolerate and even immerse ourselves in this phenomenological process, what arises are associations. When we stop interpreting and explaining and trying to fix, the natural and creative force of associations begins to bubble up into consciousness. Remember, Sigmund Freud went after associations through talking. Conscious Moving practitioners go after associations by moving. Associations occur naturally in the central nervous system (CNS). A stimulus comes into the CNS, and before anything else, areas of our brain compare that stimulus to our previous experiences—our stored memories of tastes and smells and actions. First, is this a sign of danger? Is it something I have really loved or hated before? What from my previous experience can I associate it to? If it is a good fit to a previous experience, we associate it with that, categorize it accordingly, and organize a motor response. This all occurs before we are ever consciously aware that we are experiencing this stimulus. We can watch this process in action when we daydream, when our reveries flit from the green field we are looking at to the green wallet we had when we were young, to the lack of money in our purse right now. Other folks would look at the same green field and go in very different directions. This process was leveraged for art's sake when Virginia Woolf and others pioneered *stream of consciousness* writing. Freud loved freely associating because it gave him access to the contents of his client's unconscious.

What happens when incoming stimuli get misattributed, or when they awaken traumatic memories, as is the case in posttraumatic stress disorder (PTSD)? What if the stimulus doesn't particularly fit any of our previous experiences? This is the stuff of art, education, and healing as well as Conscious Moving. Associations are invited in via high-quality attention to our present-moment experience, and rather than being interpreted, they are simply braided into the ongoing experiences we are having. This braiding of sensory associations tends to activate motoric responses, or what we call *movement impulses*. Our attention and our associations want to move us, often in unexpected ways, because we are not controlling them.

Back to the this-can-be-harder-than-you-think comment. Associations and their movement impulses are not necessarily sweetness and light. Often we have kept them out of our normal awareness for good reasons. This is why CM (and other disciplines) uses strategies for keeping things like shame, self-criticism, and dissociation at bay during this time of altered consciousness. This is often why CM needs a facilitator to be there so that we can stay associated rather than dissociated from our lived experience. This is why we have teachers, therapists, and art mentors.

All this is to state the obvious—Conscious Moving is experiential. While there are moments of talking about experiences, the most profound work is often accomplished at the level of doing. When doing is paired with high-quality attention, particularly open attention to oscillations and micromovements in our bodies (Caldwell 2019), direct experiences of knowing, creativity, and healing arise naturally from within and from the relational spaces around us.

Principle 5: Sensation Is a Type of Movement

Sensation occupies all life forms in some way, and sensation can be seen as a specialized type of movement that life uses. One of the features of life is that organisms gather information about their inside and outside conditions. One of the common definitions of life is that it involves *adaptation*—the ability to change in the face of changing conditions. In order to adapt, an organism needs to know what is happening so that it can organize a response. Single-celled organisms retract when poked. Sunflowers turn to follow the arc of the sun. But most animals have evolved nervous systems to accomplish adaptations. Nervous systems always involve a loop, called the *sensorimotor loop*. Stimuli excite sensory neurons and these neurons always hook up either directly or indirectly to motor neurons. We sense, and we act on what we sense. While most people say that the response is some kind of movement, Conscious Moving asserts that sensation is also a kind of movement that the body does, just like all our other cellular moving. The sensorimotor loop is a loop of movement that connects experience with action.

When we look at the moving human body, we can never exclude sensation. Sensation is such a special and important kind of moving that we work with intensively and extensively in CM. The movement of sensations makes feeling and emotion possible; I feel a clench in my gut, and I organize an emotion as a way to address that feeling. This realization that movement underlies emotion (e-motion = move out) likely explains why we read each other's emotions through our bodily actions, and why so many forms of therapy pay attention to Conscious Moving as a way to explore our emotional lives and our relationships.

Principle 6: Movement Generates
Bodily Authority

In our sixth principle, we challenge some old notions of what power is and how to use it. In CM we get curious about movements we are already doing, and rather than try to modify them or figure them out, we occupy them deliberately. For instance, by paying open attention, I become aware of a micromovement at my mouth—a slight pursing of my lips. I turn my attention to it further and notice tiny details of it. Perhaps it's a bit stronger on the left side, or it seems related to some tightness in my jaw. As a method of inquiry, I do the same thing deliberately that I was once doing automatically. This brings up an association, a memory of my mother, who did much the same micromovement. I braid in the image of my mother with my felt experience of my mouth as it purses. This causes my mouth to begin moving on its own and to start to form what I call a *body narrative*. It is a story that my mouth needs to tell about something I feel and remember that my conscious self wasn't tracking or interested in. Conscious Moving takes off.

Our final CM principle, one that many disciplines practice, begins with this idea of deliberateness. It comes down to this: when we identify an automatic or unconscious action we are already doing and then replicate it consciously and respectfully, we change it from being done automatically to being done deliberately, and this means we are consciously choosing that movement. We are empowering the movement, and the movement in turn empowers us. We are taking ownership of that movement and allowing its voice to be heard. We are awake and attentive as it happens, and this allows its story to be expressed. We can, over time, integrate its voice into our ongoing chorus of identities. This fluid identities notion is expanded on by Laia Jorba Galdos in Chapter 7. Laia talks about how identity shifts and adapts according to who you are with and the social context you are embedded within. Identity moves with your moving body. Where power is located—along a continuum from personal to systemic locations—influences your sense of self.

All movement involves power of some kind. When we study our movement, we empower ourselves. We feel more powerful within our various identities. I am moving in this way; it is me that is doing it; it is me that is producing this movement. Physics tends to define power as the ability to do work, or the rate at which work is done. Defined more socially, power tends to have a bad reputation, implying an action that uses force to dominate or control. This reputation is well deserved, as history is replete with instances of the abuse of power. But in the moving body, it arises simply as the ability to do something. Engaging with power during Conscious Moving, working with what we want to do, what we don't want to do or can't do, and what we are already doing, we have an opportunity to work with our relationship to power—with our memories of feeling powerless or times when we abused our power, as well as our longings to be able to do something more. The effective use of power begins at home, in our moving bodies.

Again, we can look to the structure and function of the human body. Our bodies are an energy system, consuming, producing, and expending energy and converting it into the ability to work (power). When this sequence of events flows smoothly, we get things done, and this helps us feel effective in our lives. There is a relationship between wanting something—such as a glass of water—and fulfilling that want by reaching, grasping the glass, bringing it toward us, and tipping it to our mouths. This completed action feels satisfying and just a bit empowering. There are also natural limits to power. I am not able to lift five hundred pounds or run at fifty miles per hour. But I can already do many things, and I can train myself to do a bit more in some instances.

The body provides a template for our study of power. We tend to think that power creates fixed hierarchies, according to who has more or less power. In the body, hierarchies are certainly present, but they are transient. Depending on what is happening at the time and what is most important, different hierarchies come and go. At one moment the liver becomes more prominent, and when circumstances change, the heart exerts more influence. Yes, the brain holds a lot of power, but not in the sense of being a master controller. Its role might best be seen as a coordinator or a moderator of all the input from far-flung areas of the rest of the body. It acts on input from all over the body and organizes responses that take into account the cooperative information sharing of the whole. It helps us create transient hierarchies.

This natural relationship to power, one that operates with transient hierarchies and multiple information cooperatives, allows us to understand power more deeply and use it more effectively. When this happens, we can say that we do things with authority. I become an authority of my own experience. Anthropologist Brigitte Jordan called it "the authoritative knowledge of the body," where we directly experience a sense of authority concerning what we feel and what is best for us (1997). We might consult professionals who are authoritative about bodies in general (physicians, trainers, etc.), but we are an authority on our own bodies and their individual ways of operating. This authoritative knowledge of our bodies can push back against people or systems that abuse power. Herein lies the foundation for social activism, beginning with our authoritative knowledge of our bodies and sequencing to our contributions in the world. Empowerment begins in the consciously moving body, and Conscious Moving gives this process special attention.

Empowered with these six principles of movement, CM moves us forward. Our next level of organization will be to map four stages onto these principles. Within these four stages, the discipline of *sequencing* figures prominently. By understanding what needs to be built before something else can happen effectively, we can navigate the terrain of our lived experiences with authority and grace. Conscious Moving guides us, but it is not a formula, an algorithm, or a recipe. What follows talks about sequencing and principles of action, but art, therapy, and education all point us to the idea that knowledge must always be tempered with improvisation, experimentation, and play. CM centralizes a process orientation and does not get overly involved in what product will emerge. Just like there is no ideal or "normal" body, particularly in terms of how it looks but also in terms of how it moves and functions, Conscious Moving trusts that what is produced at the end of a session is an organic expression of the process of living into direct experiences.

References

Behnke, Elizabeth. 1997. "Ghost Gestures: Phenomenological Investigations of Bodily Micromovements and Their Intercorporeal Implications." *Human Studies* 20, no. 2 (April): 181–201.

Caldwell, Christine. 1996. *Getting Our Bodies Back: Recovery, Healing, and Transformation through Body-Centered Psychotherapy.* Boulder, CO: Shambhala.

——. 2016. "Body Identity Development: Definitions and Discussions." *Body, Movement and Dance in Psychotherapy* 11, no. 4 (February 2016): 220–34. https://doi.org/10.1080/17432979.2016.1145141.

——. 2019. "Micromovements: Filling Out the Movement Continuum in Clinical Practice." In *The Routledge International Handbook of Embodied Perspectives in Psychotherapy: Approaches from Dance Movement and Body Psychotherapies,* edited by Helen Payne, Sabine Koch, and Jennifer Tantia, with Thomas Fuchs. New York: Routledge.

Csikszentmihalyi, Mihaly. 1990. *Flow: The Psychology of Optimal Experience.* New York: Harper and Row.

Csordas, Thomas J. 1993. "Somatic Modes of Attention." *Cultural Anthropology* 8, no. 2 (May): 135–56.

Fogel, Alan. 2009. *The Psychophysiology of Self-Awareness: Rediscovering the Lost Art of Body Sense.* New York: W. W. Norton.

Frank, Ruella, and Frances La Barre. 2011. *The First Year and the Rest of Your Life: Movement, Development, and Psychotherapeutic Change.* New York: Routledge.

Freud, Anna. 1963. "The Concept of Developmental Lines." *Psychoanalytic Study of the Child* 18: 245–66.

Hannaford, Carla. 2005. *Smart Moves: Why Learning Is Not All in Your Head.* Arlington, VA: Great Ocean Publishers.

Jacobson, Edmund. 1967. *Biology of Emotions: New Understanding Derived from Biological Multidisciplinary Investigation: First Electrophysiological Measurements.* Springfield, IL: C. C. Thomas.

Johnson, Will. 1996. *The Posture of Meditation: A Practical Manual for Meditators of All Traditions.* Boston: Shambhala.

Jordan, Briggitte. 1997. "Authoritative Knowledge and Its Construction." In *Childbirth and Authoritative Knowledge: Cross Cultural Perspectives,* edited by Robbie E. Davis-Floyd and Carolyn F. Sargent. Berkeley: University of California Press.

Kabat-Zinn, Jon. 2005. *Coming to Our Senses: Healing Ourselves and the World through Mindfulness.* New York: Hyperion.

Nachmanovitch, Stephen. 1990. *Free Play: Improvisation in Life and Art.* New York: Putnam.

Nhat Hanh, Thich. 2017. *The Art of Living: Peace and Freedom in the Here and Now.* New York: Harper Collins.

Pollak, Seth D., and Stephanie Tolley-Schell. 2004. "Attention, Emotion, and the Development of Psychopathology." In *Cognitive Neuroscience of Attention,* edited by M. I. Posner. New York: Guilford Press.

Ray, Reginald. 2018. *The Practice of Pure Awareness: Somatic Meditation for Awakening the Sacred.* Boulder, CO: Shambhala Publications.

Ruff, Holly Alliger, and Mary Klevjord Rothbart. 1996. *Attention in Early Development: Themes and Variations.* New York: Oxford University Press.

Schore, Allan N. 1994. *Affect Regulation and the Origin of the Self: The Neurobiology of Emotional Development.* Hillsdale, NJ: Lawrence Erlbaum Associates.

Williamson, G. Gordon, Marie E. Anzalone, and Barbara E. Hanft, B. (2000). "Assessment of Sensory Processing, Praxis, and Motor Performance." In *Clinical Practice Guidelines,* edited by the Interdisciplinary Council on Developmental and Learning Disorders, 155–73. www.icdl.com/dir/bookstore/icdl-clinical-practice-guidelines.

Woollacott, Marjorie, and Anne Shumway-Cook. 2002. "Attention and the Control of Posture and Gait: A Review of an Emerging Area of Research." *Gait and Posture* 16(1): 1–14.

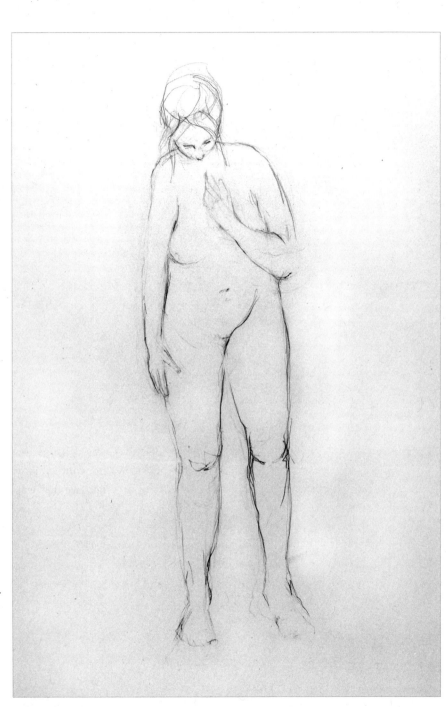

Drawing by Page Zekonis, 2023

2

The Awareness Phase of Conscious Moving

Instructions for living a life: Pay attention. Be astonished. Tell about it.

—POET MARY OLIVER

We only see what we look at. To look is an act of choice.

—JOHN BERGER, IN *WAYS OF SEEING*

Awareness is medicine.

—ALAN FOGEL, IN *THE PSYCHOPHYSIOLOGY OF SELF-AWARENESS*

Attention shapes the self, and is in turn shaped by it.

—MIHALY CSIKSZENTMIHALYI, IN *FLOW*

These next four chapters guide us through the four phases of Conscious Moving (CM), phases that show up similarly in art-making, contemplative practice, therapy, and learning. In order to avoid getting too rigid, we may want to begin with an image—that of an ocean wave as it approaches the shore. All waves go through phases: the water swells, a peak forms, the peak breaks over the front face of the wall of water, and after some time, the churning fizzles out, and that particular wave gets absorbed back into the ocean, the sand, and the air. There is both a thrill and a comfort in the repetition of ocean waves. Yet we can also say that no two waves are alike. Each one swells, breaks, burbles, and recedes differently, with different shapes, sizes, and rhythms. That is what the phases of Conscious Moving are like. We can make some general predictions about where things are going, but the individual dance of each CM experience can be exquisitely detailed in its individuality.

The idea that sensorimotor experiences occur in a phasic manner is not unique to Conscious Moving. We can see echoes of this idea in the somatic psychotherapy practice of Hakomi, which uses what they call the Sensitivity Cycle, the phases of which are called clarity, effectiveness, satisfaction, and relaxation (Weiss, Johanson, and Monda 2015). In the discipline of Body-Mind Centering, movement phases are looked at in terms of how the body organizes core movement sequences. Interestingly, they call it the Satisfaction Cycle, which contains the sequence of yield, push, reach, grasp, and pull (Hartley 1995). Psychologists Mihaly Csikszentmihalyi and Howard Gardner felt that the process of creativity occurred in five steps: 1) Preparation: an immersion in ideas; 2) Incubation: where ideas churn below the threshold of consciousness; 3) Insight: called the *aha!* moment; 4) Evaluation: deciding what is worth pursuing; and 5) Elaboration: putting it into a form in the world. Similarly to what we see in CM, all these systems pay attention to the feeling of satisfaction when a movement experience is seen through to completion.

In the field of education, David Kolb developed *Experiential Learning Theory*, which is based on the assumption that people learn through direct experiences (learning by doing) and these experiences come in a four-stage learning cycle: having an experience, reflecting on the experience, learning from the experience, and trying out what you have learned (Kolb 2014). Joana Debelt will discuss Kolb's work in Chapter 9, in particular how it relates to a kind of triangle that gets formed when we alternate between work, play, and rest, and another triangle formed by the cooperative actions of breathing, moving, and sensing. When children are exposed to "learning by doing," Kolb's four phases reveal themselves, and when a teacher can actively cooperate with these phases, learning is enhanced.

Others, such as psychologist Fritz Perls, who developed a here-and-now experiential therapy called Gestalt, enjoyed talking about psychological processes through the metaphor of digestion. First you bring the food/experience into your mouth and get to know it and chew on it. Then you decide to own it by swallowing it. This experience is now you/yours. Then you digest it, by working with the experience and transforming it into a form that diffuses out and nourishes your whole body, expelling what can't be used. Clearly, this idea of experiential stages possesses some gravitas.

Take a moment right now to observe your breathing. Just be aware of your breathing, without trying to control, judge, or analyze it. Be with it, noticing particular details of the action; what parts of your body move and what sensations are happening. You are now breathing more deliberately, attending to something you weren't attending to a few minutes ago. Stay with it a bit longer, and notice the moments when it is just you breathing, nothing more. There is just this action—*breathing*. You are your breath, just for a moment.

Breathing is a kind of wave: it builds, crests, falls into gravity, and peters out. The next one comes on its own. It embodies Principle 1 from the last chapter— the fundamental oscillations that permeate our world. It has phases, yet there are different details and rhythms in each individual breath. Paying attention to our breathing, just being with it, witnessing it, and participating with the wave of it and its myriad details embodies the first phase of Conscious Moving, *Awareness*.

If there is one idea that all education, art-making, healing, and contemplative practice share, it's an abiding focusing on how to become more aware and how to be more deliberate about what we are aware of. Think of a beam of light, and then what that light illuminates. In Buddhism, the word *Buddha* translates into "one who is awake," and being unconditionally awake generates enlightenment. To become more awake, we need to practice, to hone our capacity to be what I call an *attentional athlete*. To use the beam-of-light analogy, we need to be able to tune and focus the beam, depending on what we want to illuminate. This enables us to access more exquisite detail and nuance in what we are attending to. The object of our attention becomes richer, fuller, and more available for us to appreciate. We can see things about it we weren't seeing before. A good analogy might be to the astronomer Galileo, who, when he made a more powerful telescope, discovered several of Jupiter's moons.

Wherever you are, take a moment to become more aware of the act of reading this book. Let's assume you are looking at the words rather than listening to them. You are holding the book/reader at a certain distance from your eyes in order to optimize focus. The tiny muscles that hug your eyeballs constantly stretch and contract to minutely alter the shape of your eyeball so that you can focus on the words. All focusing involves muscular action, similar to turning a knob on binoculars in order to see something clearly at different distances. The Awareness Phase of Conscious Moving involves practicing the athleticism of focusing so that the muscles of attention (both literally and figuratively) are more exercised, more toned, and more graceful.

What tones when we can athletically focus our beam of attention is called the *figure/ground relationship*, first described by early experimental psychologists, and it involves the ability to bring some object or sound or touch into focus as it stands out from the background. When you look out over a crowd of people and you pick out your friend in that crowd, you are making them figural, and the rest of the crowd becomes the background (like in a *Where's Waldo* book). The figure is what is important to pay attention to at this moment. Newborn human babies can only focus their eyes at a limit of about eighteen inches. Interestingly, that's the approximate distance between their eyes and their mother's eyes during nursing or caregiver bottle feeding; this act of mutual gazing may be one of our first trainings in visual focusing, and this focusing on each other can be seen as one of our most important human bonding experiences. As the infant grows, ongoing and varied visual experiences extend their focal distance and sharpen the ability to create figures against backgrounds. This figure/ground athleticism predicts the ability to attend to particular stimuli while backgrounding others, a critical skill for learning, where a school child must tune out other sounds in a room in order to pay attention to their teacher's voice or see a written word as distinct from the words around it. This skill remains underdeveloped in children with learning disabilities, and, interestingly, is involved in challenges with resisting temptations (Ruff and Rothbart 1996).

To extend sensory-based attending into art-making, perhaps one of the most central skills of an artist is their ability to see things differently and to help us do the same. An artist wants us to question how we look at things by using light, color, sound, shape, movement, or words in an unusual and provocative way. They mess with our figure/ground relationship by making something figural that wouldn't have occurred to us. They upend our habitual way of experiencing a tree or a person or an action. Experiencing art can activate our ability to be awake in our world.

Most meditation practices work with altering consciousness through the practice of deliberate attentiveness, which works on our patterns of attention rather than contents of it. The following quote (Epstein 1984) speaks to what is called *bare attention*:

> *Bare attention is defined by two technical paradigms: a particular form of deploying attention and a particular management of affect. Cognitively, attention is restricted to registering the mere occurrence of thought, feeling or sensation exactly as it occurs and enters awareness from moment to moment, without further elaboration. One attends to the process of thoughts, feelings, and sensations as they come and go in consciousness, not to their content. Affectively, stimuli are attended to without selection or censorship and without reaction—without preference, comment, judgment, reflection, or interpretation. If physical or mental reactions occur, they themselves are made the objects of bare attention.*

Intriguingly, much the same process can be channeled within any of the healing arts. The joke, attributed to Rita Mae Brown, about the definition of craziness as doing the same thing over and over again and expecting a different result, carries a strong element of truth here. Many of us go into therapy when we are stuck—when we can't change or get the world to change. Therapy often helps because it involves changing how we pay attention as well as what we pay attention to. We noted before that this started long ago, when early practitioners experimented with hypnosis, looking at dreams, and free-associative speaking. These days, modern Western psychotherapists are opening up to psychedelics as an effective treatment for PTSD, anxiety, and depression. Several newer forms of therapy, such as Dialectical Behavioral Therapy (DBT) and Cognitive Behavioral Therapy (CBT) specialize in helping clients to challenge and push back against thought processes that are invasive, recurring, and outside of the person's ability to control.

All these therapies are going after a similar result—changing awareness, both the ability to focus the beam of attention and to be more at choice about where it lands. An analogy lies in the origin of the word *addiction*. It comes from a Latin root meaning "devoted habits." One of the primary features of addiction is that it sucks up all your attention—you are less and less aware of anything other than the substance, the behavior, the way it makes you feel, and how to get more of it. This topic is explored in more detail by Rachelle Janssen in Chapter 8, where she works with folks experiencing addictions in a way that helps them alter not only their actions, but their attention. In a related way, we could see anxiety as a kind of helpless devotion to fear, and long-term depression as a devotion to a sense of powerlessness. We get stuck in a washing machine of certain thoughts or get sucked into a whirlpool of certain emotions. Healing can be seen as an exit ramp from the deep groove of limited or habitual attention. Our awareness operates best when it is both free to play across inner and outer sensorimotor landscapes, and free to withdraw from something in order to become aware of something else.

Learning, contemplation, therapy, and art all involve altering our awareness in order to strengthen it. Apocryphally, it has been said that Albert Einstein, when asked how he saw such novel and counterintuitive solutions to existing problems in physics, quipped that you can't solve a problem in the same state of awareness that the problem arose in. He used thought experiments that pulled his concentration outside the restricting box of classical physics. Indigenous healers use psychedelics, trance dancing, and other rituals to alter states of consciousness in individuals, families, and communities. Hypnosis puts you in dream-like states. Free association shortcuts some of the momentum of what you are usually thinking, thus allowing unthought material from the unconscious to emerge. Meditation works by enabling us to sustain and withdraw attention at will, thus accessing an altered state where we are simply inhabiting the present moment (Epstein 1984). Feeling our feelings allows us to be moved by them, moved to a different place, a different consciousness. All these examples point to Principle 3 in the previous chapter—the principle that attention structures and determines experiences. It all addresses this central issue of working with the skill of being increasingly awake to our inside and outside worlds in productive and playful ways.

Awareness of Micromovements

At this point we want to introduce one important way to support and encourage what we can pay attention to as we work with awareness deliberately. This attentional practice takes the form of recognizing and caring for micromovements.

Many diverse people have noticed that we tend to make small, often unconscious movements when something hits home, or when we are right at the edge of some emotion. Philosopher Elizabeth Behnke (1997) wrote about them, as did Anna Freud (1963), researcher Paul Ekman (1997), and others, including myself (Caldwell 1996, 2019). Micromovements can occur anywhere in the body, but many occur in the face. They are often missed, either by the micromover or the witness, since they can be quite small, and it is in their nature to stay as quiet as possible. They are closely related to *tells* in poker games. They could be a slight squeeze of the eyes, a small pursing of the mouth, a quiet rubbing of the thumb against the index finger. They occur when we are responding to something that moves us (usually emotionally) and we are not yet aware of what we are feeling, or when we don't want to broadcast what we are feeling. We can be quite aware of our micromovements or clueless of them.

In Conscious Moving, we subscribe to the idea that we are multiple selves (Caldwell 2016; Laia Jorba Galdos's Chapter 7), that some of these selves are more public while others are more private, and that some are more supported while others are marginalized. We tend to internally oppress aspects of our identities and emotions that have been persecuted or neglected. We "bite back" emotion that may not be appropriate in current conditions, but that emotion remains present in a tightening of our jaw. Micromovements often occur when associations arise during an experience that have some charge to them. They need care, support, and encouragement. One way to get down below our normal, habitual consciousness and our usual defenses is to identify and care for micromovements and support them to do what they want to do. They are usually the leading edge of an impulse to move in some novel way that hasn't yet been acknowledged or supported. This caring for micromovements can uncover wounds, but they also uncover information and creative impulses. By working with them, we can access powerful resources.

The Awareness Phase as a Way to Begin an Athletic Practice

How do we cultivate these altered states of consciousness that allow our awakeness to strengthen? Picking up ideas from our six principles in Chapter 1, we can construct three basic Awareness Phase practices. Playing with these practices distinctly—like practicing throwing and catching a ball before playing a game of baseball—can help us put together an Awareness Phase that speaks to our learning, healing, art-making, and contemplative life. These practices are not unique to Conscious Moving; many have their origins in meditation and psychotherapy, for instance. They are included in CM because they have a long history of being effective for broad populations of people.

Practice 1: Oscillating Attention

This first practice does consciously what we are already doing unconsciously. By doing it deliberately and precisely, we increase our ability to do it better. The particular type of oscillation we are going to practice here is the oscillation of attention. These practices work well when we use our eyes but can be applied to any of the senses.

IN AND OUT

Begin by having your eyes open or closed. Take some time to just notice what it's like in there or out there. Then change it—open to closed or closed to open. Notice the details of what you are experiencing, landing your attention on something specific inside or outside your body. Just go back and forth, open eyes to closed eyes and back, for a minute or two. You can follow it as it occurs naturally, and you can do it deliberately. Focus on the act of doing it.

Eyes open gives you data about the outside world, and eyes closed foregrounds information about your inside world. Both locations are important sources of safety, discernment, and interest. By oscillating in and out, you tone the attentional muscles that allow for a balance between them. We get out of balance when we pay too much attention to ourselves for too long. We also get out of balance when we spend too much time monitoring the outside world. By oscillating deliberately, we athleticize our ability to play across both inner and outer landscapes and to minimize getting stuck in either location.

PANORAMIC TO NARROW

Let's begin with eyes open, not looking at anything in particular. This tends to create a broad field of vision. The center of your vision is no more important than your peripheral vision. Just allow a general sense of color, shape, movement, and atmosphere to emerge. Then oscillate to looking at some small object quite particularly. When you attend to that one thing, details about it can emerge. Go back and forth deliberately a few times, and then just notice moments when it happens naturally.

This second attentional oscillation can be illuminated through the analogy of a flashlight. We can create light with a wide beam, one that takes in a broad expanse but doesn't illuminate much depth or detail. We can also create a narrow beam, like a laser, that homes in on small details, dropping out of the panorama. Both are sources of safety and discernment. By oscillating from panoramic to narrow, you tone the attentional muscles that allow for a balanced life. We get out of balance when we only see the big picture, and we get out of balance when we get stuck in details. By oscillating deliberately, we athleticize our ability to play across tiny specifics, as well as take in the entire scene, and minimize getting stuck in either location. We tone our figure/ground capabilities.

Other types of oscillating attention are available to us. You might want to try practicing an oscillation between different senses, switching deliberately from using your eyes to using your ears, or from your sense of taste to your sense of smell. Although humans are a visually dominant species, we can still access important information from all our senses, and this tends to create enriched experiences of ourselves and the world.

IMMERSION AND OBSERVING

Let's start by observing something going on inside your body. It could be a painful or pleasurable sensation, or it could be neutral (try them all at some point). When observing inside, you create two selves: one that is in the experience of the sensations and one that is observing the experience. This is your oscillation. Take a few moments to be in the experience without thought, evaluation, or commentary. Then take a metaphoric step back and observe yourself having that sensation. This observing self will likely come up with words, images, sounds, new sensations, memories, or emotions as a way to express what is being observed (this can be hard to do descriptively—without judging, evaluating, or critiquing—just do your best). Take a few more minutes to oscillate between being in and witnessing different experiences.

This oscillation can be very challenging to pull off, and very rewarding when it happens. It athleticizes two capacities: the first tones our ability to be more at choice when we are immersed in something, and the second capacity enables us to be a bit detached from it. In a sense, it's like oscillating between being an experience and having an experience, between "this experience is me," and "this experience is not me." Both those realizations can be useful for learning, art, healing, or contemplation. I can give myself over to an experience completely, like moments during good sex, while listening to an amazing piece of music, or when taking the first bite of a juicy orange. I can also step back from experiences while still seeing them in context, like the moment when I experience being angry while also realizing that I am not my anger, that it will come and go, and that I want to express my anger with care for others. I can also describe my experience to myself and others.

This ability to immerse in an experience develops our capacity to share states with others directly, body-to-body, and to feel connected to others and the world. Our ability to witness ourselves within an experience allows us to swim in an experience and not drown in it. It gives us ways to work with the experience. However, this swimming requires a companion athleticism spelled out in the next practice.

Practice 2: Pushing Back against Judgment, Control, Analysis, Criticism, and Meaning-Making

We have looked at the idea of immersion in an experience and then oscillating into witnessing it. In immersion, we embed ourselves, and in observing we take a step back. We could say that in the first practice, we don't think—in fact, we push back against the urge to think about what is being experienced—we just *are* that experience; philosophers call this being *pre-reflective*. In the second practice we engage in reflection, but we push back against any thinking that critiques or categorizes the experience; we use associations rather than explanations as a way to reflect. This can be hard to do, and this is why most practitioners see these practices as needing to be done for the rest of our lives, much like exercise, meditation, and staying socially connected. The saving grace is that they can be quite satisfying, and can increase well-being almost immediately.

Much like the immersion exercise in Practice 1, we take some dedicated time with simple, direct experiences like breathing, sensations, or simple movements. We actually immerse unconsciously all the time, calling it *spacing out* or *zoning out*. When problematic, it is called *dissociation*—as when therapists see clients exit the here and now and get sucked into traumatic memories. In this practice, we are attentive within the immersion, much like artists and athletes report when they are in the midst of painting, dancing, sculpting, tumbling, and swimming. The psychologist Mihaly Csikszentmihalyi (1996, 2008) called these conscious immersions *flow* states. In flow states, we enter into the action and inhabit that action consciously. In flow states, we become more creative, and our creativity spills over into our productivity.

Just Immersion 1

As a meditation, take a few minutes to find a quiet spot, and let your body become quiet. Notice the bare details of what your attention lands on—the pressure of your body against the surface of a chair, the movements of your breathing, and the color of the sky outside the window. Whenever you notice yourself thinking—no matter what—just acknowledge that and bring your attention back to your direct experience. Start out with a few minutes, and work your way up to as many minutes as feels right.

Just Immersion 2

Find a space you can claim for yourself, either indoors or outside. Start in any position, and bring your attention to your body. Notice small details of your sensations. Just notice, being aware that some sensations can be pleasurable, some painful, and some neutral. Practice not favoring any one of those sensations. They all have equal weight in your attention, and they are just there, like a voice. Be with each one without prejudice. If you notice yourself making a sensation right or wrong, just notice that and go back to simply sensing your body as it is. If you notice yourself thinking about any of these sensations, just notice that and go back to being within that sensation. Start out with a few minutes, and work your way up to as many minutes as feels right.

Just Immersion 3

Create a space where you can move around easily. Start with simple movements, like shrugging your shoulders, wagging your finger, or lifting up a leg. Just experiment with moving, for no particular purpose, just seeing what comes. It could be a gesture, a shiver, or a dance move. One movement sets you up for the next movement. When you notice that you are thinking about the movement, planning what comes next, criticizing what you just did, or explaining what it meant, just notice that and go back to playing within the movements.

Just Immersion 4

With one or both hands, make a fist. Take a few moments to look at your fist, and notice small details about it—the feeling of the muscles working, the feeling of pressure—the original details of it. You might notice an association to some emotion coming up. This association is fine, but see if you can put it to the side and just let it be a fist. You might notice different associations coming up; just acknowledge them, and go back to holding the details of making a fist.

The trick of these four exercises is to choose to be awake within an ongoing experience and to push back against thinking of any kind because it causes us to begin separating from that experience. And once we begin to separate from it, we have a strong tendency to evaluate, to criticize, and to categorize. Nothing is wrong with these mentalizations; it's just that they take you away from direct experiences, and they often chatter about the experiences in ways that have more to do with your wounds and biases than with your actual ongoing being.

You might notice that all four of these exercises sound a lot like versions of meditation practices. Most contemplative traditions use meditation as a means of training attention toward the reduction of suffering—the suffering that comes from investing mental energy in the mind's tendency to gossip, brag, tear down, point fingers, puff up, and misconstrue direct experiences. Being able to choose direct experience and to sustain it for periods of time hallmarks art-making, learning, and healing as well as many spiritual traditions. Immersion in experiences taps into places inside of us that inspire, teach, challenge, and illuminate.

Now we will work with oscillating deliberately between being in the flow of direct experience and reflecting on that experience because sooner or later we all need to think about things, and we might as well get that as clear as possible. Some psychologists and philosophers have talked about these practices as the cultivation of the *observing self* (Deikman 1982), or our *witness consciousness* (Albahari 2009). In CM, we say that I am oscillating among immersing in ongoing experiences, observing them, and then describing them. Description tends to be thought of as something that anyone would say about what they were experiencing or observing, something that is unarguable and only tries to get at the features of it. For instance, the book is blue with white edging. The shoe is red and is missing a shoelace. If I say that the sunset is pretty, I am not describing it, I am saying something about how I experience it. Sunsets can be quite pretty in anyone's experience, but what we are after here is relating to something that literature calls *original detail*. Have you ever read a book in which the author described something, like snow falling on cedars, in such a rich way that you felt like you were there?* That's the power of original detail. Too often we skip over

---

* *Snow Falling on Cedars*, by David Guterson, 1994.

the richness of simply describing something, closing off details that don't align with our interests, or not even realizing that our reflections about something are suffused with self-interest and pockets of blindness. Descriptive detail fleshes out an experience and gives us more access to its true nature.

REFLECTION 1

Staying in Description: Take a few minutes to play with one of the preceding immersion practices. Then, choose to reflect on this experience by putting it into words that are as descriptive as possible. We are playing with finding words for things because that is what humans do. You can keep the words in your head, or you can say them out loud, or write them down. Keep at it until finding more details feels challenging. Notice when you slip into interpretation or categorization or critique, and just turn your attention back to the original details that any of your senses pick up about that thing you are observing. Try this both with something you notice inside your body as well as something in your outer environment. Notice which things are easy to describe and which are more challenging. We often find it more challenging to describe things we care about.

REFLECTION 2

Describing an Ongoing Experience: This exercise is more easily done with a partner but can be adapted to being solo. Sit facing your partner. Taking turns, describe one thing you are seeing about your partner (their head is tipped to the left, let's say), and one thing you notice in yourself (my throat is tight). Alternate describing these details for a few minutes. Be as precise as you can about unarguable, original details. Then talk about what that exercise was like. Did you feel like you wanted to argue with some of your partner's descriptions? Was it a bit boring? Did you notice that some of the descriptions related to each other? Did you feel seen, or examined? Did you feel nervous or calmer?

Often an exercise like this can surface attentional wounds that we might not have realized we had. I can remember having to practice not cringing when people looked me in the eye, especially women. When I worked on this in therapy, I uncovered an association of how my mother would look at me over her glasses right before she would criticize something I had done, or how I looked. Being seen equaled being criticized. By practicing description we can really see the details of a tree before painting it, experience emotion as it is before dancing it, or rest into the richness of an orange before we peel and eat it. We can also paint or dance how we feel about the tree, but then it is a dance about feelings, and the tree becomes symbolic of the feeling.

Versions of the next exercise are often used in psychotherapy, and we can see it used extensively in body-centered and experiential disciplines. I use it in the Moving Cycle and have seen it used in Hakomi, Focusing, Sensorimotor Psychotherapy, and Somatic Experiencing, to name just a few. It involves oscillating between immersion and reflection so that we don't get swept away by either, and so they companionably inform and enrich each other.

REFLECTION 3

Describing a Challenging Experience: This exercise is best done with a partner who you trust to hear you and who cares about your well-being. Choose an experience you have had that was challenging (please don't pick something traumatic or intense) that you are willing to talk about with your partner and that doesn't take long to describe. Begin by closing your eyes and remembering the event, taking some time to recall the details. Notice any emotions or reactions that might come up. Now open your eyes, and alternate between describing the event and describing what you notice in your body as you retell the event. Stay with that oscillation for a bit, and then if you feel willing and able, go to the more challenging level of describing your emotions, both then and now. Let yourself feel the sensations and possibly the emotions for a bit, and then deliberately shift your attention to verbally describing the experience, so you go back and forth between experiencing and describing the experience. Be on the lookout for making any part of the experience right or wrong. If at any time you can't manage the oscillation between experiencing and describing, stop the exercise and take care of yourself by doing something else with your partner, something relaxing, fun, or nourishing.

Being able to have one foot in the here and now and one foot in the there and then, and to both feel and describe these places as we alternate between them without critique or extrapolation, underlies the skill of being able to learn from our experiences and make something creative or educational or healing out of them. We need immersion and distance, closeness and separation. We can cultivate an athletic ability to enter a state that can enrich us as well as exit a state that overwhelms us, giving ourselves the power to make productive use of them. By staying in description when we talk about them, we push back against emotional and cognitive distortions that sap our power to learn, to be creative, and to heal. Staying descriptive also makes us better partners in our relationships. We are less likely to wound with our words, and more likely to communicate our willingness to see others clearly and accompany them in their experiences.

Practice 3: Sustaining Attention on Present-Moment Experiences and Welcoming the Ensuing Associations

We have noticed before that when we simply pay attention in an open and relaxed way, our experience can begin to shift. Associations arise. Have you ever been brushing your teeth, and all of a sudden that person's name you couldn't remember from yesterday in the grocery store just pops into your head? That's because of associations that are going on subconsciously. In CM we use these associations to explore more deeply what we are experiencing, to the point of bringing up material from parts of the brain that aren't conscious. It involves noticing what comes up when you hold something in particular in your awareness and staying curious about it.

WELCOMING ASSOCIATIONS 1

Begin by focusing your attention on something or someone that you care about. Take a few minutes to sustain your attention there, coming back to it/them whenever your attention wanders. Stay attentive to anything that comes up—it could be a color, a sound, an emotion, a memory, or a sensation in your body. It could seem strongly related or it could seem like some random, weird association (why when I remembered their name did I see the color blue?). Now braid that association into what you are attending to; trust that something is there to explore (that person's name and the color blue). It could be that nothing seems to come up. In that case, "nothing" is the association. Take a few minutes to let this associative process go wherever it wants to go. Each sound or image or feeling that comes up is included, as you trust that somehow the person/thing you care about is associated with what is coming up. Don't try to figure out the connection, just welcome each association as it arises in a creative jumble. Let it be a jumble rather than an organized thing.

This exercise is a training in enriching our perceptions of someone or something. The associations that come up can be used for contemplation and reflection, or they can be an inspiration to draw a portrait of your cared-for person in blue colors. Who knows where it can go? Our subconscious can be immensely fertile and creative, and this exercise works to welcome associations that arise in ways that allow us to explore and play with more than the everyday obvious. We often think of knowledge or information as a resource that exists outside of us, and we have to pull it in. Authoritative knowledge is also within us, and we need methods for accessing it. Importantly, we postpone putting this knowledge to use; we first assemble associations without interference. Later, we will find ways to shape what we know into usable forms. We do this even when the associations that arise make us uncomfortable.

In the early 1900s a developmental psychologist named Lev Vygotsky (van der Veer and Valsiner 1994) asserted that we learn best when we are in a state of mild discomfort. He called it the Zone of Proximal Development. The idea is that when you are super-comfy, like when you are on the couch in your jammies with a glass of wine, you're not learning anything. You are doing other important things, like resting and recuperating, but you are not working at accessing something new. Psychotherapists notice this as well; when a client tries to stay in their comfort zone at all costs, they tend not to confront challenges or explore alternatives.

You don't learn when you are far away from your comfort zone either. If you are scared or stressed or really sick or in over your head in a situation, learning goes out the window and things like defense, protection, or survival become most important. The sweet spot for learning (and for healing and creating) is when you are a bit on alert. Your senses are active, you are attentive, you care about what's happening, and your body is neither too tense nor too loose. This is also the zone where associations emerge. How do we find this zone? Practice may be our best bet, but in addition, we need to develop skills for when painful associations show up so that they don't take us too far away from the comfort of what we know and where we feel safe. If we have strategies for dealing with painful associations, then associating can be a friendly and rewarding experience.

WELCOMING ASSOCIATIONS 2

Pick an experience that was uncomfortable for you. Please don't pick anything intense, unless you do this with a therapist. Take a few minutes to remember the experience in as much original detail as possible. In order to work with this memory effectively, use your skills of oscillation to alternate between being in the memory and then oscillating to describing it. You can also oscillate between attending to the memory and shifting your attention to something or someone else, like your therapist or friend, or a tree outside the window. The important thing is to feel that you have control over your oscillations such that you feel the memory but don't get stuck in it. Notice what associations come up—sounds, images, sensations, emotions, and different memories. Just include them and hold them in your attention without trying to figure them out or do anything about them. The associations that arise can be clues to how you have positioned this memory within your worldview, and they also form seeds for the cultivation of learning, making art, healing, and leading a reflective life.

I remember well the first time a friend told me I was beautiful. My knee-jerk response (old motor plan!) was to say, "No, you're wrong. You're just being nice." But when I was able to oscillate out and really look at him—at the expression on his face—I realized that he looked quite sincere, and I allowed for the possibility that he was being honest with me from his vantage point. This shook up my worldview, one that had constellated around a belief that I was homely. It was actually a painful experience because I realized that my worldview required that I mistrust my friend and that I continue to feel bad about my looks.

When we really stay with our experiences, when we postpone our typical responses and really take in the associations that come up (in this case, flushing of the cheeks, embarrassment, feeling very young and fragile), these associations provide an exit ramp from old, reflexive attitudes and actions. We empower ourselves and occupy the present moment, where change, creativity, learning, and being awake reside.

Painful experiences are a part of life, and when we empower ourselves to work with them directly, we enable them to be our most powerful teachers. This process cannot be rushed, and it cannot be manualized. You know best how to work with your own suffering. The first stage of working with any experience, from the mundane to the dramatically intense, is to wake up to the exquisite details of it and allow it to access resources buried within you and around you.

PUTTING AN AWARENESS PHASE TOGETHER: PRACTICE EXAMPLES AND AN OPEN RECIPE

Let's put all these exercises together in a more practical way and play with what the Awareness Phase of Conscious Moving might look like in different conditions. We can begin with some examples from my work that have been generalized for privacy's sake and collapsed a bit for brevity's sake. These examples represent the beginning minutes of a CM session.

EXAMPLE 1: A THERAPY SESSION

The client and I are sitting facing each other. The client has told me they are experiencing mixed feelings about an upcoming visit with family members.

Me: Just take a moment and notice what's happening in your body as you talk about this.

Client: My chest feels tight.

Me: Yes. I notice too that your hands are rubbing your thighs a bit.

Client: Yup, that too.

Me: Let's assume that your chest and your hands are saying something about this family visit. Would it be OK to pay attention to your tight chest and your rubbing hands? Just let them do what they are already doing, trying not to judge them or make sense of them.

Client: I feel nervous.

Me: Yeah, "nervous" comes up. Can we experiment with that? Would it be OK to keep doing the tight chest and the hands, and the feeling of nervousness, and see what else comes up?

Client: When I do that, a memory comes up. I'm about six years old and I'm waiting for my father to come home from work. I'm excited, but I'm also scared of him. And now I feel like I can't breathe.

Me: Would it be OK to look at me for a moment, and take some time to pay attention to your breathing rather than the memory?

Me: We are here now. We are breathing, and we can either stay with breathing or go back to the memory, or both.

Client: I think I want to talk about my father.

Me: Yep, let's do that, and just take care of your breathing at the same time. Make your breathing just as important as talking about your father.

Do you see the oscillations, the original details, and the associations embedded in this Awareness Phase?

EXAMPLE 2: A DANCE CHOREOGRAPHER

Artist: The piece I want to make is about gender. About when it is defined rigidly and when it is fluid.

Me: Would it be OK to begin by standing here in the studio space and taking a moment to alternate between noticing the space you are in and noticing what is going on in your body?

Artist: I know this space so well, I feel comfortable in it.

Me: Take a moment to just be with that feeling—comfortable.

Artist: I feel safe here. In some spaces, I don't feel safe.

Me: Ah, so the experience of safety may be a part of the dance.

Artist: Yes.

Me: What do you notice when you pay attention inside?

Artist: My feet hurt a bit, and I notice my upper body is swaying slightly.

Me: Let's work from the small hurting and the swaying and the sense of safety in this space. Holding these in your attention, what happens when you say the word gender to yourself, either interiorly or out loud?

Artist: My toes are curling and I feel unstable, like I might fall over.

Me: That's it, just let your body feel all that and see what wants to happen next.

Artist: I want to play with feeling off balance.

Me: Yeah, trust that. See where it takes you just to play with "off balance." Every so often you might want to check in with your feet.

Did you notice the descriptiveness and the postponing of meaning? As a dancer, this person tends to form physical associations in the form of bodily actions.

EXAMPLE 3: A FIRST-GRADE CLASSROOM

Teacher: What do you notice about this letter O you are writing here?

Student: I can't get the beginning and the end to hook up. It keeps being open. Uggh!

Teacher: Yeah, what does the open O remind you of?

Student: It looks kinda like a teapot and all the water could pour out.

Teacher: Oh, cool image. Is there something you would like the O to look like?

Student: My mom and I are reading this book where a snake figured out how to roll down a hill by putting its tail in its mouth.

Teacher: What a cool image! Can you draw that?

Student: There, the snake is munching on its tail.

Teacher: I'll say, and it looks like a perfect O.

Did you notice the reframe from making the letter wrong to making it into a descriptive association? Associations can function as skills bridges.

AN OPEN RECIPE FOR AWARENESS

Conscious Moving is designed fairly loosely in order to embrace lots of different people, situations, and contexts. Trust your own bodily authority in terms of how CM operates for you. The assumption here, and in the next few chapters, is that you will find it and work with it within yourself first. Chapter 16 will be devoted to how it can be applied to working with others.

The following is a recipe that you can try, one that includes the elements spoken about earlier in this section. But first a note of context for this idea of a recipe. A recipe is a guide for making something. In a cooking recipe, if you follow the instructions exactly, you will likely get a nice loaf of banana bread. With more practice, you will start playing with the recipe, adding or substituting ingredients. Further on, you will know how to make banana bread without the recipe because you have internalized it. And even further on, you may find yourself developing recipes for others to try. The following recipe is like that. It is assumed that with practice, you will play with it and make it yours.

In CM, there are two ways to start a session. The first is called the HERE & NOW practice. It involves staying in the present moment with your bodily state, noticing what is happening in any of your senses. You might notice the pressure of your feet as you stand, a gurgling in your belly, or tightness in your throat. The idea is to hold these sensations in your attention, coming back to them whenever you catch yourself in thought or distraction. When you hold your ongoing states with high-quality attention, associations begin to emerge—they could be other sensations, or images, sounds, words, emotions, memories, and so on.

The second way to begin is the THERE & THEN practice. This involves bringing in a topic you want to work on or study. You start by describing the topic to yourself or someone else. It's important not to go on and on in your description of the theme—just a bare description is best. It could be something like "I want to choreograph a dance about gender," or "I'm worried about an upcoming family visit."

BEGINNING WITH EITHER PRACTICE

▶ Take a moment to find a quiet space where you won't be disturbed. Decide where in the space you want to be, and whether you want to start standing, sitting, or lying down (just be careful with lying down— don't do it if you get sleepy and have trouble paying attention).

▶ Decide whether you want to do a HERE & NOW practice or a THERE & THEN practice. Make the call by noting how you are feeling right now, and what circumstances you are in; for instance, "I only have 15 minutes."

HERE & NOW:

▶ Begin by following your breathing for a minute or so. Notice your inhale and exhale. You can play with just observing it the way it is or altering it a bit.

▶ Next, pay attention to the details of your bodily experience. You can oscillate in or out to do this, but the most information will come when your eyes are closed and you are paying attention inside. You can do this systematically, like starting at your toes and checking in to each successive body part up through your head. Or you can do it just by making your focus more panoramic and noticing what sensations stand out. Both strategies have upsides and downsides, so please experiment. Make sure to pay attention to all kinds of sensations— pleasurable, painful, and neutral—without prejudice. Sometimes it can help to put your noticings into words, but sometimes it's better just to be with them wordlessly.

▶ With each sensation you notice, allow your attention to linger, and hold the sensation in your attention without trying to do anything about it. Notice the original details of the sensation. Pay particular attention to sensations that may be a bit novel or intuitively interesting. It may be more intuitively interesting to linger on the tightness in your chest as opposed to the way your clothing feels against the side of your leg. But who knows?

▶ As you do this you might notice that associations emerge—colors, sounds, words, urges to move, feelings, and so on. Braid them in— including them alongside the sensation itself. Example: "I am aware of a tightness in my chest, a bit stronger on the left than on the right. As I pay attention to this, I feel like I want to rotate to the left." Over time you might notice that one sensation, along with its associations, is getting more of your attention. Go ahead and choose this particular experience, taking your time to let things emerge and more associations to show up.

▶ When it feels right, take a moment to acknowledge the experience you had, and take a few moments to oscillate your attention in and out, gradually letting yourself be more out. You can write down details of this experience, or you can relate it to someone. Don't analyze or try to make sense of it.

THERE & THEN:

▶ Begin by identifying a theme. For the purpose of this exercise, it should be short, simple, and not too intense—something on the order of "I lost my keys for a few minutes this morning, and it almost made me late for work."

▶ Take a few conscious breaths to help establish your bodily presence.

▶ Take a few minutes to focus on the details of the theme. You can do this by using words, or wordlessly. Flesh out the memory or theme a bit with small details.

▶ Now, oscillate your attention back and forth between the theme and how your body responds to the theme. You can use words if you'd like, such as "When I recall looking in the closet for my keys, I notice that my hands are making fists, and I hear the sound *ugh!*" Give plenty of airtime to your bodily response to the theme, and to any associations that emerge. Check into parts of your body that you might not normally check into. If you don't notice anything, not noticing anything is the association.

▶ When it feels right, take a moment to acknowledge the experience, and take a few moments to oscillate your attention in and out, gradually letting yourself be more out. You can write down details of this experience, or you can relate it to someone. Don't analyze or try to make sense of it.

Remember, this is not a full CM session, but just how it starts. As we progress in the next few chapters, we will add more to the session until it is complete. The following is a shorthand version of the Awareness Phase, for easy access.

A SHORTENED OPEN RECIPE
FOR THE AWARENESS PHASE

▶ *Begin by tuning in, either to your interior world or the world around you, or a combination.*

▶ *Be deliberate about what posture/position you want to be in.*

▶ *Take some time to just noodle around with your attention until you find some experience/sensation you want to focus on.*

▶ *Turn your attention in a concentrated way to this sensation, and come back to it when your attention wanders.*

▶ *Notice the details of this experience, without commentary. Just be with it as it is.*

▶ *Notice if any words, images, memories, other sensations, movements, or emotions come up as a result of this open concentration, and welcome them. Be particularly attentive to any micromovements that might be present. Just be with them.*

▶ *End the exercise when it feels organic to do so. You can take a few minutes to move around, draw, or write if that feels right.*

In general, the Awareness Phase is about waking up to more than what you were paying attention to before and using these new elements to consciously move so that your bodily experiences give you the resources to learn, grow, make art, and lead a reflective life. In the next chapter we see how working with sensations and associations naturally facilitates movement impulses to emerge and be supported. These movement impulses carry their own associations and enhance our ability to respond to what we sense and feel, which in turn helps us understand what we want to do with what we experience, and how our experiences generate our body stories.

References

Albahari, Miri. 2009. "Witness Consciousness: Its Definition, Appearance and Reality," *Journal of Consciousness Studies* 16(1): 62–84.

Behnke, Elizabeth. 1997. "Ghost Gestures: Phenomenological Investigations of Bodily Micromovements and Their Intercorporeal Implications." *Human Studies* 20, no. 2 (April): 181–201.

Caldwell, Christine. 1996. *Getting Our Bodies Back: Recovery, Healing, and Transformation through Body-Centered Psychotherapy*. Boulder, CO: Shambhala.

———. 2016. "Body Identity Development: Definitions and Discussions." *Body, Movement and Dance in Psychotherapy*, 11(4): 220–34. https://doi.org/10.1080/17432979.2016.1145141.

———. 2019. "Micromovements: Filling Out the Movement Continuum in Clinical Practice." In *The Routledge International Handbook of Embodied Perspectives in Psychotherapy: Approaches from Dance Movement and Body Psychotherapies*, edited by Helen Payne, Sabine Koch, Jennifer Tantia, and Thomas Fuchs. New York: Routledge.

Csikszentmihalyi, Mihaly. 1996. *Creativity: Flow and the Psychology of Discovery and Invention*. New York: Harper.

———. 2008. *Flow: The Psychology of Optimal Experience*. New York: Harper.

Deikman, Arthur J. 1982. *The Observing Self: Mysticism and Psychotherapy*. Boston: Beacon Press.

Ekman, Paul. 1997. *Emotions Revealed: Recognizing Faces and Feelings to Improve Communication and Emotional Life*. New York: Holt.

Epstein, Mark D. 1984. "On the Neglect of Evenly Suspended Attention." *Journal of Transpersonal Psychology* 16(2): 193–205.

Freud, Anna. 1963. "The Concept of Developmental Lines." *Psychoanalytic Study of the Child* 18(1): 245–66.

Hartley, Linda. 1995. *Wisdom of the Body Moving: An Introduction to Body-Mind Centering*. Berkeley: North Atlantic Books.

Kolb, David. 2014. *Experiential Learning: Experience as the Source of Learning and Development*. Upper Saddle River, NJ: Pearson Education.

Ruff, Holly Alliger, and Mary Klevjord Rothbart. 1996. *Attention in Early Development: Themes and Variations*. New York: Oxford University Press.

van der Veer, Rene, and Jaan Valsiner, eds. 1994. *The Vygotsky Reader*. Cambridge, MA: Basil Blackwell.

Weiss, Halko, Greg Johanson, and Lorena Monda. 2015. *Hakomi Mindfulness-Centered Somatic Psychotherapy: A Comprehensive Guide to Theory and Practice*. New York: W. W. Norton.

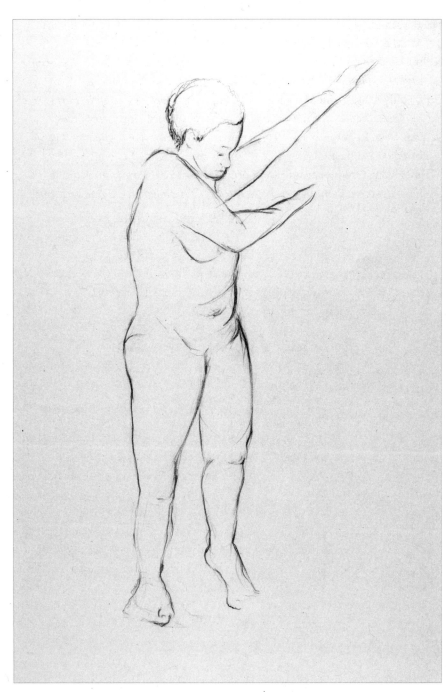

Drawing by Page Zekonis, 2023

3

The Owning Phase of Conscious Moving

Some twenty years ago, my husband and I learned to canoe. Because we live in the Rocky Mountains, that meant whitewater canoeing—paddling down rivers. Whitewater canoes, because they are built to navigate churning, fast-moving water, are designed to turn on a dime, requiring the people paddling them to lean both their bodies and the canoe into the very waves that they instinctively want to recoil from. Needless to say, within a few minutes of my husband and me trying this out, we flipped over and took a swim, learning experientially one of the main principles of couples therapy—no matter who made the mistake, you both get wet.

Aside from this handy life lesson, learning to canoe has also helped me understand and navigate this next phase of Conscious Moving. One of the most basic instructions in whitewater canoeing is "keep your paddle in the water." You may not be able to do anything about the fact that rocks stud the whole width of the river, causing crazy currents that want to suck you under, but if you keep your paddle in the water, you can do something about your situation. If you work with what you've got, paddling into the best position to take advantage of what the river is already doing, you have the best chance of staying relatively dry and warm. You could even get a thrill out of it! It's not a guarantee—even the most experienced canoers take a swim now and then, even when they haven't made any mistakes and have given it their best. But by paddling during the ride, you ensure that your boat is under power, and being under power gives you a say in the outcomes you get.

We have built a beginning to Conscious Moving by changing how we pay attention and what we pay attention to. Whether we are in a classroom, a studio, a therapy office, or a meditation room, first we pause some aspects of daily life and oscillate our attention within and around us in an open and curious way. We work to suspend meaning-making and critique while we hold and care for our ongoing experiences, allowing richer details and stored associations to emerge. We braid all these aspects of our ongoing experience together while we remain invested in our task, whether it be learning, healing, growing, or creating. We embed ourselves within the present moment, while at the same time, we open up to past experiences as they are evoked.

Organically, what happens next and alongside this concentrative experience is that we start responding. As was mentioned before, humans live in a loop of gathering input and outputting responsive behaviors. This chapter, which unfolds the second phase of CM, articulates the actions that naturally show up as a result of paying high-quality attention to our ongoing experience. The tasks of the Owning Phase revolve around keeping our paddle in the water of ongoing experience. Life requires actions, and actions always involve movement of some kind.

We call this second phase of Conscious Moving the Owning Phase because as experiences emerge and take shape, by moving consciously with them we incorporate them into our sense of self. "I am the one doing this movement. I own this." In this phase, we literally generate a sense of empowerment by claiming our experiences. "I am not only feeling this, but I am also powering my way within it and through it." We don't just observe experiences—we participate with them. By actively participating in what's coming up, we have the potential to ride it out and even shape it for future use. Yes, there are givens in this river, like calm stretches and rocky outcroppings and huge waterfalls. But by keeping our paddle in the water, we can work with our life events to the best of our ability. That is Owning—keeping our paddle in the water. To understand "paddling" from a Conscious Moving standpoint, we can take a more detailed look at movement itself, from the vantage point of several of the principles outlined in Chapter 1.

We noted before that movement lies on a continuum or gradient from fairly fixed to fairly free. At one end we have reflexes, and at the other we have improvisation. Another companion movement continuum involves tiny micromovements inside the body all the way to large locomotions. In general, we are less aware of and less in control of the smaller and more fixed movements we make and more aware of and more in control of larger actions (Rosenbaum 2010). A third movement continuum covers very interior bodily actions, such as the beating of your heart, all the way to the external, communally shared actions across groups of people (think of thirty people all doing the same moves in a line dance at a local bar). These three movement continuums tend to map onto each other so that interior movements are usually smaller and less under conscious control, and larger movements tend to be more deliberate and influenced by others. The Owning Phase is going to deliberately mess with the relationship between all three continuums for creative purposes.

First, let's flesh out a few more details about influence. Large movements and smaller ones influence each other; we could also say they are interdependent.

Fixed motions influence what motions can be freely made and vice versa, and interior actions influence and are influenced by more external public ones. Imagine a vigorous wave of your arm as you unexpectedly see a friend across the street. That large, voluntary motion will stimulate several muscle groups to stabilize your trunk so that your waving doesn't cause you to fall over. Your small core muscles are "waving" just as much as your arm is. Each end of a movement continuum is interdependent within itself and interdependent with the other two. It's this interdependence that we will leverage in order to move more consciously.

It might be useful for you to put down the book, or turn off the recording, and simply play a bit with these three movement continuums. Let yourself investigate large to small, in your whole body, or in one part. Just notice what associations or judgments might arise. Does it feel freeing to get big, or perhaps a bit scary? Does getting small bring up images of a child huddling in a corner, or curling up to take a nap in the sun? Playing with more fixed motions can be tricky as by definition you are not in control of your reflexes, but you can approximate them by doing actions like shivering, blinking, or deliberately unbalancing yourself so postural reflexes get activated. Notice how you feel. What associations come up? Then go to the other end of this continuum, and move as freely as possible, working to not be able to predict what will happen. Lastly, oscillate your attention to the inside of your body, and just be with some small movement you notice there, like your heartbeat, or a tension in your shoulder. Alternate that with some moves that are very visible. Do images or sounds or colors or memories or emotions arise anywhere along that continuum? Just greet them, welcome them, and work to not interpret, analyze, or explain them.

Body Oscillations and Attunements

We have talked about body oscillations before—heartbeat, breathing, and peristalsis. Here we will add just a bit more detail. Moving back and forth can often be interior, small, and fixed. Our metabolism uses lots of different oscillations. If we skate across the movement continuum to more spontaneous movement, we can also see oscillations, which are usually deliberate and shared with others, often as a way to feel connected to others or to some larger event. Melissa Walker, in Chapter 10, calls this *embodied somatic resonance* and uses it to work with couples in therapy. At this end of the movement continuum, oscillating often goes by the name of *rhythmic movement*. If a piece of music has a rhythm to it, we almost can't help moving in time with it. We create dances where everyone makes the same moves, loving the feeling of turning, stomping, and clapping in unison.

Rhythm bands together related parts (or people) into a unified whole (H'Doubler 1946). To see a powerful example of this, go to YouTube and look for the Balinese trance dance called Kecak. Here you can even see the blurring of individuality as a single group movement takes over.

We can move to feel more separate and also to feel more connected, a crucial oscillation in any social species. Embedded within this oscillation lives the concept of attunement. Technically, attunement involves harmonizing with someone or something else. From a psychological perspective, attunement occurs when we allow our internal state to shift as we resonate with the inner world of another person (Wallin 2007). Attunement forms the basis of empathy because of this. How that operates involves allowing our movement to be influenced by the movement of someone else. Often this process is quite unconscious and can involve harmonizing with another's micromovements, movements that can barely be observed but are nonetheless responded to in a way that helps the other person feel that "You get me" (Westland 2015).

In developmental psychology, attunement creates the foundation for attachment. All infants need to form a secure physical and emotional attachment to their caregivers, and the formation of this attachment occurs via nonverbal exchanges between the infant and their loved ones. Decades ago, when psychologists began to analyze films of mother-infant interactions frame by frame, these wordless exchanges became quite visible (Schore 2012). In a secure attachment scenario, the mom waits for her baby to do something (like look at her or purse their lips) and then she responds sensitively and often playfully, often doing some version of what the baby had done. It's not necessary that the parent's actions be the same as the baby's, only that they are harmonizing with the baby's actions. In repeated acts of attunement, the baby feels secure. The caregivers in these filmed interactions were not instructed to attune and were not consciously aware that they were doing it. That's how deep down this behavior is.

Attunement lies at the connecting end of the oscillation between closeness and separation. We can also see it as related to the oscillation between immersion and reflection. I immerse in another's experience, and then I take a step back and notice what I feel and I think. In body-to-body attunement, my movement is not just my own but is shared with others and influenced by rhythms around me. Both personal and shared movements are required for a secure relationship. Attunement tends to be seen as a person with a person, but there is no reason not to see it as an act you can do on your own, attuning, for instance, to your own heartbeat. Or to your dog. Attunement also manifests in our relationship with the world. We have all felt transported by a sunset, an amazing work of art, or a sense of our embeddedness in the cosmos. We can appreciate that the oscillation between closeness and separation necessitates movement all the way from micromovements to large public events. With that, let's turn back to the Owning Phase.

Body Narratives

In the Owning Phase, we are not trying to expand our movement repertoire. More is not better. We are instead investigating where our stories lie and how we can own them by moving with and powering through them. Different locations on any of the three movement continuums hold what I call *body narratives*, movement sequences that literally enact our relationship to present and past events (Caldwell 2016). Body narratives awaken when we pay attention to the associations we have within our experiences. When we carefully attend to a constriction in our chest, and as a result we notice fear coming up and we hear the word *No!*, these associations begin to surface the elements of a story the body wants to tell, a story that is wordless and narrated through emerging actions. At this point we are speaking our first and most native language, body language (Knapp and Hall 2006). Infants of any species that involves parental care must use their bodies to communicate what care they need and when. An attuned caregiver, whether it's a chimp mother or an elephant father or a human grandmother, reads their infant's body to know when to feed, to cuddle, to play, and when to give some space. In the Owning Phase, we are going back to that original language of cries, waving hands, tension and relaxation, and looks on the face, not as a way to regress, but as a way to include more. We don't just go into our thoughts to find stories because some of our most meaningful and powerful stories imbed themselves along our movement continuums and in our earliest nonverbal experiences. We are, at our roots, physical storytellers, moving and being moved by all that we experience.

The events of our lives leave physical traces, not just in our thoughts and attitudes but also in our posture, our breath patterns, our gestures, and in mundane actions like reaching for a glass of water. As we reach for that glass, we are in the present moment with our thirst, and we are also enacting and re-membering our long history of reaching. The point here is that our bodies are not telling the truth of what happened before. They are telling stories about memories of what happened with longstanding perspectives, biases, cultural influences, and social constraints (Koch et al. 2012). Neuroscientists are fond of informing us that all memory is a reconstruction; that the act of remembering something is an act of changing that memory (Squire and Schacter 2002). This is because when we commit something to memory, we also absorb the context in which that event occurred. If I was tired and hungry when my dad shouted at me, I remember the event somewhat differently than if I was feeling energetic and playful. Tired and hungry will, for me, be associated with fathers and shouting so that I have a tendency to think of him when I am tired or hungry, or when I think of him, I feel a bit tired.

When we re-member (bring an event back through the body, the "member"), the memory alters slightly because the original details have changed. My body has changed. If I remember my father when I am not hungry and feeling energized, I will also shift my memory of him slightly. Psychotherapy leverages this process deliberately. If I was abused as a child by a shouting father who would trap me in a corner, an attuned psychotherapist would sense that a calmer, quieter voice, and a chair next to the door or an open window would support me to remember something traumatizing and not be overwhelmed by it because the circumstances are now different. It doesn't make a difference for the therapist to say, "You are safe now."—the body needs to know that experientially by *being* in different and safer circumstances. Only then are our body stories able to emerge and express themselves.

Let's start with the Awareness Phase, where we begin to pay high-quality attention to what is going on, just for the sake of being with it. By opening up to more physical details about our inner and outer world, we begin to experience associations. I might notice that my shoulders are tight. I listen to that sensation and notice that there is also a sensation of heat there. I stay with the tension and the heat. I notice that my upper chest seems to want to go down. I explore that and as my chest goes down I start to feel sadness. If I stay with my chest, I feel the sadness, but if I bring my attention back to my shoulders I notice the tension in them wants to pull my chest back up. I deliberately pull my chest back up and the sadness diminishes. As I notice that, I hear a male voice in my head saying, "Buck up!" I have a memory that my father used to get mad at me for crying when I was a child. I stay with that memory and begin to alternate between pulling my chest up and letting it drop down, between feeling and taking away the sadness. For no discernible reason, my chest now starts to arch back, causing my head to tip back. I take a big breath there. Without trying to control or explain the movement, I arch back deliberately, and then my hand seems to be going to my chest as I rotate to the side and come back to my chest falling forward. I rest here for a bit, and then the sequence starts again, shoulders tensing, back arching, breath, torso rotating as the hand goes to the chest, and I come back to the center.

As I feel complete with the experience for now, I notice I feel lighter and a bit more energized. I don't feel so sad or so tense. One way to understand this event is that by supporting small impulses to move consciously, I can access states just outside that old pattern of tension and sadness. I kept my paddle in the water and was able to work with it and through it, not getting pulled into it in what Freud might have called a "repetition compulsion." On a pragmatic level, I began with awareness and attention, this stimulated responsive movement impulses and associations, and I trusted them and consciously *inhabited them from within* (Behnke 2018), helping them transition from a well-worn movement habit to a full sequence of movements that incorporated and then went beyond the body memory, becoming a body narrative that was enacted in present-moment circumstances with present-moment resources. I paddled through the experience consciously and got a different result.

The process looks a bit like this:

▶ Body experienced as is

▶ More original detail and associations

▶ Responsive movement impulses

▶ Movement sequences

▶ Body narratives

Body narratives are not reenactments of what happened before. They don't mimic. We can't use them to determine definitively who did what to whom. They unfold as creative renderings of how we live with and ultimately shape the events of our lives. They reflect what we learned from events and how we have come to organize our lives because of them. Similar to a movie that tells a certain story, body narratives are inspired by true events.

Unconsciously repeated and reinforced body narratives reduce our choices. They lock us into stereotyped ways of moving in response to life events and more black-and-white explanations of events. These stereotyped actions in turn generate bodily predispositions toward certain emotions and thoughts. We start quite literally doing the same thing over and over again while expecting different results. Ultimately, when we are captured by old body narratives, we lessen our capacity for learning, creating, and reflecting. Because we respond more automatically, we don't feel that we are under power during challenging circumstances; we feel more helpless, more powerless, less creative, and less curious.

The answer to an ingrained habit of moving through the world is not to attempt to stop doing it, or to do the opposite. If I am caught in a pattern of tension and collapse, I don't just muscle myself into raising and expanding my chest and pushing my shoulders down. That's just another forced action, and it disrespects the events and circumstances that laid down that pattern. Conscious Moving begins with exploring the details of the movement habit. We have a body story to tell, and the body habit is holding onto that story until we are ready to work with it consciously. So we inhabit the pattern consciously and deliberately. We respect it by listening to what it is doing and where it wants to go. What Owning does is shift "my shoulders are tight" into "I am tightening my shoulders." This active tightening puts our paddle in the water.

The tightening in my shoulders represents something my shoulders want to talk about. I don't have to translate that tightening into a verbal explanation. The tightening is a legitimate act of physical storytelling. If I listen by doing (rather than listening by thinking), the doing of the tensing brings up associations and movement impulses that allow the story to emerge and shape itself into a coherent action or sequence. That action, because it deeply attunes to the original detail of my experience, generates a sense of "Ah, there I am," which in turn creates a sense of self-coherency and a sense of secure attachment, in this case, an attachment to my own bodily integrity and my own bodily authority. I now have an increased capacity for learning, healing, reflecting, and creating.

Body narratives tend to show up as various movement impulses, seemingly random actions that come through the body in a jumble, similar to associations. When I followed my chest's urge to collapse, I had an image of a baby come up, and my hand started to clasp as I did it. I know that instead of trying to come up with an explanation for the image and the action, I simply welcome the baby and the clasping and braid them into what I am already doing. It may be helpful to bring in a bit of neuroscience to better understand the processes going on at this point.

Most of us know that our brains have two sides, or hemispheres. The left hemisphere specializes in the three L's—linearity, literalness, and logic. The left hemisphere likes to order things into sequences so that it has a sense of what happened first, second, and third, giving us a sense of past, present, and future. It also uses words and thoughts to make the world predictable and logical. It puts a time stamp on events and creates explanations for them that help the world make sense. On the other side, the right hemisphere holds no time stamp. As far as it is concerned, everything it is processing is happening right now so that an emotional memory feels exactly the same as an emotion arising from current conditions. It specializes in organizing our bodily actions and emotions. It works with images and sounds and sensations more than words. The right hemisphere immerses and feels. Both modes of processing, left and right, ideally work together to help us lead a balanced life (Lambert and Kinsley 2005).

Our modern, industrialized lives have a tendency to work well when our left hemisphere becomes more dominant. Certainly many tasks require left hemisphere dominance, such as creating a grocery list. Some experiences are best given to the right hemisphere, however; experiences such as sex and play and feeling one's feelings. In left hemisphere dominance, we memorize a line of poetry, and in right hemisphere dominance, we are moved emotionally by that line of poetry. A good life balances both. You would think that making a decision would be the left hemisphere's job, but studies have shown that we also need the right hemisphere to let us know how we feel about something in order to make good decisions. Neuroscience shows us that unbalancing the left and right hemispheres for very long can result in stress and illness (Siegel 2007). In excessive and sustained left hemisphere dominance, we tend to become detached from our feelings, rigid in our thinking, and isolated from the messy connectivity of relationships. In excessive right hemisphere dominance, we tend to get depressed and feel less in control of our lives. The answer to this imbalance is oscillation.

Oscillating between left and right hemisphere dominance—what we have been calling immersion and reflection—seems to unlock multiple resources for creativity, learning, healing, and contemplative practice. In the Owning Phase of CM we are in a slightly altered state of consciousness, which allows associations to bubble up and previously suppressed material to be welcomed. This altered consciousness and open attention stimulate the right hemisphere to become temporarily more dominant by removing left hemisphere chatter and time stamps. We are more in the here and now, the playground of the right hemisphere. We are foregrounding bodily states, another playground of the right hemisphere. This right-side dominance surfaces movement impulses—seemingly random, short, and fairly simple actions—as a way to begin processing our experiences. We don't want them to make sense yet because we don't want the left hemisphere to bully the right hemisphere with its need to explain and compartmentalize.

The work of the Owning Phase has to do with supporting movement impulses so that they gradually self-organize into movement sequences. They become more ordered and coherent because we have created the conditions for the left hemisphere to work with the right hemisphere in a cooperative and respectful way. Movement impulses, like tensing shoulders and slightly collapsing the chest, morph into a spiral that rotates the torso. A coherent sequence self-organizes into a body narrative, a body story that emerges from the right hemisphere and is supported and made sensible by the left hemisphere in a cooperative dance. This body narrative possesses its own aesthetic; it often feels and looks graceful. This cooperation between left and right accesses body-centered resources, while also shaping the experience into a beginning, middle, and end. By finding an organic ending, one that has given voice to buried or unprocessed material by telling its story, I move with and through this sequence, can experience a satisfying sense of completion, and can then let go and move on. How the experience has moved me puts me in a position where I can then shape it for further use in my learning, my art-making, my contemplative life, and my healing.

Working with Overwhelming Experiences

The previous paragraphs described a simple and somewhat idealized process. What does it look like when things get sticky? What happens when the associations that emerge are scary, overwhelming, or traumatizing? Not all movement sequences are easy or immediately workable; some can arise like demons or ghosts. Or, we can find ourselves experiencing something that is so novel or strange that we just don't have the wherewithal to work with it. A short answer to this problem is to have someone there who can support and guide us. This is who therapists and mentors and teachers are. If we could do it ourselves, we would have. Some experiences are bigger than we are and need more than one person to hold them. In an attuned and secure relationship with someone, we can rest into the support of folks who have been there before. We will look into this companionship in more detail in Part III, but now we will unpack the details of the Owning Phase when things get sticky.

The first time I encountered a class-three rapid while canoeing, I froze, with my paddle in the air.* I think my husband might have yelled for me to do a specific stroke so we could negotiate it as a team, but I'm just not sure because I was shocked into insensibility. As we got buffeted around, I recovered and at least got my paddle in the water to do some kind of stroke. Miraculously, we got through it, likely from a combination of dumb luck and my husband keeping his paddle in the water for both of us. This moment holds interest as an Owning Phase metaphor because months later, with practice, I was going through class-three rapids like a champ. What had been a Holy Shit! experience had become a thrilling ride. What are our guides and practices for paddling through the Owning Phase? Again, we turn to principles like oscillations and balancing.

---

* A class-three rapid features waves up to four or five feet tall that will crash over the bow of the boat.

This first practice I thought I had invented myself, but then I looked around and realized a lot of different folks had already been using it. I call it *entering and relieving*. This practice relates to the oscillation of immersion and reflection we worked with in the Awareness Phase. The first reference I can find to it is over two thousand years old and comes from Buddhist psychology. There it is called *touch and go*. The idea is that some emerging experiences need to be approached and "touched" with care and in small doses. If I am caught up in an overwhelming fear (like my first class-three rapid), the fear takes over and drives my behavior down the movement continuum to the fixed area of reflexes (in my case a freeze reflex), where I am not able to work with what is in front of me. This happens any time there is a substantial gap between what I know how to do and what I need to do; as Vygotsky would say, I am outside my Zone of Proximal Development. In education this might look like being given a test for which I have not studied, involving concepts I just don't get (the ingredients of many classic nightmares). In psychotherapy, this happens with clients suffering from trauma. It happens when our worlds fall apart, or when demands far exceed the resources we have to deal with them.

Entering and relieving works much the same as touch and go. You step into the difficult experience just a little, work with it as best you can for a bit, then step back out of it and take a rest. You challenge yourself, then you rest, in a back-and-forth oscillation of attention. I remember many years ago working as a psychotherapist with a man who had been brutally traumatized by both his parents as a child and who was at that point both suicidal and homicidal. He once said to me, "Who I am hurts people." His memories were so awful that he would freeze and go blank if he began to remember much of anything about his childhood. Teaching him to breathe, along with other strategies for calming, did not seem to help. At this same time, I found out he was a football fan, rooting for the Denver Broncos. His face would light up when he spoke of watching a game. In subsequent sessions, he would begin to call up a particular childhood memory. When he began to freeze, I would lean forward and gently say, "How 'bout them Broncos?" He would come back, look at me, sigh, and smile. He had entered a bit and had exited the trauma under his own power, going to a place of recovery where he would extoll the virtues of his team for a bit.

This story is a bit odd, as I know of no other therapeutic situation in which sports talk has been employed as a trauma work strategy. But it nicely describes entering and relieving. The key is the deliberateness of it—the conscious movement from one state to another. It was important to work with his memories, especially to share them with someone else, but more importantly, he was, over time, able to be more in control of his state so that he was able to leave it when he needed to and enter it when he felt ready. That attentional muscle—that ability to land your attention on something deliberately and then just as deliberately withdraw attention from it—builds the bones of a home where you can live, the home of your ongoing experiences. You no longer need to be afraid of what is inside you or around you, and what is there can be a source of learning, creativity, and reflection.

In other trauma therapy systems, this practice has different names, but the principle is much the same. Somatic Experiencing (a trauma-based body psychotherapy) calls it *pendulation*, like the swinging back and forth of a pendulum (Levine 2008). Sensorimotor Psychotherapy, another trauma-informed body psychotherapy, calls it *titration* (Ogden and Fisher 2015). The experiences that are worked with are respected and valued, but the real healing comes from the act of practicing—a specific kind of keeping one's paddle in the water—a skill that can be used for lots of subsequent rapids.

This rhythm of immersion and taking a break echoes in education and contemplative practice. Studies have shown that kids who have regular recess at school actually learn more than kids who are kept at their desks (Hannaford 2005). In meditative practices, sitting meditation is often alternated with walking meditation. During month-long retreats the Zen Buddhist monk Thich Nhat Hanh used to have "lazy day" once a week, where doing much of anything useful was frowned upon. In art-making, in problem solving, in decision making, you can feel when your immersive concentration and efforts hit a wall, and the deliberate act of walking away and taking a break actually seems to support nonconscious processes to work with the problem in the background, allowing a fresh perspective when you come back to work (Csikszentmihalyi 1996).

I would add a third activity to the oscillation of work and rest, which might create a spiral of empowerment. The third activity—play—creates a triangle. We oscillate between three elements, work, play, and rest. Unfortunately, modern psychotherapies (with the exception of play therapy) tend to undervalue play as a healing force. Contemplative traditions also underuse this resource. But education and art-making may have more going on here. Both creativity and educational research have demonstrated the power of play to foster intelligence, adaptability, problem solving, and experimentation (Brown and Vaughan 2009). Joana Debelt will go into this triangle of work, play, and rest in Chapter 9.

A solid grounding in a playful childhood helps us to be more socially engaged and relationally savvy (Landreth 2012). We tend to think of play as a childhood pastime, but humans and other animals play throughout their life spans. We could even posit art, sex, and games as forms of adult play. A playful life helps us be nimble, resilient, and adaptive. My client, cited earlier, experienced my "How 'bout them Broncos?" question as a play signal. One of the few times he could be safely playful was when watching a Broncos game and talking about it with me. He was getting a part of his childhood back.

Now a second triangle used in the Owning Phase shows up because it supports a sense of balance within the unbalancing forces of difficult experiences. It has to do with the physicality of Owning. To introduce it, perhaps an exercise would be useful.

Take a moment now to move around a bit, in whatever way works for you. But as you move, hold your breath. Just notice what it is like to move while holding your breath. Now do the opposite—make your body as still as possible, and breathe faster and deeper. Notice what that's like. What associations come up? Now, move around while distracting yourself with thinking about something else, like a problem you are having. Don't track the sensations that occur as you move. Do the same with breathing—put your attention somewhere else while you breathe deeply. These actions are purposefully unbalancing three physical actions that work best when they weave together. Now, just take a minute to do all three together, consciously. Notice the details of your breathing, and notice the details of the small movements that occur as you breathe. If you want, you can move a bit more—like dancing around—just enjoying the feeling of breathing a bit more to balance the increase in moving, and sharpening your senses as a way to keep track of it all.

BALANCING SELF-REGULATION

Figure 2: The Breathing-Moving-Sensing Self-Regulation Triangle

Breathing, moving, and sensing all support one another toward an outcome of well-being. Unbalancing them over time tends to cause distress and ill health. This is because moving (contracting muscles) requires oxygen, yet too much oxygen that doesn't get used up by muscle contraction causes your acid/base balance to unbalance, which in turn causes metabolic stress. And if you don't pay attention to the signals coming from that, you can't make changes to get back into balance. The balanced triangle of breathing, moving/expressing, and sensing/feeling (see Figure 2) can be seen as one of our most fundamental sources of ongoing health, and the source of spare energy that can be used for learning, reflecting, and art-making. Expressing is added to moving to include sounds and words. Feeling associates with sensing because sensations form the ground of emotion.

The *breathing-moving-sensing self-regulation triangle* enters a CM session deliberately and is often used as a means of keeping the Owning Phase workable and productive. Because, when things get sticky, one of the angles in this triangle stops functioning properly. When we enter an experience that is too challenging for our current resources, we disturb our breathing, or we disturb our moving, or we mess up tracking sensations. This destabilization can set off metabolic alarm bells and can actually make us think we are under threat when none is there. Unbalancing this triangle likely sits at the root of many panic attacks. It can nudge you to think you are in the midst of a trauma response, when all that is happening is that you have a habit of holding your breath when things get sticky. With enough practice, we can come back to balance by ourselves, but we often need help from a teacher, a therapist, or a mentor to notice what is going on and get back on the triangle. Feeling balanced within the challenges of a stressful experience enables us to feel that the experience is workable and instructive and points us to a feeling of more wholeness, both hallmarks of a successful Owning Phase.

One of the paradoxical elements of Conscious Moving and many related practices is the commitment to tolerate some uncomfortableness in order to learn, heal, and grow. Calling on the educator Lev Vygotsky, we venture a bit outside our comfort zone in order to gather previously inaccessible resources and skills and then bring them back and integrate them into our sense of self and into our aspirations. This is why the Owning Phase *should* get sticky. We put one foot into the landscape of the less known and the less predictable because the known and the comfortable contain no new resources.

Getting Control of the Gas and the Brake

Most muscles come in pairs. On one side of a bone, like in the upper arm, a muscle contracts to produce an action, like the biceps flexing the arm, and on the other side of the bone, the opposite action occurs, like the triceps extending the arm. In a smooth action, one contracts while the other stretches; one works while the other lets go, a very basic and powerful oscillation. Both actions are required in order to produce many of our movements, especially the bigger ones.

Our movement tends to get clumsy when this pairing gets out of sync. Tension, from this perspective, can be seen as both the flexor and the extensor contracting at the same time, much like having your feet on the gas pedal and brake pedal at the same time. There's work going on, but it's likely not accomplishing much, and, like in cars, it can cause damage if done too often. To drive across town efficiently, we oscillate between our foot on the gas and our foot on the brake. Much the same happens with bodily tension. There are plenty of reasons to hold tension in the body temporarily in order to accomplish a task (like lifting a heavy object or freezing in place), but we want to let go of that pattern of effort as soon as the action is finished. Judith Aston-Linderoth, of Aston Kinetics™, calls this *functional holding*, the tension that lets go when the function is completed. Judith also talks about *structural holding*, tension patterns in the body that are so ingrained that we can't release them (Aston 2019). The stiff neck, the raised shoulders, and the tight lower back are all examples of tension that had to be there for some reason and then became habituated and automatic. The back-and-forth oscillation of contraction and release diminishes, and we get bound up. We chronically overwork in some parts of our bodies (and our lives) while collapsing (underworking) in other parts. We unbalance and become more vulnerable to illnesses, accidents, and upsets. We tend to feel frustrated or powerless because our ability to act effectively diminishes.

Our next Owning Phase oscillation now unfolds. How do we transition from having both feet on both pedals into alternating go and stop, gas and brake? The answer lies in the control of attention and the actions of muscles. The Awareness Phase teaches us to pay attention to the tension and refrain from criticizing or analyzing it. Just be with it and welcome the details of it. This allows associations and responsive movement impulses to show up. The body starts to talk about the tension in a free-associative kind of way. Now, as the Owning Phase appears, we can use deliberate movement to allow the story to be told with increasing levels of active coherency. We do this by consciously tensing, consciously supporting and enacting what we were doing habitually before. Judith Aston-Linderoth calls this *matching*. We match an action we were doing automatically so that now we are Owning it; we are intentionally doing it. Elizabeth Behnke (2018), you might remember, calls this "inhabiting the movement from within." This practice of intentional tensing in order to decrease tension was pioneered in the 1930s by a physician named Edmund Jacobson, who called it *Progressive Relaxation* (1974). The idea was to help the tense person to gain control of the ability to let go by first increasing the muscle contraction and feeling the details of it. In order to take your foot off the brake, you first feel the braking, own the braking by doing it on purpose, and possibly discover its original purpose by listening to the associations that arise. By consciously doing the tension we not only give it a much-needed voice but we create more capacity for letting go.

In this practice we respect the tension and the letting go, allowing that they both carry legitimate voices about our experience. We also leverage entering and relieving by gradually oscillating a bit more into tension, then a bit more into letting go, all the while balancing our breathing, moving, and sensing. What can show up is a movement sequence that embodies a bit more consciousness, a bit more creativity, a bit more information about the details of our lives, and a bit more feeling of empowerment within our lives. It also helps us to drive across town more gracefully.

The alternation processes cited previously expose the organization of the movement centers of the brain. Our brains have many different areas that assemble movement. We have a center in the brain whose only job is to plan complex movements. We have another center that specializes in initiating movements, and another whose job is to inhibit movements (Rosenbaum 2010). Lots of different kinds of movement require not only that certain muscles contract to produce an action, but that other muscles contract to inhibit unrelated actions. Parkinson's disease tends to erode the brain area that inhibits extraneous actions, which is why we see tremors and other unrelated movements in these folks. To move in one way, we need to inhibit other actions that might interfere with that movement. Part of what happens in CM is that we not only pay attention to how we are already moving but also to how we are already inhibiting movement. Part of what makes any movement efficient and easily executed is the coordination of enabling and inhibiting movement.

A more visible analogy might bring in our ideas about decision making. At work, I might get mad at my boss and feel the urge to punch her in the nose. If I suffer from low impulse control, I have trouble deciding not to do that action—it just erupts like a reflex. Inhibiting actions not only makes complex movements more efficient but also enables us to make and stick to decisions. It can be a really good decision to inhibit certain impulses. This inhibition skill is not yet developed in young children, which is why they have tantrums and feel emotions so intensely and unrestrainedly. The course of childhood development gives them practice at controlling some impulses while supporting others. For many of us, this maturational process worked fairly well, and for others the development of this skill has been disturbed or ignored. As adults, we have opportunities to work on these impulses as a means of turning away from actions that harm ourselves or others, while moving into actions that promote healthy relationships and a balanced life. The Owning Phase helps us to consciously inhabit the inhibition of movements as well as their expressive opposites. Given all these Owning Phase elements, let's transition to specific practices that can support Owning and then add Owning into a CM session.

Practices for the Owning Phase

We have already gotten a start on some of these practices. Make sure to adapt them as you know best, and trust that you know how far to take them. If any practice feels like too much, you may want to do it with a friend, a therapist, a teacher, or a mentor. In all these practices, make sure to put yourself in a space that feels comfortable and that allows you to move around a bit.

Practice 1: The Sensorimotor Loop

This practice helps you get a feel for the linkage between gathering information and acting on it. You can begin with either sensing or moving, but this example begins with sensing. Often an exercise like this begins by turning your senses inward. You can start there, or you can begin by attuning your senses to the outside world.

Let's assume that you are starting inward. Land your attention on some specific sensation. Take a few moments to just rest into the attending, noticing small details and pushing back against thinking about your experience. Notice any associations that arise and welcome them. It may happen that a movement impulse naturally arises as a result of this attention. If so, go with that and support the movement to do what it wants to do. Or, you may want to nudge the process by asking yourself, "What does this sensation want to do? What comes next when this sensation is invited?" Be patient; the answer doesn't always come right away. And watch out for moving in a way that tries to control the sensation, for example, noticing tension and then stretching to relieve it. Any movement that tries to change a sensation comes from trying to manage your experience rather than be with it. To be with it, it's important to find how the sensation actually wants to move you. For instance, noticing a tension and aligning with it require you to support the tension as is. I am tense here, I am tensing here. The tension may actually want you to curl up a bit. For a few more minutes, just experiment with the idea that each sensation is a movement that wants to organize and emerge. Notice the movements that show up may stimulate more associations and different sensations. Play with this idea that sensations are tiny actions, ones that often want to move us in larger ways.

Variations on the theme:

▸ *You can attend first to movement, to start the ball rolling.*

▸ *You can attend outside your body as a way to begin.*

▸ *You can pick a pleasant sensation to work with.*

▸ *You can pick a neutral sensation to work with.*

▸ *You can pick a painful or uncomfortable sensation to work with.*

Practice 2:
Micro- to Macromovement, Interior to Exterior

Take a minute to notice some small, interior movement going on inside. Your heartbeat or your breathing are good places to start, but any movement will do. Now find a way to move with that action in a slightly more full-bodied way. It may be that the movement of your breath gets just a bit bigger, or that you tap your finger on your leg in time with your heartbeat. Gradually play with it, getting more inclusive of more of your body, which will also make it more visible until it takes up as much of your bodily action as you feel comfortable with. At this point, it pretty much becomes a heartbeat dance or an inhaling and exhaling dance. Notice what associations arise. Notice what emotions arise. Is it fun to dance in this way? Is it a bit scary to be this visible? Take it back down to the original, interior movement, and notice the possibly changed details of that.

Practice 3:
Attunement—Closeness and Separation

This exercise can be done by yourself or with someone else. If you do it by yourself, you'll want to find something in the room to attune with: something alive, like a plant; or something moving, like curtains wafting in the breeze at your window or music. You can also do this with a pet, or with a friend. Babies can be especially helpful partners in this exercise.

Begin by taking some time to observe this other thing or action or being. Notice the details of it without commentary. When you're ready, begin to take on aspects you have noticed about the other. It may be their shape, or their rhythms of movement, or some action they are doing. You don't have to do the same thing, but it might be a way to start. The idea is to be in your body in a way that is a bit more plant-like, dog-like, roommate-like, or six-month-old niece-like. If the object or being is moving, be with the movement in a way that your body feels good about. Just be with it and move with it in a way that feels like you are more together.

Then take a bit of time to step back from this togetherness, and pay attention just to yourself. Come back to yourself. Notice any small ways you may feel different because of your attuned interaction, and just hold them in your attention, and move with those differences so that you feel like yourself. Then you may want to observe the other and just notice any small natural oscillations of closeness and separation from it/them.

Practice 4: Matching

This practice can be done with many different states, but in this case we will explore a tense place.

Begin by purposefully putting tension into your hand, either contract your fingers into a fist, or extend them into an open hand. Now take your other hand and put it onto this hand, shaping it as much as you can around the tense hand. This could look like clasping the tense hand with the same quality of tension, for instance. Just match the shape and the tension as much as you can. Notice what associations come up as you match the tension rather than try to get it to go away. A variation would be to notice or put some tension into your shoulders, and then match as much of the qualities of that as you can, using your hand. It is as if your hand is showing you what your shoulder tension looks and feels like. Notice what associations arise and welcome them. What tends to happen in this practice is that the tension becomes more foregrounded. This is important for your ability to work with it in some way. As a balance, find an area that is relaxed, or get into a relaxed position, and match that letting go process in other parts of your body as much as possible.

Practice 5: Movement Impulses to Body Narratives

Begin this practice with attention to a sensation that feels interesting, one that you want to explore. Attend to the sensation in a way that allows it to move responsively. Welcome this movement impulse and play with it a bit if you want; you're not trying to change it, just be with how it feels. At some point work to follow a movement impulse that interests you, and see where it wants to go. The important thing here is not to assume anything about where it will go or should go. If you can predict where it's going next or if you feel impelled to do some specific movement, pause and listen further. Let the movement itself take the lead—it knows where it wants to go. If you want to give it a bit of encouragement, you can ask, "What does this movement want to do now?" Expect the unexpected. Our emerging right hemisphere body narratives are actually more creative than our left hemisphere comments about what should happen next. This practice might be called "the dance without a dancer"—the body is dancing itself. The dance becomes a non-verbal story, told in motion. Be sensitive to when it feels complete for now, and be with this ending consciously. Notice afterward how you feel and what associations helped support the dance.

Practice 6: Entering and Relieving

In this practice, pick something that is bothering you—please no traumas or intense situations. It could be someone you are irritated with or some small fright that got resolved, like falling off your bike but you were OK afterward. If for some reason something unmanageable shows up, back out of the practice and only try this with someone there to support you.

Begin by picking some mildly upsetting situation you want to work with. Now enter this by remembering it and finding small descriptive details of it. Work to step away from the rabbit hole of blame by saying to yourself, "Now I notice I am blaming." See what associations as well as what movement impulses come up. Now, deliberately exit this process, and notice something different, something pleasant or aesthetically pleasing. It could be looking at the tree outside your window, or at a framed photo of a loved one. Or it could be the steady rise and fall of your breathing. Rest there for a bit. If you want to, oscillate into and out of this entering and relieving. It's not about resolving the issue particularly; it's about toning the muscle of your attention so that it can enter and exit states under your own power.

Practice 7: The Triangle of Work-Play-Rest

This practice doesn't need a special time or place, and in fact it can best be done in the midst of your day. It simply involves consciously moving between phases of work, of play, and of rest. They don't have to be in perfect thirds. In fact, during a workday, the work angle can be more prominent. At the end of the evening, rest becomes more foregrounded. It can be as simple as pausing to tell a joke in the break room, or stepping back from your desk every hour and stretching and breathing. The play angle can look quite different for different people; for some, it's playing cards, sports, or music. My only caution would be not to count anything on your phone or laptop as playing or resting. By moving easily between all three phases, each one can be more effective. By valuing each angle of this triangle, we support a balanced life.

Practice 8:
The Triangle of Breathing-Moving-Sensing

We got a start on this last exercise within Chapter 2. The idea is to strengthen our ability to stay in balance with these three angles because they need each other for ongoing support, and because their imbalance constitutes dissociation—exiting the present moment and not being able to keep your paddle in the water. One of the best ways to exercise the ability to balance the three is to unbalance them deliberately, and then find your way back to balance under power. Doing this deliberately strengthens the muscle of attention, but it also strengthens the literal muscles of turning into and away from different movements. In the deliberate unbalancing version of this practice, we consciously hold back one element— breathing, moving, or sensing—and study what happens when we do. We then reintroduce that angle and study what happens when the balance returns. Deliberate unbalancing happens naturally at times and presents no problems. What we are working with here are habituated or predictable exits from balance that we do unconsciously, automatically, and habitually, habits that interfere with our well-being, our learning, and our creativity.

Tune into bodily movements going on right now. They could be big or small. It could be that you are walking to work. Be awake to the sensations of moving and breathing as you go. Just notice how they relate to one another and enjoy that experience. Put your attention to it carefully and with ease. Consciously practice their interwoven relationships as you go so that it becomes more familiar and easier.

....

PUTTING AN OWNING PHASE TOGETHER:
PRACTICE EXAMPLES AND AN OPEN RECIPE

We can now apply Owning Phase concepts and standalone practices into distinct areas of daily life. How does taking ownership of the depth and breadth of bodily experience translate into specific domains? The following examples are generalized and collapsed a bit for brevity and privacy.

PRACTICE EXAMPLE I: IN A CLASSROOM

In a third-grade classroom, the teacher brings out large pieces of paper, each one large enough for a student to lie down on. Students pair up, and while one lies flat on the paper, the other draws an outline around the edges of their body. Now each student has a large page with an outline of their body on it. With a number of crayons and markers, the teacher begins the lesson by showing the class images of the interior structures of the body—bones, organs, muscles—and asking each student to draw that structure where it belongs inside their outline. The teacher gives examples of what several structures do, and asks the students to give a voice to that structure, either verbally or by writing it on paper. It could sound like "I am Keisha's lungs. I inhale and exhale. I bring air into her and let it back out. That's good for all the parts of my body." As an ending, all the students do a breathing exercise together where they feel their inhale and exhale. In a fifth-grade classroom, perhaps some details about oxygen and carbon dioxide could be added.

In this example, learning is embodied. The lungs are not just out there in a book and you have to memorize where they are and their functions. You have lungs, they do these things in your body, and they support you to run and do lots of other things. You give them a voice and listen to that voice.

PRACTICE EXAMPLE 2: IN A THERAPY ROOM

The session begins as the client talks about their grief from their beloved old dog dying a few weeks ago.

Therapist: As a way to just be with the sadness, would it be OK to take a minute and notice how that feeling lives in your body?

Client: I notice the tears, and my eyes are squeezing to hold them back, and I notice a tightness in my jaw.

Therapist: OK, just stay with those sensations as they are for a bit, and let's see what happens.

Client: (pausing for a few moments): I feel both the urge to cry—just wail—but I'm embarrassed to do that in front of you.

Therapist: So, part of you wants to cry and part of you wants to hold back the crying?

Client: Yes.

Therapist: And you have this feeling but don't want to show the feeling?

Client: Well, a little bit of feeling is OK, but a lot of feeling is not OK.

Therapist: Would it be OK to repeat that statement and see what comes up as you say it?

Client: "A little bit of feeling is OK, but a lot of feeling isn't OK." Oh. When I say that, I hear my older brother's voice. He would tell me all the time not to be such a baby.

Therapist: Yeah, just take a minute with that memory and see if there is anything that your body wants to do with it.

Client: (Her jaw tightens visibly, her hands grip at her sides, and her brow furrows.)

Therapist: That's it, just be with what your hands and your face want to do. It could be a little, or a lot. Get a feeling from your hands and your face exactly what the volume of the feeling wants to be, right now.

Client: (Her fists shake a bit, and she makes a low growl.)

Therapist: Keep breathing as you do that.

Client: (takes several audible breaths while growling and shaking her fists)

Therapist: Would it be OK to look at me while you growl and make a fist?

Client: (takes a few quick glances at the therapist while shaking her fists)

Therapist: (leans forward slightly and says "yeah" quietly a few times, while fisting her hands quietly in her lap)

Client (dropping her hands and relaxing her face, takes a big breath and lets it out on a sigh): It was hard to look at you.

Therapist: Yeah, I bet. I appreciate your willingness to try that. It wasn't easy.

In this therapy example can you pick out the moments of attunement and the work to stay on the breathing-moving-sensing triangle? The session also could have gone in another direction, where client and therapist played with entering the grief and finding ways to relieve it. At the time it seemed more figural to take ownership of the empowerment encased in the patterns of tension. Could you also see the simultaneous gas and brake, and then the foregrounding of the brake as a way to separate the actions of crying and holding back tears? This turns a stuck simultaneity into a sequence, which then generates the ability to get somewhere. Also present was the practice of doing something slightly uncomfortable (looking at the therapist) as a way to carefully lessen the grip of an old body memory of looking away as a way to lessen the upset at a bossy and rude older brother.

PRACTICE EXAMPLE 3: WHILE READING A CONTEMPLATIVE BOOK

This is a report from a friend who was reading a book by Thomas Merton, a Christian contemplative philosopher, while sitting on the couch during a snowy day.

Every few paragraphs I would have to put the book down and gaze out the window at the snow. What Merton was saying was so powerful that I would have to take some time to digest it before reading on. He was talking about God as a quiet presence, a presence that you could distract yourself from or open up to. There were moments, looking out at the snow, where I could feel this presence very distinctly. Sometimes it made me want to cry because it felt so overwhelming, and at others it just felt so simple and easy. At one point I realized that I had forgotten to eat lunch, and when I sat down to my sandwich I realized that God was a quiet presence inside me as well, in my hungry belly as well as in the act of eating the sandwich. It later struck me that a good definition of prayer would be this opening up to the presence of God in these ordinary moments.

This short email poetically describes an immersive experience in multiple acts of owning. They (their pronoun) deliberately oscillated by entering and relieving the act of reading, creating a workable rhythm that enhanced the experience by shaping it to be both a mental and a sensory act. It became an immersion and then a reflection, according to inner-felt dictates. It both challenged and soothed them. It opened up learning and a kind of aesthetic participation with immediate experience that might be said to be full of grace.

OPEN RECIPE FOR AN AWARENESS AND OWNING PHASE

As in the previous chapter, the recipe that follows can be engaged with as is, or played with in minor or major alterations. Be aware that it is only going to coach the Awareness and Owning phases, so it might leave you hanging a bit at the end. Do what feels right to complete the experience.

- ▶ *Begin by tuning in, either to your interior world or the world around you, or a combination of both.*
- ▶ *Be deliberate about what posture/position you want to be in.*

- ▶ *Take some time to noodle around with your attention until you find some experience/sensation you want to focus on.*
- ▶ *Turn your attention in a concentrated way to this sensation, and gently come back to it when your attention wanders.*
- ▶ *Notice the details of this experience, without commentary. Just be with it as it is.*
- ▶ *Notice if any words, images, memories, other sensations, movements, or emotions come up, and welcome them into your focus of attention.*
- ▶ *Focus on how this experience and the attending associations want to express themselves. How might you already be moving with this experience? It could be a small gesture or a face you are making. It could be a sound that comes up, or it could be a feeling of tension somewhere. Try not to make anything up or assume how your body would want to move. Be patient, and wait for the movement to arise organically. Be alert to the tiniest of movements—they are often the most relevant ones. Support them to happen as they are, and if you notice yourself trying to control or shape them, just go back to being with your experience.*
- ▶ *If you want to nudge it, ask yourself what this experience wants to do right now.*
- ▶ *As you focus on moving, pay attention to how your breathing and your sensing support that. If you notice one element falling away, take a moment to reestablish it consciously.*
- ▶ *Allow the movement to keep going where it wants to go and surfacing new associations.*
- ▶ *Notice the sequence of events that accompany the moving. You could even support this by asking, "Where does this want to go next?" It may help to repeat any sequences that develop so that they can be tweaked or refined.*
- ▶ *If any disturbing or challenging associations come up, practice entering and relieving—touch into the power of the association, then rest away from it, attending to and doing something else. Your body will start moving back into the immersion when and if it's ready.*
- ▶ *Trust when it feels complete for now.*
- ▶ *Take some time to breathe, notice both inside and around you, and perhaps wiggle around a bit. How can you use the triangle to enter back into ordinary life?*
- ▶ *If it feels interesting, take a few minutes to draw, write, sculpt, or something similar about the exercise.*

References

Aston, Judith. 2019. *Aston Postural Assessment: A New Paradigm for Evaluating Body Patterns*. Edinburgh: Handspring Publishers.

Behnke, Elizabeth. 2018. "On the Transformation of the Time-Drenched Body: Kinaesthetic Capability Consciousness and Recalcitrant Holding Patterns." *Journal of Consciousness Studies* 25(7–8): 80–111.

Brown, Stuart, and Christopher Vaughan. 2009. *Play: How It Shapes the Brain, Opens the Imagination, and Invigorates the Soul*. New York: Penguin Books.

Caldwell, Christine. 2016. "Body Identity Development: Definitions and Discussions." *Body, Movement and Dance in Psychotherapy* 11(4): 220–34. https://doi.org/10.1080/17432979.2016.1145141.

Csikszentmihalyi, Mihaly. 1996. *Creativity: Flow and the Psychology of Discovery and Invention*. New York: Harper.

Hannaford, Carla. 2005. *Smart Moves: Why Learning Is Not All in Your Head*. Arlington, VA. Great Ocean Publishers.

H'Doubler, Margaret N. 1946. *Movement and Its Rhythmic Structure*. Madison WI: Kramar Business Service.

Jacobson, Edmund. 1974. *Progressive Relaxation: A Physiological and Clinical Investigation of Muscular States and Their Significance in Psychology and Medical Practice*. Chicago: University of Chicago Press.

Knapp, Mark L., and Judith A. Hall. 2006. *Nonverbal Communication in Human Interaction*. Belmont, CA: Thompson Wadsworth.

Koch, Sabine, Thomas Fuchs, Michela Summa, and Cornelia Muller, Eds. 2012. *Body Memory, Metaphor, and Movement*. Philadelphia: John Benjamins.

Lambert, Kelly G., and Craig H. Kinsley. 2005. *Clinical Neuroscience*. New York: Worth Publishers.

Landreth, Garry L. 2012. *Play Therapy: The Art of Relationship*. New York: Routledge.

Levine, Peter A. 2008. *Healing Trauma: A Pioneering Program for Restoring the Wisdom of Your Body*. Boulder, CO: Sounds True.

Ogden, Pat, and Janina Fisher. 2015. *Sensorimotor Psychotherapy: Interventions for Trauma and Attachment*. New York: W. W. Norton.

Rosenbaum, David A. 2010. *Human Motor Control*. Amsterdam: Elsevier.

Schore, Allan. 2012. *The Science and Art of Psychotherapy*. New York: W. W. Norton.

Siegel, Daniel J. 2007. *The Mindful Brain: Reflection and Attunement in the Cultivation of Well-Being*. New York: W. W. Norton.

Squire, Larry R., and Daniel L. Schacter. 2002. *Neuropsychology of Memory*. New York: Guilford Press.

Wallin, David J. 2007. *Attachment in Psychotherapy*. New York: Guilford Press.

Westland, Gill. 2015. *Verbal and Non-Verbal Communication in Psychotherapy*. New York: W. W. Norton.

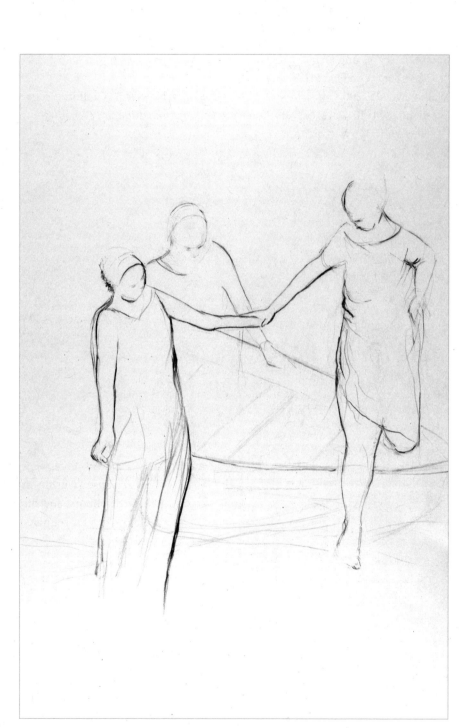

Drawing by Page Zekonis, 2023

4

The Appreciation Phase of Conscious Moving

We can be clear about confusion. It is wild, random energy. We can use that energy. We can convert it into force. We can make it into sense. Writing makes sense. It makes experience into form.

—S. LEONARD RUBINSTEIN, FROM *WRITING: A HABIT OF MIND*

The psychiatrist and author Dan Siegel specializes in how the physiology of the brain, as it processes childhood and ongoing adult experiences, becomes not only more complex but also more integrated (2007). His work posits that our brains not only need lots of neurons in order to grow and be healthy, but also those neurons need to connect to and influence each other by forming a neural network. Early childhood development starts with a profuse overproduction of undifferentiated neurons, and as we grow and interact with the world, these neurons learn to specialize and connect to one another, and connections that are reinforced are strengthened and connections that aren't used will die off (called *pruning*). Our brain's neurons grow toward multiple neighbors, and the more neighbors they connect with, the more options the brain has for sophisticated sensorimotor experiences and actions. Siegel calls this *neural integration* and champions the idea that neural integration lies at the heart of healthy functioning and meaningful relationships (2011). Siegel states that a failure of these neural nets to develop and complexify equates to mental and emotional illness. Neural integration aligns with the saying "It takes a village." It takes a village to raise a child, and it takes multiple neural villages to raise a healthy human.

Elsewhere in the body, we also find integration at play. *Praxis*, the ability to plan and sequence unfamiliar actions, reflects sensory integration. Quite literally, all the different sensations associated with a complex movement must work together to get that movement to happen—what your eyes tell you has to match up to what your ears are sensing, which has to coordinate with your proprioceptive sense of where you are in space and the level of tension in your muscles—when this comes together, you can get the basketball in the hoop (Williamson,

Anzalone, and Hanft 2000). When this sensory integration fails, learning and language disabilities often ensue.

The Appreciation Phase might be seen as a process of integration, metaphorically akin to neural or sensory integration. New experiences have occurred through Awareness and Owning, much like new neurons being produced in the brain, and in order to stick around, these experiences need to integrate with other previous ones, as well as be reinforced by practice or be deliberately allowed to wither. This allows experiences to continue to support a nuanced and enriching quality of life, even in situations of challenge and suffering.

We could also compare this neural and sensory integration metaphor to our sense of self. We might say that knowing who we are is composed of lots of smaller structures, a myriad of continuing experiences that leave their traces in our body memory, some just a whisper and some a shout. These experiences also connect to one another, forming networks of associations that can be recalled through activating any part of the network. These networks may be equivalent to my sense of who I am—I am the person that fell off my bike and broke my arm when I was ten, I am the person who likes to eat chocolate chips out of the bag, and I am the person who has chronically tight shoulders—lots of different experiences network together to compose my identity. My identity is made up of lots and lots of different elements, lots of different selves. Laia Jorba Galdos will write about this in Chapter 7, where she notes the different selves that show up in different social contexts, and that our identities are mapped onto our movement patterns.

One way to work with Conscious Moving (CM) begins by holding multiple and varied experiences because they are all me. Part of me wants to have that doughnut for dessert and part of me doesn't. One part of me wants to stay in this relationship and another part wants to hit the road. By holding and owning both of these wants, by supporting all of my voices without judgment, and by alternating my attention to their voices, my subsequent decision to eat or not to eat the doughnut can include more of who I am. I feel more at choice, more myself. I have strengthened the inhibition of reaching mindlessly for the doughnut. This is what the Appreciation Phase strives for.

In the Owning Phase, we immerse into and rest out of unfolding experiences, stepping into challenging associations and finding out which associations are networked with these experiences. We move within these experiences. In Appreciation we create an increased sense of self-coherency by integrating those experiences consciously and deliberately. By doing that we enable creativity, self-reflection, and learning.

Remember old radio dials, where you would manually turn them and in between stations there would be this scratchy static, and when you landed on a radio station, all of a sudden you were hearing voices, or music? Both the static and the music are radio waves, but in static the waves are jumbled. At the station they are lined up so that they make sense, they become music. Another way to put it is that when we drop into a radio station, incoherent waves become coherent. What was insensible becomes sensible. The potential for information transitions into usable information. One of the definitions of the word *coherent* is "the quality of forming a unified whole." In the Appreciation Phase, we spend some time developing and reinforcing this feeling of a unified whole.

This increased coherency gets its start in the Owning Phase, as movement impulses cohere into body narratives. What remains for the Appreciation Phase to accomplish is to integrate those right-brain–dominant movement coherencies into identity coherencies (Caldwell 2016). We are shaping the experience for use by asking the left and right hemispheres of the brain to begin to work cooperatively with what has emerged and been expressed. We integrate the experiences into our identity, thereby changing our sense of who we are just a little. By other names, this would be called learning, healing, or growing.

Up until now, we have been pushing back against meaning-making as a way to invite in possibilities that exist outside our old way of making sense of things. In the Appreciation Phase of Conscious Moving, we gradually invite new meanings to arrive organically as a result of our embodied experiences. We form new coherencies as a result of dialing into new stations and accessing new music, new news, and new podcasts (to belabor the metaphor a bit). These new meanings take shape as a result of our engagement with our bodily authority. By trusting the physical processes of our bodies as a means of exploring, uncovering, challenging, and playing, we access creativity right here at home. Originality emerges organically from original detail, which then gets supplemented with original responses, which then get networked together into original coherencies. The word *originality* harkens us back to the idea of origins. Originality, one of the synonyms for creativity, brings us back as close to square one as we can get, back where potentialities live.

As a professor for over thirty-five years, I have read and graded my fair share of term papers, master's theses, and doctoral dissertations, a task at times blissful and at other times excruciating. One of the main elements that separate a blissful from an excruciating paper is whether or not it is coherent. Many, many evenings I would find myself scratching my head at what read like a student's stoned rap, only able to discern meaning from occasional words or phrases. This act of not making sense can also be seen in couples or family therapy, where two or more people say things to each other that fundamentally don't make sense to the other. Head scratching ensues. "They don't get me" ensues. One of the most powerful moments in couples therapy is when one partner says something like "I feel invisible to you!" and I might step in and gently ask, "Are you being visible?" Frequently, the other partner has not even realized that their lover feels they have been sending coherent signals, but the signals are in the form of static noise. The task is to help each partner shape their movements—their expressions—into communications that are sensitive to the receiver and therefore land and are interpreted correctly.

In the Appreciation Phase, we are leveraging our newly won internal coherencies into narratives that can be spoken, written, sculpted, or presented in a boardroom, ones that emotionally move others and make sense to them. The Appreciation Phase first rests into our inner wisdom and then oscillates out into being understood more externally. How can we begin to share our narratives, such that they can be meaningful to others? This requires a kind of shaping or polishing. Most artists want their work to be seen and engaged with. They want people to be moved by their work. Teachers want their lectures or activities to land in a coherent way for their students. The priest in the pulpit and the Zen master on the cushion hopes that their talks inspire, move, and assist the people present. The shaping or polishing required to accomplish those external connections often oscillates back inward and increases internal coherencies as well. Our polishing generates integration, both with internal and external systems.

What does coherency feel like? How do we know it when we see it? My personal opinion is that it looks and feels like grace. Isn't it interesting that the word *grace* has two distinct meanings, one for movement (LeBron James's layup was so graceful), and one for spiritual experiences (Hail Mary, full of grace)? Perhaps those two processes are related? When some physical action is first attempted— when LeBron first picked up a basketball—his motions of grasping and aiming and throwing and bouncing tended to show up in a jumble. It took time and practice with each one separately, and then time and practice to coordinate them so that the ball had a good chance of going through the hoop. Not only does each individual action need to be learned, but the multiple actions required to shoot the ball must be linked to one another in a coherent sequence. When that happens, we start to see grace. We watch basketball games not only because we want our team to win but also because we want to feel the awe of seeing folks like

LeBron execute some of the most graceful movements possible. Just to be in the presence of that grace moves us because we subtly attune to it. We feel just a little bit of our own bodily grace.

This grace has its origins within LeBron, as a result of his years of effort and play. But it also results from his interaction with his teammates; when they move together as a group, they all approach the basket in a kind of gorgeous synchronization, one that may reach its conclusion through LeBron, but was enabled by the whole team (even by the other team). Even those of us attending the game contribute to the team. Grace travels in groups as well as individuals. Antje Scherholz will speak to this interactional synchrony and group coherence in Chapter 12, as she discusses her Moving Cycle–based psychotherapy groups in Germany.

Is there a contemplative equivalent to this? Likely. One equivalency has to do with the fact that one of the central features of almost every religion is that it can be practiced either alone or with others. When it occurs alongside and among others, the attunement we feel to each other helps our own practice feel more supported and more graceful. Think of singing together, of praying or chanting out loud together, of sitting in meditation next to others doing the same. These communal actions lift us all up and help us experience moments of contemplative grace. The same logic applies to classrooms; we create an atmosphere that allows us as students to oscillate between the material to be learned and our own responses to it as well as the presence and engagement of other students around us.

But the basic equivalency of grace between practicing a sport and contemplative practice lies in the initial jumble of simple elements—new, undifferentiated neurons, separate parts of complex actions, separate words that will later form sentences—and the resulting coherence when they line up and work together. We might begin a prayer with the feeling that we are just calling out. But after some time with it, we may feel a sense of presence, a sense of being held or cared for. We could be sensing that presence as a deeply internal experience or as coming from outside of us. We feel connected, whether to a divine presence, a higher consciousness, or the whole universe. This sense of holding and caring as an experience of grace occurs in the Appreciation Phase of Conscious Moving.

This coordination of basic actions into graceful sequences gets its start in Owning, as movement impulses begin to link together into coherent sequences of motion called body stories or body narratives. As a therapist and educator, when I witness a student or client begin to coordinate their experiences into coherent actions, I do feel a bit of awe. How does the Appreciation Phase support this awe? Previously we talked about the importance of owning what arises in us by moving experiences as they are. Now we will talk about caring for what has arisen as a kind of long-term connecting device between the discrete elements of experience that engenders a sophisticated feeling of coherency that can be replicated in daily life.

Neuroscience has long known that one of the best ways of committing something to long-term memory is to care about it and to have an emotional experience of it (Squire and Schacter 2002). Caring does not have to be gushy happiness; it can involve fear or anger, as any of us who have ever held a grudge can attest to. Emotions fill out the details of a body story in ways that facilitate its endurance. Likely the body narratives that produce gifted athletes like LeBron James get their start in the sheer joy of doing the action, in loving the act of drawing a tree, or yoga, or singing a song. Anger and fear, in the long run, are so physiologically expensive that they don't always support effective or graceful action. But they can endure, at a cost to ourselves and others. Emotions like fear or anger are crucial capacities in any human, but hopefully can be rare, and can be let go of when the need for them ceases. Paradoxically, one of the reasons we do Conscious Moving is to find the body story of our anger or fear, and by caring for it as it is, gradually shape it into productive and positive identities, as well as powerful art pieces, essays, and community actions. By doing so we both respect and use these feelings, as well as enable them to feel satisfyingly complete and therefore able to be let go of, transitioning to a stored memory and a potential for future action.

Emotions anchor experiences so that they endure in memory and can be retold and changed slightly with each care-full retelling. This storing, calling up, and retelling reinforce a sense of open identity, all the way from the personal to the communal. In Appreciation, we deliberately and consciously hold our body narratives and polish them a bit with our caring. We do this by taking some time to deliberately oscillate between holding the experience carefully and talking about it carefully. Fogel (2009) talks about this specialized kind of speaking as *evocative language* and invokes Eugene Gendlin's Focusing technique (see interview with Ann Weiser Cornell at www.consciousmoving.com) as an explanation of the difference between regular speaking and this kind of embodied verbalizing; in evocative languaging, "words are used to evoke a concrete internal experience, felt directly and in the moment. When used this way, words will 'resonate' in the felt experience of that person: they will sound 'true' or 'deep' or 'powerful.' Words spoken by other people that similarly address our embodied state can also resonate" (2009, 32). Another way to put it might be that in evocative languaging, our left and right brain hemispheres are working together to communicate experiences. In the previous chapter, we worked with an example of raising the shoulders deliberately and then letting the chest fall deliberately because we became aware that this was what we were already doing, in a clunky way. What gets us into the Appreciation Phase is our conscious support of these actions while braiding in emerging associations; this allows a spirilic movement sequence to develop and this sequence to feel coherent and even a bit graceful. Now it is time to use evocative languaging to begin to share it as a way to polish it.

First, let's look at an artistic equivalent. A dancer goes into their studio with the intention of choreographing a dance that can be performed for an audience. After warming up (often with classic, well-practiced dance moves), they begin to improvise, just playing with different movements that come up as a result of paying attention to a theme they have chosen, or perhaps that arise from open-movement play. They start to repeat moves that feel interesting or right, perhaps changing them a bit as a way to refine the sense of rightness. Then they begin to string different interesting moves together to form what dancers call movement phrases. They repeat the phrases and keep playing with them, refining them and helping their body remember them. They may occasionally look in a mirror as they move as a way to get a sense of how the phrases might look to others, hoping that the emotions they feel as they dance can be visible. They also might show it to other dancers. These phrases evolve into whole stories, ones that can be told as a named piece of choreography. As they begin to refine the movement story with an eye toward performing it in public, an artistic Appreciation Phase ensues.

A similar sequence occurs in music-making. A few strung-together notes become a phrase, and different phrases are played with and strung together and further refined to become a coherent song with a beginning, middle, and end. After singing and playing the song a number of times and performing it for various audiences, the musician commits to recording a version of it that will be released to the world. Musical Appreciation Phases occur as the song is prepared for recording. It's in the studio, getting ready for the larger world. Gretl Bauer works this way, as she writes about in Chapter 11. You can listen to some of her songs via the links she has provided on the www.consciousmoving.com website.

The therapeutic equivalent in Appreciation work happens when the client feels complete (for now) with their explorations, and begins to oscillate between being with their experiences and talking about their experiences, typically with the therapist. The ability to talk about one's experiences could be said to be equivalent to showing one's art to others and polishing it before taking it out into the world. Within these often-tender moments, the therapist often models how to hold and care for what happened during Owning by offering supportive observations such as "I noticed that when your chest came down, that seemed to be when you felt the sadness you are talking about most intensely." The movement story is held and cared for by being witnessed very care-fully, and then it is shaped into a meaningful experience. Meaning-making arises creatively and organically through a balancing of left- and right-hemisphere processing. The act of caring in this way integrates the experience into ongoing identity, thereby enriching it.

Now that we have all these Appreciation Phase elements in mind, let's see how this looks in freestanding practices and CM sessions. I have hesitated to use the word *love* as a part of this phase, fearing a kind of mushy, sappy association to the word. But what I realize is that this phase *is* about love, but not in the way we usually use that word. When we say we are in love, we typically mean with someone or something. Our love has an object it connects us to. In the Appreciation Phase, the love we feel does not often land on an object. We are *in love* the way we are in an environment. We are occupying love, embedded within it. Love in this sense is a field, like a magnetic field, that simply exists and does not have to be confined to locations, objects, or people. An awareness and owning and appreciation of this field may constitute our experience of grace.

Standalone Appreciation Phase Practices

These exercises can be done on their own and don't need to be integrated into experiencing Appreciation as a part of the phases of Conscious Moving.

Exercise 1: Improvisation to Polished Piece

Put on some music and enjoy a few minutes of moving freely to it, just attuning to its rhythms and messages. Now, repeat some of the movements you have done, with deliberateness and care. String them together, with the idea that you could teach them to someone else so that they could do them too. Feel them as a sequence, with a beginning, middle, and end. Notice how it feels to do this small bit of choreographing. If you want to extend this exercise, you could actually teach this tiny dance to someone else and see how it feels for the both of you to do it together. You can also do the equivalent for making your own music or other performance arts.

Exercise 2: Stream of Consciousness to Small Essay

Write out a small event that you can remember, like running into an old friend at the grocery store, or accidentally dropping and breaking a plate on the kitchen floor. Just write enough detail to jog your memory of the details of the event. It doesn't have to be complete sentences. Now imagine that you are going to publish this small story in a magazine. Take some time to imagine other readers, readers who have different associations to this event. How would you refine this story so that you could help them see the experience from your perspective, as a result of your associations? Work with just a few sentences, or the whole thing, as a way to get this sense of shaping for use and for caring about the experience enough that you want to share it with others.

Exercise 3: Knowing How to Do It to Teaching It

Think about something you know how to do quite well, like riding a bike, making spaghetti, or memorizing your times tables. If you were to teach this skill, how would you do that? Construct a map, from beginning to middle to end, of what you would do first, and then what would build upon that, all the way to the end of the process. Was the map you created coherent for someone else? How might the construction of this map help you to understand the skill more deeply?

Exercise 4: Caring for Whatever Comes

Choose some small instance in which you did something you now regret, such as saying harsh words to your child, or committing some minor thoughtless act with a friend. Take a few moments to recall the event as best you can, and push back against the tendency to get distracted by self-criticism, justification, or shame. Just be with the details of it, breathing, moving, and sensing as you recall. Now, take a few minutes to work at actively caring about those details. There is a subtle but important difference here between caring for yourself and excusing yourself from responsibility. It tends to feel something like "I did that, it hurt my friend, and I am holding myself and them in a caring way about it." In this sentence, I care about myself and I care about my friend as well, and I care about the effects of my actions. I care about it all.

PUTTING AN APPRECIATION PHASE TOGETHER— PRACTICE EXAMPLES AND AN OPEN RECIPE

In Appreciation, caring for one's experiences creates a kind of glue that holds the experience together as a unit, creating an inner state of increased coherency. This coherency allows for connection of the experience to other experiences that have formed our identities, establishing a more integrated system. We are thus slightly changed by what happened, and that change is integrated through our conscious efforts. The following are some stand-alone exercises for the development of Appreciation.

PRACTICE EXAMPLE 1: AT A MEDITATION RETREAT OR ON THE STREET

Many of the world's religions have some way of helping people care about themselves, each other, and their world. In Buddhism the practice is often called Maitri, or loving-kindness practice. The word *Maitri* also translates as goodwill, active interest in others, and wanting others to be happy. It develops as a result of our unconditional acceptance of ourselves. Maitri practice typically takes place during sitting meditation and goes something like this:

Begin by calling up some way that you dislike yourself (something small). Now, hold that dislike in a loving way, much the way a parent might hold a crying infant. Just keep returning to this act of self-kindness, to the feeling of it rather than the thought of it, even if you get distracted. If you find that you are incapable of this good will toward yourself, then work to hold your inability to do it in a loving way.

The next step in this practice is to choose someone that you dislike (a mild dislike), and hold this dislike of that person in a loving way. Work to feel the feeling of loving-kindness toward them, and if that seems undoable, hold your inability to do it in a loving way.

In these practices, you don't absolve yourself or others from responsibility for their actions. It's important to acknowledge harm and be accountable for it.

A Christian version of this practice was taught to me in high school, loosely called Christ at the Door. It comes from a story about Christ showing up at someone's door in disguise. You never know; it could happen to you! Simply put, whenever you meet someone, at your front door or on the street, you imagine they could be Christ in disguise. Christ is giving you an opportunity to practice Christianity. How would you treat Christ if you met him? He would want you to be that way with everyone.

A social version of this practice can be found in the Truth and Reconciliation Commission that formed after the apartheid government in South Africa fell. The idea was to heal the wounds of apartheid by getting the perpetrators and victims together in an ordered and public space, and having the perpetrators tell the truth of what they did, and having the victims tell their stories of what happened to them. Ideally, they would listen to each other and be moved by what they heard. In this way, the trauma and suffering could be healed and integrated into society going forward. A version of this in other countries' judicial systems is called restorative justice.

In these examples, notice how the act of caring creates a holding environment for coherencies to reverberate inward to our sense of self and outward into our relationships and communities.

PRACTICE EXAMPLE 2: IN A THERAPY ROOM

A client has been working with feelings of anger and resentment toward his romantic partner who slept with someone else while in their monogamous relationship. In the Awareness phase, he became aware of tension in his gut as well as all up and down his arms. After focusing on those two areas of tension, he noticed they seemed to hold different associations. When focusing on his belly, the client reported fear coming up, along with an urge to shrink back. When he touched into his arms, he had an association to movement—he wanted to aggressively fist his hands and push his arms downward. We worked with those two actions and sets of feelings, first allowing the fear and shrinking and then allowing the aggressive and quick pushing of his arms toward the floor.

Client: When I stay in touch with my gut, I want to cry. I feel really young, like I hear this little boy saying "Don't leave me!" But when I focus on my arms and fists, I feel really angry, and I want to shout "Fuck you!" as I stomp on the floor.

Therapist: Let's trust that both of these reactions have a voice and want to be heard. Would it be OK to alternate between the two, in your own timing, for a bit? See what else develops when you support those two reactions.

Client: (For about 10 minutes he spends time fleshing out the two sets of impulses, finding a sequence in his belly that included raising his arms up in a pleading gesture, and crying. In the arms, the pushing down developed into a pushing away gesture. When both these sequences emerged, he felt a sense of recognition of an old action that a previous boyfriend had accused him of, a pattern he called "Come here, go away.")

Therapist: Let's spend a bit of time with both those actions. As you attend to the "come here," just be with it in as friendly a way as possible. If you were to be a friend to it, what would you want to do?

Client: (His hand rests on his chest, and he rubs it gently.) I wish someone had comforted me all those times when people left.

Therapist: (Rubbing their own chest) Yes, is there anyone you would have wanted to ask for comfort?

Client: Yes, my dad.

Therapist: Would it be OK to imagine your dad here now? What would you have wanted to say to him? Say it as if he is here.

Client: Dad, I wanted you to give me a hug, I wanted you to tell me I would be OK when Uncle John died, and when Grandma died. (Takes time to feel the sadness.)

Therapist: Does it make sense now to shift and do something similar with the angry arm movement? Or should we work on that next time?

Client: Let's do that next time. This feels so tender right now.

Therapist: Yes, tender. Take a few moments and see if it feels OK to give some of that tenderness to yourself right now, in your current situation.

(The session progresses with the client imagining his partner in the room, and talking about his feelings of loss—loss of connection, loss of exclusivity, loss of intimacy.)

Notice the associations that come up through the body in this session, and how the client's capacity to greet them and work with them allows for a deeper truth-telling to emerge, one that he might be able to take home with him in the Action Phase. There is also a developing coherency between the client's past and present situations, and an oscillation between different body narratives.

PRACTICE EXAMPLE 3: IN A CLASSROOM

The students in a suburban high school take a trip to a local nature preserve, where they hike up a hillside to sit and look down on the local river that goes through their city. Their art teacher begins by asking them to draw the scene before them, paying special attention to the curves in the river and to the vegetation. He asks them to do several versions according to how they feel about being there. Their science teacher then points out the layers of rock strata, and talks about how different geological processes deform the strata so that it curves as well. She also helps them calculate the relationship between the length of the hike and the elevation gain and the number of calories they used as they walked. After lunch, the science and art teachers lead a discussion about how the students felt about what they were looking at, and what they knew about the relationships between rock, water, vegetation, and animal life. As a homework assignment, they are asked to form groups that will study the history of their city and this river, how the water is used by the city, and issues of water safety and conservation.

Notice how learning can be integrative, just as experiences when being in a particular environment are holistic. As well, experiential education, because students embed themselves in an experience, creates an atmosphere conducive to caring and to realizing that things are connected (that there is a relationship between this scene before them and the water that comes out of their tap).

OPEN RECIPE FOR AN AWARENESS, OWNING, AND APPRECIATION PHASE

Appreciation navigates sensitive and challenging terrain, helping us to use feeling and caring as a means of discernment; learning firsthand the difference between forgiving and forgetting, between caring and enabling, between regret and self-hatred. By moving consciously and care-fully with these states, we ready ourselves and empower ourselves to take action in the world. The following example illustrates a possible journey from Awareness to Owning and into Appreciation.

- ▸ *Tune in, either to your interior world or to the world around you, or a combination.*
- ▸ *Be deliberate about what posture/position you want to be in.*
- ▸ *Take some time to noodle around with your attention until you find some experience/sensation you want to focus on, and come back to it when your attention wanders.*
- ▸ *Notice the details of this experience. Just be with it as it is.*
- ▸ *Notice if any words, images, memories, other sensations, movements or emotions come up, and braid them into the experience.*
- ▸ *Begin to focus on how this experience and the attending associations want to express themselves. Try not to assume how your body would want to move. Be patient.*
- ▸ *Be alert to the tiniest of movements and support them to happen as they are.*
- ▸ *If you want to nudge it, ask yourself, "What does my body want to do right now?"*

▶ *As you focus more carefully on moving, pay attention to breathing and sensing. If you notice one element falling away, take a moment to reestablish it consciously.*

▶ *Allow the movement to keep going where it wants to go and surfacing new associations that you include.*

▶ *Notice the sequence of events that accompany the moving—where does this want to go next? It may help to repeat and tweak any sequences that develop.*

▶ *If any disturbing or challenging associations come up, practice entering and relieving—touch into the power of the association, then rest away from it, as often as feels right.*

▶ *Trust when it feels complete for now; when it is coming to an organic conclusion for now.*

▶ *Take a few minutes to go back over the events of the experience, and acknowledge them. "I did that, and then that came up, and then I felt a bit fearful." You can also talk about them to a friend or write them down.*

▶ *Take some time to actively care for what came up, especially the parts that were challenging. You can help this along with gestures, if that feels right, gestures like putting your hand on your heart or lightly caressing your arms.*

▶ *Take some time to breathe, notice both inside and around you, and perhaps wiggle around a bit. How can you use the triangle to enter back into ordinary life?*

References

Caldwell, Christine M. 2016. "Body Identity Development: Definitions and Discussions." *Body, Movement and Dance in Psychotherapy* 11, no. 4 (February 26): 220–34. http://dx.doi.org/10.1080/17432979.2016.1145141.

Fogel, Alan. 2009. *The Psychophysiology of Self-Awareness: Rediscovering the Lost Art of Body Sense.* New York: W. W. Norton.

Siegel, Daniel J. 2007. *The Mindful Brain: Reflection and Attunement in the Cultivation of Well-Being.* New York: W. W. Norton.

———. 2011. *Mindsight: The New Science of Personal Transformation.* New York: Bantam Books.

Squire, Larry R., and Daniel L Schacter. 2002. *Neuropsychology of Memory.* New York: Guilford Press.

Williamson, G. Gordon, Marie E. Anzalone, and Barbara E. Hanft, 2000. "Assessment of Sensory Processing, Praxis, and Motor Performance." In

Clinical Practice Guidelines edited by the Interdisciplinary Council on Developmental and Learning Disorders, 155–73. www.icdl.com/dir/bookstore/icdl-clinical-practice-guidelines.

Drawing by Page Zekonis, 2023

5

The Action Phase of Conscious Moving

Practice means to perform, over and over again in the face of all obstacles, some act of vision, of faith, of desire.

      —DANCER AND CHOREOGRAPHER MARTHA GRAHAM

I could've spent 15 years in therapy talking about my reluctance to be intimate. Guess what? I just did it and got better. Once you say—"This is just a muscle that is weak in me—if I developed it I'd feel better"—once that's clear, it's common sense. Push the weight.

      —KELLY BUTLER, FOUNDER OF LIVING ON PURPOSE

All song forms that have grown up to stir mankind to mass action, and concentrate the efforts of human physiological power, are based upon the rhythms of muscular action.

      —MARGARET H'DOUBLER, IN *MOVEMENT AND ITS RHYTHMIC STRUCTURE*

When we walk out of the classroom, therapy office, or art studio, we reenter our daily lives, with all their sharp edges and quiet comforts. One of the values of Conscious Moving is its attention to applying the work to our daily lives. How do our experiences in these special circumstances (classrooms, studios, mosques, etc.) make themselves useful in our relationships, our work in the world, and our society? We take time at the end of a Conscious Moving experience in order to create and support this link, because no healing, no art-making, and no learning make a lasting difference if they are not applied and shared. This chapter delves into the art of using movement to help make our experiences useful in some way, from simply making our lives a bit easier or more beautiful, to social activism.

We have spoken before about Conscious Moving being shaped for use; in the Action Phase, we learned to understand this shaping from a social perspective. Human beings are a social species; we thrive when we are connected to each other, and we fail to thrive in conditions of social isolation (much like neurons and sensory experiences). The work we do in specialized places—such as studios, classrooms, and chapels—needs to be integrated into our daily lives, and this takes special practice. The Appreciation Phase integrates our new experiences into our sense of self and can begin to integrate these experiences into relationships. The Action Phase integrates our work into our relationships, our families, our work in the world, and into society at large. It is here, for instance, where action becomes activism. It is here where we can change the world.

I once had a psychotherapy client who was seeing me because she had been in a devastating car accident that had almost killed her and had left her health an ongoing concern. She was coping fairly well with the physical changes and challenges that had happened as a result of the accident, but what brought her to therapy was her sense of rage and helplessness because the accident had been caused by a defect in her car, and the car company was denying this and laying the blame on her. She had seen online that other people were reporting this same defect in the braking system of that particular model, but this did not seem to sway the car company. She felt powerless, mistreated, and ignored, and this was causing her to feel depressed and suicidal. She didn't want others to go through what she had been through.

Our work over a series of months focused on how her body experienced powerlessness and power, the overarching question being how she could get her power back. She spent a lot of time allowing her body to collapse and feel heavy while studying the associations that emerged. Then she would allow what she felt were more powerful movements (often associated with anger) to energize her and help her feel like she could accomplish things. Her Action Phase work began as she used these practices as an inspiration to "go up against the Goliath." By supporting both the collapse and the energizing rage, she glimpsed the possibility of transforming the "dead weight" of her body into a sense of letting go and of rest. But she knew she wouldn't be capable of that until she had also transformed the helpless rage into efforts that got something done in the world.

She began to research this car model, creating a website that published records of complaints and reports about brake failures. She invited others to share their stories about their accidents. She made up flyers with links to her website and she put them under the windshield wipers of this same car model when she spotted them in parking lots. The people she gathered to her banded together and initiated a class action lawsuit against the car company. Right after this, the car company finally recalled this model and repaired the brake systems. The lawsuit was settled out of court years later, and although my client was not allowed to share the details of the settlement, she glowed as she told me "We won!"

This example dramatically illustrates an Action Phase, one that made a substantial contribution to my client's well-being as well as the well-being of others as they drove. Not all action stories are so bold, or so clearcut, or have such satisfying endings. Not all of our behaviors rise to the level of action movies, though this one certainly could have, reminiscent of Erin Brockovich. Most Action Phases are quieter, more personal, and more nuanced.

In an educational environment, action often takes classic forms, such as handing in term papers at the end of class, or taking the bar exam after graduating from law school. Ideally, exams and tests not only demonstrate that you learned something but also that you can apply that learning to life's challenges because it is not enough that you went to school; you also have to demonstrate that you can practice what you learned in real-life situations. This is often why many professions have internships (medicine, law, different kinds of therapies, plumbers, electricians, and teachers). Internships give you time to practice your actions in real-life settings, under supervision. In this sense, the Action Phase looks like a kind of mini-internship.

In art-making, the Action Phase holds the transition between being creative and producing art that will be published or performed, or simply shared. While the Appreciation Phase polishes creative processes into a piece, the Action Phase sets up shows, performances, social media postings, and publications as a means of showing the piece and having it influence the world. It's a bit trickier to talk about the Action Phase in contemplative practice, but it seems visible in dharma talks and sermons, where longtime practitioners tend to offer guidance on contemplative practice as they address everyday problems and challenges.

Moving and Acting Along the Continuum from the Personal to the Political

As we know from our movement continuums, not all actions are large and visible. The same goes for the Action Phase of CM. Bigger is not necessarily better. Small actions can be just as powerful, sustainable, and enduring as large ones. They are also just as important and impactful as the big stuff. For instance, my friend and colleague Rae Johnson (one of the interviewees for this book) has published a book called *Embodied Activism* in which they offer the term *microactivisms* (2023). A relative of micromovement, and an answer to *microaggressions* (Sue 2010), microactivism comprises small acts that contribute to social and environmental justice and equity. It could be that you take a bus one day instead of driving your car. Or you speak up when a person in the room has been subjected to a microaggression due to some aspect of their identity. It could be the tiniest little thing, but it matters because it tones your body toward taking action in the world, it keeps your paddle in the water of the systems we all live in, and it makes an ever-so-slight difference in the world. The cumulative effect of microactivisms cannot be understated.

In Conscious Moving trainings, we work with the power of *the witness*, for instance. At times simply being there and being attentive to someone without judgment or analysis and with curious and compassionate intentions can make all the difference in the world. We also see the power of this witnessing of another's movement in Barbara Dilley's work, called Contemplative Dance, as well as a type of dance therapy called Authentic Movement. In CM trainings, we frequently work in pairs where one person is called the mover and the other is dubbed the witness. The mover moves, and the witness sits off to the side and holds the mover in a beam of high-quality attention. We train the skills of *seeing* and *being seen* as being fundamental to any subsequent capacities, such as making interventions in the process. Witnessing could be called a microactivism since it uses such quiet and respectful actions. But witnessing someone or something can also create huge effects. Quakers have used it as a way to bring various forms of social violence out of the shadows. Bystanders using their cell phones have created personal and social accountability in cases of violence and the abuse of power. Bearing witness can save lives and hold people and systems responsible for their actions. We use the simple yet powerful skill of paying attention as a form of influencing action.

In the Action Phase we experience our movements as within us as well as shared with others in a back-and-forth oscillation of influence, an oscillation that connects us all with each other and the world. From this vantage point, all movement lies on a continuum from the personal to the political, from the individual to the systemic. There are times when we move just for ourselves and times when we move for and with others. Yet both these movement locations influence each other ongoingly. We all have experience with how uplifting it can be to be in the presence of someone who is cheerful, and how difficult it can be to remain cheerful in the presence of someone who is relentlessly grouchy (Goleman 2006). Lots of research over the years has confirmed that when we are interacting with someone we like, we gesture similarly to them with similar timing. We unconsciously move with the emotions of others. When we hold an infant to our chest, their heartbeat and breathing start to link up with ours. When someone's movement clashes with ours, we tend to give them more space (Knapp and Hall 2006). In so many ways we are all in this together. Another way of putting this is that we are all influencers; we all possess the power to influence the world around us via our actions.

At times we hold our movement close and oscillate our attention and actions inward so that movement can reverberate through our flesh and bones and blood and assist in an experience of inner coherency—a kind of knowing ourselves as well as altering ourselves—that empowers us and orients us toward what feels right, right now. And there are times when our inner reverberations form the infrastructure of more external, public, and socially influential movements, movements that, because of their visibility, have an opportunity to make a difference in the world.

Have you ever noticed yourself sitting up straighter in the presence of someone with good posture? I am amazed at how my spine aligns and lengthens when I am in the presence of Judith Aston-Linderoth. Have you ever noticed how a spiritual teacher, just by the quality of their embodied presence, affects your ability to be awake? I have felt this intensely during times when I have been fortunate enough to share space with Thich Nhat Hanh and the Dalai Lama. Teachers of all kinds are—whether they track it consciously or not—teaching with their bodies. One of their most fundamental skills lies in their ability to maintain their bodily integrity and authority even when people around them are not able to do so yet. This same skill holds true in the therapeutic relationship, the child-caregiver relationship, and in the creative process. Our bodies are our own, yet they also belong to, embed in, and shape the public sphere, where the personal presence of another being—often on the level of micromovements—calls out to our bodies in a back-and-forth reciprocity, one that alters our identities and alters our actions and activisms. This is why working on the level of microactivisms and micromovements can be such a powerful means of working in the world.

Of course this embodied activism can go in destructive and hateful directions as well. Being with someone who is depressed, critical, tense, or aggressive challenges us to make a decision to either move toward them in a gesture of helpfulness or to retreat from them in an act of self-preservation. How we move at that moment depends on how empowered we are; how much bodily integrity and authority we are able to sustain (Johnson, Leighton, and Caldwell 2018). Can we be the ones who use their energy in this encounter as a form of activism that stands up to and contrasts with what others are doing? Or, in the interest of safety or the conservation of energy, do we get some distance so that we are not battered by the toxic actions of others? By engaging in movement practices that athleticize our sensorimotor awareness, that tone our ability to include novel or challenging experiences, and that strengthen our capacity to appreciate and integrate new self-coherencies, we can position ourselves to make informed and effective decisions about our actions in the world.

All this talk of action relies, however, on a foundation of bodily authority. Repressive social systems want to keep us physically docile so that we will work where and when they want us to work, buy what they tell us to buy, question our own experience so as to defer to authoritarian power structure, and fail to question abuses of power. By working with our body's signals and ongoing actions, by trusting them to be an important part of how we make decisions and how we support ourselves and others, we counteract the body insecurity that can be bred into us by consumer culture, repressive social systems, and authoritarian regimes.

The Action Phase of CM carries the dual functions of helping us apply our learning and healing to our own lives, as well as helping us apply our own contemplations and creativities to more social locations. Our actions radiate out as well as in, a kind of oscillation of influence. What comprises an individual action becomes the same stuff as activism as it radiates outward. Action and activism arise from the same movement impulses and sequences. As we shape movement sequences into body narratives, and from there learn to care for and polish them, they tend to specialize as contributions in one direction or the other, though action in any direction influences all other directions. In action, we make a difference in the world, that world that lives within us and outside of us.

Another piece of good news comes to us from the movement continuum because taking conscious action as a result of our Conscious Moving experiences sets up good action habits. Being responsible in the world can be like riding a bike—you never forget how to do it, how to consider others, how to put your money where your mouth is, how to turn off the light when you leave a room— the action becomes semiautomatic. We tend to be amazed and entertained by big, heroic, singlehanded acts, but the cumulative effect of small contributions forms its own kind of everyday heroism.

Another result of taking action after stepping outside of special Conscious Moving experiences occurs as a result of the phases of the Conscious Moving cycle. Taking action stimulates and links to new Awareness Phases. Our actions reverberate into new capacities for being awake, and the cycle starts again, this time at a different location on the spiral of our development and evolution. The more we take conscious action, the easier it gets to be just a bit more aware, and to discover new experiences we can use to make art, grow, and learn. This can take the form of simple movement acts, like noticing tightness in your chest, working with movement impulses and associations so that some old fear or creative block surfaces, working with these surfacings to find that conscious breathing helps you listen to the issues and organize their body stories, and telling those stories by moving them and caring for them. In the Action Phase, the breathing you used is practiced, perhaps with some challenging circumstance in mind. At the very end of the session, you craft a standalone breathing practice that will help create a new and more supportive breathing pattern. Over time, as a result of that new breathing practice, you find that some experiences you used to find challenging aren't so challenging anymore, and you realize that doing this kind of breathing when caring for your small children helps everyone in the room take a breath.

In the example of my client who had been in a car accident, we started small, local, and personal. She murmured during one session, "They don't want me to do anything about this." I asked her, "What does your body want to do right now?'" She found an impulse to clench her fist. By supporting that it developed into a shaking fist and the statement, "I'm not going to take this lying down!" The Action Phase from this session ended up with the simple practice of her committing to literally not reading about the car company while lying down. Subsequent sessions began to involve standing up, as she worked with a new metaphor of "standing up to the Goliath." Once she started standing up during sessions, she gradually found practical action plans for dealing with her longing for justice.

In a contemplative application, action begins when we walk out the door of the meditation hall or church or our own quiet space, and realize that what we did there is connected to what we do out here. How does the Golden Rule—do unto others as you would have them do unto you—play out at a school board meeting or while waiting in line at the grocery store? It's not enough to just know they are connected; what are the practical ways we can link one to the other? The Action Phase helps us to engineer that link. We begin to craft that link while still within the session by practicing with our therapist, teacher, or mentor (like an internship). We then might take the action home and practice it with those we love and who have our backs and who can give us feedback. Then we might take it into more challenging circumstances and more far-reaching applications.

The same goes for art-making. On a very literal level, movements during a CM session can be shaped into a dance that might be shared with others. With an eye toward how you want to be seen, you might start with a shaking fist and see where it wants to go. Where it goes can be elaborated and practiced and shown to others, who then can have their own experiences of how shaking their fist feels and moves them. This process can assist individuals and whole communities in making meaning out of their lived experiences, meaning that arises organically from inhabiting the experiences from within rather than passing on meanings internalized from dysfunctional systems.

My friend and colleague Rae Johnson and I engaged in a research project some ten years ago. We interviewed people who identified as belonging to various marginalized social categories, and we asked them to talk about how marginal-ization or oppression felt in their bodies. Their visceral descriptions of daily life were so powerful that we realized it would not feel right, respectful, or complete just to write an article about the research and publish it in a professional journal. We asked people who were willing to work collaboratively to create a perfor-mance at my university's yearly Somatic Arts Concert. Several graduate school somatic counseling students plus several of the interviewees/co-researchers par-ticipated, and working from the audio recordings of the interviews, folks played with how the spoken words felt and moved their bodies. These movements were polished and integrated into a public performance piece that was shown in the spring. The resulting project felt like an important way that we all learned about taking action that arose from direct experience. We didn't do it perfectly, but we worked hard to use the process of choreographing, rehearsing, and performing as a way to give voice to people whose voices were not being heard. We used transient hierarchies, conscious movements that arose from lived experiences, and feedback from co-researchers as our means of making art. The process and the product were crafted using the values of bodily authority and the inclusion of the phases of Conscious Moving (Johnson 2017, 2020). On another occasion, I paired up with my transgender colleague Owen Karcher and worked in much the same way; he and I staged a performance from our research (Karcher and Caldwell 2014). These are other examples of a large and elaborate Action Phase. Again, large and elaborate actions take a lot of time and energy and are not nec-essarily the best way to feel complete with your conscious movement. Microac-tions can prove just as effective.

Both large and small actions in the world generate new Awareness Phases, as we said before. The other result of taking conscious action comes from our will-ingness in earlier phases of the cycle to postpone meaning-making. By valuing description over evaluation as long as possible, we enable a novel and perhaps more effective sense of meaning to coalesce through the actions that show up in our world. In the therapeutic story cited earlier, if my client had just stayed with her experience of her body as dead weight and her statement that "they don't want me to do anything about this," those meanings would have likely kept her in a sink-hole of powerlessness. By holding those experiences differently, neither believing them nor disbelieving them but simply letting them have a voice, they could metamorphose into resources for action. And from these resources new meanings can emerge, meanings that contribute to creativity, inclusion, learning, and reflection. By postponing old, inherited meanings and working with the raw data of lived experience, then richer, more nuanced, and more effective meanings can blossom. A fresh and perhaps challenging perspective can be experienced by engaging with art forms that live outside received pearls of wisdom (though art that expresses received wisdom does have its place). Contemplations that push back on explanations rooted in blame and powerlessness, giving ourselves time to simply breathe, feel, and sense your inner and outer worlds, allow for a more spacious and clutter-free relationship to those worlds. This action means something useful. This is an action that helps us to feel complete with something and able to move on to the next thing.

One of the most important features of any Action Phase is the sense of completion it can engender. A sense of completion can be a powerful reward for all our hard work. Why not feel complete at the end of something? We all know how frustrating it can be to not feel finished with something, to not have the option or the know-how to accomplish that completion. CM uses bodily experiences of moving until something feels complete, at least as complete as it can get today, as a means of linking endings with a sense of satisfaction and closure whenever possible. In the Owning and Appreciation Phases of the session this may take the form of playing with effort and the release of effort, or noticing how movement sequences have a natural beginning, middle, and end. Or it can start as an experiment in noticing when you are not exhaling completely, not letting go into gravity as the air falls out of your body such that you are holding too much air in your lungs each time you breathe. What are the associations that come up when you notice that? These practices act as a microcosm for learning how to navigate larger endings. The Action Phase foregrounds the idea that it takes Conscious Moving to make sure that we feel as complete as possible with experiences.

In art-making, this idea can be echoed by the perennial question: How do you know when a painting/sculpture/book is complete? Does it need just a few more daubs of paint, or will that take me into another painting that is different than this one? Should I add one more paragraph about a related topic, or am I done? Doing conscious work to craft an ending helps us mitigate the stress of these kinds of questions and access our felt sense of completeness as a guide.

At the end of things, evaluations commonly occur. We look back and decide what was helpful and what was not so that we can get better at that thing next time. Evaluating an experience also helps us feel complete with it because it oscillates us from looking back to looking forward. This oscillation from past to future creates a bridge that allows a crossing, a walking from the bank of the river we have been on to the other bank where we will be as we step back into our daily life. This bridge exists in the present moment, in the details of the Action Phase, where we consciously decide what we will take with us into the future. It can be as simple as asking—how did that work? What happened and what does that mean to me going forward? It can help us to learn from two different sources—from what went well and what went badly. Acknowledging these events as we overlook them from our position on the bridge can contribute to our feeling of completion.

All this is to say that at the end of things, we enter a transition. We are in a small in-between moment between sacred and ordinary, between altered and normal, between what was and what will be. Transitions can be as commonplace as leaving the house or finishing a meal, or as fraught and complex as the breakup of a long-term romance or a funeral for the dead. Transitions carry within them a suspension between two things, a moment when there is no ground underneath us and we have to reorient to find the new ground. Most parents will tell you that children have a tendency to melt down during transitions, and most therapists will tell you that clients seek therapy because of painful, powerful, or traumatizing life transitions. By spending conscious time with the Action Phase's ending, we learn to anticipate and perhaps welcome that state of suspension during a transition and increase the athleticism of moving through transitions with as much grace as possible.

Standalone Action Phase Practices

Several of these practices will feel familiar and like no-brainers. What this speaks to is the enduring power of coming to a satisfying conclusion. Feeling complete with a project in a way that makes it visible to yourself or the rest of the world carries within it a deep human urge to see things through until the end, much like the motor plans we discussed in the Movement Continuum. Ultimately, this can lessen some of our existential fears, such as of death or loss. Many people, as they approach death, seek to tie up loose ends. We feel more at peace with endings when we feel complete with the processes coming toward that end. Serenity, in this sense, may be defined as feeling complete as an ending approaches.

There is an apocryphal story that Socrates, as he lay on his deathbed, was asked by his students what was his most important teaching. As the story goes, he simply said, "Practice dying." We take this to mean that our lives hold many endings, large and small, and learning to do what it takes to feel (as much as possible) complete and satisfied at those ends creates a sense of meaningfulness and grace.

Example 1: In an Elementary School Classroom

A teacher works with their students to learn about various wild animals. In science class, this looks like discussing the difference between wild and domesticated animals. In art class, this involves drawings of various wild animals, and in gym class students become various wild animals and dance their movements. The teacher enlists parents to help some of the students make wild animal costumes that they can wear in their community's yearly parade.

Example 2: In a Church, Mosque, or Synagogue

A sermon or talk is given to the community on the practice of giving to those in need. At the end of the sermon/talk, handouts are left at the exit of the building that list various charities and resources for helping people in need. The community also organizes a support group for people volunteering in their town.

Example 3: In an Art Studio

A writer finishes a book, a memoir on their journey from being able-bodied to being in a wheelchair. At the end of the book is a whole section on resources for folks in wheelchairs. The author also arranges with their publisher to give out free copies to folks in VA hospitals.

....

PUTTING AN ACTION PHASE TOGETHER: PRACTICE EXAMPLES AND AN OPEN RECIPE

PRACTICE EXAMPLE 1: IN A COUNSELING SESSION WITH AN EIGHTEEN-YEAR-OLD WOMAN

Therapist: So today we worked on the grief of losing your grandmother, who meant a lot to you. Is there anything else you might want to say or do about that before we end today?

Client: I realize that she meant a lot to my brother as well. I just had a thought that I could call him and just talk about her with him sometime. I'd like that.

Therapist: Would it be OK to take a few minutes right now to imagine yourself on the phone with your brother, talking about her? Would it be OK to role-play that a bit, as if he was here and you were talking?

Client: OK. "Hi, Jim. Do you remember that time that grandma brought us to the baseball field across town, and we watched the local team play? Do you remember how loud she was? How she yelled at the players and we were so embarrassed?" (Client tears up a bit, and laughs.)

Therapist: How do you think your brother might respond to that?

Client: I think he would laugh too. I hope he can tell some stories about her too. I want to remember.

Therapist: Yes, you want to remember. Take a breath into that. Perhaps that's an intention you'd like to set.

Client: Yah. It just occurred to me that I could make a photo album of her, and of us with her.

Therapist: I'd love to see that!

Therapist: Is there anything else from the session you'd like to take a look at before we go?

Client: No, I'm good.

Therapist: OK, maybe we could just make a transition here. The session is over and you are going back out into daily life. Would it be OK if we just stood up together, and faced the door?

(Client and therapist stand up, shoulder to shoulder, facing the door.)

Client: As I stand here, a thought occurs to me—I have to go back to school now to a theater club meeting. I don't want to cry in front of everyone.

Therapist: Yeah, some feelings can be more private. What do you want to do with your body to help keep these feelings private in that setting?

Client (playing around a bit with her breathing and moving): If I breathe deeply, I want to cry, but if I stand like this (feet wider apart, hands by sides, a bit more tension in her body), I feel more like I can be there without losing it.

Therapist: Great. Sounds like you found a good strategy for both feeling it with your brother and holding it privately when the time's not right.

Did you notice entering and relieving as a way to manage daily encounters? The therapist and the client really took the time to plan for how she would be in the social world while feeling the loss of a loved one. Notice how experiential it all was; she didn't just talk about it—she literally practiced it. These are all features of the Action Phase. The session also used the relationship with the therapist as a bridge (Vygotsky would say *scaffold*) for going out into the world, and the client herself came up with actions that would feel helpful to her grief and her love of her grandmother.

PRACTICE EXAMPLE 2: AT A MEDITATION RETREAT

Meditation Teacher: OK, so we are coming to the end of the retreat. We have a bit of time now before we go to see if anyone has any lingering questions or comments on the retreat. We have about an hour, then we will go to lunch, then everyone packs up and goes home. What feels important to say as we come to an end?

Participant: This was a very powerful experience for me. I almost didn't come because it sounded so boring to just sit here all day! I struggled a lot with that, but there were moments when I found this utter place of peace, just being here, even with the junk that came up. Even with the backache.

Several Other Participants: (Express gratitude to the teacher, complain about the long line at the food tent, express what they got out of the retreat.)

Meditation Teacher: Thank you for all your comments! I will make sure to pass your comments about the long lines on to the food service folks. Long lines suck, but long lines also happen. So in the days ahead, notice that you now have more of a choice about how you experience the long lines in life. Be aware of your urge to control the experience you are having. You can meditate while standing in line as well as on a cushion during a retreat. You can show compassion to yourself for your irritation and show compassion to the others who are waiting with you. You can practice relaxing into the experience, since there is nothing you can do about it. You can speak compassionately to people who could make a difference in how long the lines are in the future.

Notice that evaluation can be an important way to feel complete with an experience—looking back over it and stating what worked and what didn't, what feels complete and what doesn't. Part of the Action Phase is seeing what wants to happen next as we go through daily life events, much like Ann Weiser Cornell talks about the body as always leaning in to the next thing in her interview for this book. The meditation teacher just cited started by stating the ending structure of the retreat so that people could plan for how much they could say and how the transition would go. Transitions are always a kind of ending, and small endings such as this one can be a rehearsal for how to manage bigger ones.

PRACTICE EXAMPLE THREE: AT A VOCATIONAL SCHOOL

Teacher: OK everyone, over to the main table and listen up. For the last three weeks, we have been working on how to make simple furniture pieces with wood. We started by cutting lengths of wood in straight lines. We've played with different ways to join the pieces of wood together, and when and how to use nails, screws, and glue. We also covered sanding, both what gauge to use and how to work with the grain. Looks like we got some benches out of this, a step stool, and a storage box. Starting on Monday we're going to add finishes. But before we call it a week, do you have any questions about what we've done so far?

Students: (One student asks about the thickness of the wood for different projects, another complains about her shoulder hurting from all that sanding, another asks when they can take their pieces home, and so on.)

Teacher: (Answers all the questions, including demonstrating how to use a sander without straining your arm.)

Teacher: OK, so next week we will finish the pieces by doing stains and finishes and adding on any metal hardware needed. Then they can go home. Going forward, we're going to make it harder by making a new piece that uses different types of wood and learning how to saw angles and arcs. Be thinking about what you want to build that has curves in it. And read the handout on different types of wood—it's important to get to know their grain and their relative hardness. Take some photos of what you have done so far to show off!

This teacher is doing a good job of what Vygotsky called scaffolding. *Scaffolding* uses the image of creating a bridge to the next thing so that learning progresses in a stable and sustainable way. Scaffolding links what has been done to what wants to happen next, and forms a vital part of any Action Phase. This way a learner feels a sense of accomplishment that is connected to how that accomplishment can be applied and extended. The teacher reviews what has been done, makes sure that students feel complete with those skills for now, and then introduces the next steps that will be taken and how the students can prepare for those steps.

OPEN RECIPE FOR THE ENTIRE CONSCIOUS MOVING CYCLE

The following practice outlines how a CM session might work. It works as a guide, not a prescription. Play around with it from your own bodily authority and your own interests.

▶ *Begin by tuning in, either to your interior world or the world around you, or a combination.*

▶ *Be deliberate about what posture/position you want to be in.*

▶ *Take some time to just noodle around with your attention until you find some experience/sensation you want to focus on, and gently come back to it when your attention wanders.*

▶ *Notice the details of this experience. Just be with it as it is.*

▶ *Notice any associations that come up and just braid them in.*

▶ *Begin to focus on how this experience and the attending associations want to express themselves.*

▶ *Be alert to the tiniest of movements and support them to happen as they are.*

▶ *If you want to nudge it, ask yourself, "What does it want to do right now?"*

▶ *As you focus more carefully on moving, pay attention to your breathing and sensing. If you notice one element falling away, take a moment to reestablish it consciously.*

▶ *Allow the movement to keep going where it wants to go, including new associations.*

▶ *Notice the sequence of events that accompany the moving—where does this want to go next? It may help to repeat and tweak any sequences that develop.*

▶ *If any disturbing or challenging associations come up, practice entering and relieving—touch into the power of the association, then rest away from it, as often as feels right.*

▶ *Trust when it feels complete for now.*

▶ *Take a few minutes to go back over the events of the experience so far, and acknowledge them to yourself. "I did that, and then that came up, and then I felt a bit fearful." You can also talk about them to a friend or write them down.*

▶ *Take some time to actively care for what came up, especially the parts that were challenging. You can help this along with gestures, if that feels right, gestures like putting your hand on your heart or lightly caressing your arms.*

▶ *Now imagine yourself back in your daily life, either what will happen as you walk out the door into your next thing, or by putting a scene with someone into your mind's eye. Take a few minutes to imagine and then practice how you might take the events of the session into that circumstance. You can practice this with a friend, mentor, or counselor, or you can try it on your own. It might be something like taking several full breaths (ones that you used in the session) as you imagine a tricky interaction with your boss at work. Or it could be a gesture from the session that you modify to use when arguing with your spouse, as a way to be more visible to them and potentially feel more understood. It might be a simple decision to do something like look up resources on the internet or practice relaxing muscles that you usually tense. Be careful not to get too project-oriented, however. Start with microactions that can be practiced and tweaked. It may happily stay at that level, or it may progress to larger actions. All along that continuum is good.*

We have now completed a full cycle of Conscious Moving. Awareness, Owning, Appreciation, and Action all progress in a way that can inform and extend our learning, art-making, and healing. In the next section, various authors show us how they apply these theories and practices in their own work. The practice of Conscious Moving is an invitation to be innovative and contributive from our own locations and aspirations.

References

Goleman, Daniel. 2006. *Social Intelligence: The Revolutionary New Science of Human Relationships*. New York: Bantam Dell.

Johnson, Rae. 2017. *Embodied Social Justice.* New York: Routledge.

———. 2020. "Body Stories: Researching and Performing the Embodied Experience of Oppression." In *The Art and Science of Embodied Research Design* edited by Jennifer Frank Tantia, 189–99. New York: Routledge.

———. 2023. *Embodied Activism: Engaging the Body to Cultivate Liberation, Justice and Authentic Connection—A Practical Guide for Transformative Social Change.* Berkeley, CA: North Atlantic Books.

Johnson, Rae, Lucia Bennett Leighton, and Christine Caldwell. 2018. "The Embodied Experience of Microaggressions: Implications for Clinical Practice." *Journal of Multicultural Counseling and Development* 46, no. 3 (July): 156–70.

Karcher, Owen Paul, and Christine Caldwell. 2014. "Turning Data into Dance: Performing and Presenting Research on Oppression and the Body." *Arts in Psychotherapy* 41, no. 5 (November): 478–83.

Knapp, Mark L., and Judith A. Hall, J. 2006. *Nonverbal Communication in Human Interaction*. Belmont CA: Thompson Wadsworth.

Sue, Derald Wing. 2010. *Microaggressions in Everyday Life: Race, Gender, and Sexual Orientation.* Hoboken, NJ: Wiley and Sons.

PART II

Applying Conscious Moving to Healing, the Arts, Contemplative Practice, and Education

Introduction

Over the years, I have been honored and humbled by the thousands of students I have taught. I have worked with young adults just out of college as well as seasoned professionals. I have taught at universities, at conferences, and in private trainings. The work of training Conscious Moving for others to take into the world has been one of the most meaningful and fulfilling actions I have ever undertaken. In the following chapters, people who have studied with me are writing their thoughts and actions as they do this work in their own way. Some of these authors are newly minted CM practitioners, and some have been studying this work for decades. For over half of them, English is not their first spoken language. They live primarily in the US and Europe. Several take this work into therapeutic directions, most take it into artistic and contemplative directions, and several use it in various educational settings. All began this project with a strong sense of their own bodily authority, using their lived experiences of the work to guide their writing. You can see their photos and contact information in the Chapter Contributors tab of www.consciousmoving.com.

This section of the book is offered as a way to see how Conscious Moving lives and works in the world. Ultimately, it might invite you to find your own way with this work, your own methods of moving consciously for some purpose, or no purpose at all but the sheer feeling of the experiences.

6

Working with Trauma and Oppression in Multicultural Contexts

AMBER GRAY, PhD BC-DMT, (*Muxkwudeheenawxkway; Saa'am So Otsi*), is an award-winning dance movement therapist, human rights psychotherapist, and authorized Continuum teacher. She has worked for twenty-five years with survivors of human rights abuses, war, torture, historical trauma, and oppression. Equally artist, advocate, author, educator, and therapist, she, her clients, and mentors cocreate survivor- and Spirit-centered, polyvagal-informed approaches to Somatic and Dance/Movement Psychotherapy for interpersonal and collective trauma that are holistic, relevant, and emergent.

Quiet friend who has come so far, feel how your breathing makes more space around you. Let this darkness be a bell tower and you the bell. As you ring, what batters you becomes your strength. Move back and forth into the change.

—RAINER MARIE RILKE

Introduction

The restriction of movement, from micro to macro levels, is an effective act of oppression. One way to define *oppression* is the suppression and repression of sovereign movement in service of the oppressors' control and power. Trauma, as a defining life experience, reshapes our bodies and its capacity to express itself through movement. With trauma, conscious movement is undermined by a wide range of often unconscious disconnected, fragmented, and distorted movement patterns arising from fear-based physiological states. Ongoing adherence to these movement patterns and fragments is what gives the oppressors—whether they are individual or collective—ongoing power. The reclamation of conscious movement is core to the restorative process with survivors of human rights abuses, violence, and long-term oppression (Herman 2015).

This chapter explores the integration of the four phases of Conscious Moving, as expressed in the Moving Cycle, with a body-, dance-, and movement-based phasic approach to working with interpersonal, collective, historic, and ancestral trauma in many contexts and with many communities. As always in this work, clients are our teachers. The work shared here reflects their steadfast courage in entering and navigating the dark corridors of fear and terror their bodies have become mined with through acts of torture, sexual violence, and individual and social persecution. Their bodies, which can feel like maps of suffering, become maps of the heart—the noblest human map. These maps are guided by Restorative Movement Psychotherapy, a somatic and dance/movement therapy clinical approach codeveloped with clients through twenty-five years of work and play together. This approach integrates the Moving Cycle, Polyvagal Theory, and Indigenous perspectives and practices. This chapter is dedicated to all who have known the pain of restricted, limited, and immobilized movement.

A defining feature of my clients' experience is displacement—displacement from land, home, family—the things that ground them to a feeling of belonging. Our sense of belonging is a filter for our attentional and our movement capacities. Whether we are displaced by gentrification, war, colonization, genocide, torture, persecution, or constant exposure to the hostility and violence of racist, phobic, cruel, oppressive, and exclusionary white societies, our movement is affected. We may have to plan our movements to stores, schools, and places of worship to coincide with emptier streets so we are not disrespected, attacked, violated, or subjected to judgmental gazes. We may have to move our family to a place that has no history of our people, no favorite corner store, no friendly neighborhood where a child can be tended to for a few hours. When our outward movement is restricted, our inner movement—breath, heartbeat—is forced to change. How we pay attention becomes how we are vigilant. We literally change our shape to accommodate the oppressor and/or the loss that defines displacement, and our inner movement and voice become lost in forced patterns from the tiniest movements to how we walk, behave, act, and express ourselves.

Working with Trauma

Trauma, a term that is used to describe the way survivors act, behave, or feel, is sometimes confused with a clinical diagnosis of posttraumatic stress disorder (PTSD). I have observed that many people can be traumatized without meeting the specific criterion for PTSD. While PTSD is defined by a specific arrangement of diagnostic criteria, being traumatized might be reflected in the inability to sleep properly, or eat and eliminate regularly for extended periods of time, without those specific criteria present. This is as distressing and disruptive to bodies as the many symptoms that comprise PTSD. PTSD is most often cited as a behavioral or affective condition. Being traumatized is often categorized as pathology, or something to fix. These are important distinctions when working in multicultural contexts and being mindful of the body as core to the restorative process.

Culture, which is inclusive of religion, spirituality, familial beliefs and ways, social norms, educational influences, and everything from home that helps shape us, becomes an internal guidepost. From a neuroscientific and, more specifically, a polyvagal perspective, it seems plausible that our *neuroception*—our autonomic nervous system's subconscious capacity to help us seek safety and scan for danger—is influenced by culture.* This is an essential idea for therapists who work in multicultural contexts, or simply with cultures that differ from their own, to understand. Because we therapists who center the body and movement in our work consciously focus on attention, and more specifically the oscillation of attention from inner and outer (interoceptive to exteroceptive; implicit to explicit), we must acknowledge that although neuroception is universal and exists below story, culture informs the expression of this inner physiological process. Neuroception informs our *interoception*—our inner voice—which in turn informs how we see the world. Hindi (2011), citing Fogel, describes a continuum of inner to outer sensing as essential to *somatic awareness*. Somatic awareness is a synthesis of *embodied awareness* (our feeling of an experience) and *conceptual awareness* (our thinking, evaluating, or talking about our experience).

To be traumatized is to be forever changed. From the perspective of the body, this is an important distinction. Both trauma and PTSD, which I prefer to refer to as "perpetual traumatic spiritual reordering," are the bodies' and the whole person's response to a reordering of their world. Whether brief or sustained, single or multiple instances, *exposure* to an event that is perceived as dangerous or life-threatening is core to being traumatized, diagnosably or not. This is the reordering of our world. How we react in the moment(s) of exposure, which is a forced shift of attention, becomes the imprint that fosters our PTSD symptoms or our traumatized state, which then manifests through the ways we move: sensing, feeling, expressing, perceiving, acting and more. Being traumatized shifts our capacity to pay attention to the continuum of human experience.

---

* The Polyvagal Theory was developed by Dr. Stephen Porges. It illuminates the role the autonomic nervous system plays in human development, relationships, and life.

This continuum of human experience is also a continuum of embodiment and conscious movement. This continuum contains an ever-evolving hierarchy of influences, which I language in ways that honor my clients' descriptions of how *they* relate to their bodies. At both the "beginning" and the "end" (a true continuum has neither) is the Mystery—Spirit, the Divine, Soul, Creator, God, Allah— however a person describes this level of experience. At the continuum's bottom, the deep subconscious evolutionary gift of the autonomic nervous system (ANS) seeks safety and scans for danger (called neuroception), and this process relies on sensation, our "key informant" (Porges 2011). Bodily sensation is always the root of what we perceive, feel, think, and how we act. Sensation comes in three branches: interoception, our inner feelings; exteroception, the stream coming in from the outer world; and proprioception, or tracking of our body's position, tone, and balance. These three branches braid together to inform how we pay attention. Impulses arise from this physiological dance and lead us to movement. Movement can be described as our *primary language*. Conscious movement is the integration and recruitment of the whole continuum, in service to moments such as when we notice the quality of light coming through a window or warmth against our skin, or when we dance across a floor in performance. It's movement that we do while paying attention. Above impulses and movement lies the neural-rich brain highway—our belly brain, heart brain, and *brain* brain. *Heart mind* refers to the Indigenous wisdom of a heart-informed brain. The simplest way to describe this is in the bio-intelligence of the fetal curl we are all in at our earliest development. Indigenous wisdom has long promoted the necessity of our embryological curl so that the brain and heart are in close proximity in order to facilitate communication between them, toward our greater and more-evolved wisdom. The transpersonal level of the continuum might best be described as our understanding of a greater purpose, and then we reach the eternal return of Mystery. The whole process, which I call the continuum of human experience, might look like this:

- ▶ Mystery
- ▶ Transpersonal
- ▶ Heart Mind
- ▶ Cognition/Brain
- ▶ Feeling-Emotion-Affect/Heart Brain
- ▶ Intuition/Belly Brain
- ▶ Movement

- ▶ Impulses

- ▶ Perception

- ▶ Attention

- ▶ Exteroception

- ▶ Interoception

- ▶ Sensation

- ▶ Neuroception

- ▶ Mystery

©Amber Gray, RRT&C, 2015

In an experience of fear or terror, our attention shifts and disrupts the continuum, truncating the fluidity of spiral sequencing or flow that we might usually experience. We either uber-focus on the danger, using a limited range of action options—we fight or flee—or, when we experience terror, we shut down. These actions arise from neural circuits of survival in the ANS. There are also many emergent, blended, and hybrid actions—that in simpler terms can be described as freeze, defensive play, submissive play, placating, posturing, appeasing, and many more (with many more culturally incongruous ways to speak about them)—that we engage in service of our survival. The balance between our inner and outer landscapes is altered. Some clients remain so internally aware that every pain, tension, or difficult breath becomes a landmine of fear, disabling their ability to connect to the world around them. Some are so focused on the external—the space around them—that they disconnect from their interior. And everything in between. For most, if not all, the fluid connection between inner sensing and the information we take in from the world around us is disrupted. This is why many survivors of trauma "lose their beat," and experience and express an imbalance between their external and internal worlds, finding the oscillation of attention very difficult.

The Work

Restorative Movement Psychotherapy (RMP) evolved over many years of work with newcomers: refugees, survivors of torture, asylum seekers, and others with a wide variety of legal statuses (and therefore, supportive social resources) within the experience of displacement and forced migration. There are many influences on this work, a primary one being the Moving Cycle, which is the emphasis of this chapter. Other influences include Polyvagal Theory, Indigenous practices from medicine teachers, my work in Indigenous communities, my own heritage, and Body-Mind Centering. These practices are implicit and are bowed to but won't be centered here.

When therapists are working with survivors of complex trauma, it's widely considered essential to use a phasic approach. Most phasic approaches begin with some form of establishing relative safety. They then work on reconnecting to resources, recovering relational connection, and processing the trauma itself, though they may differ in the order in which these occur. RMP's phasic approach might be considered a mirror of the Moving Cycle. The concept of *mirroring* is an important and auspicious one, and it is at the heart of many children-centered, developmental approaches and dance/movement therapy itself. Mirroring is how we learn to be seen and how our being seen is reflected to us, in service of our development toward holism. In my own spiritual tradition, everything is considered a mirror. For every feeling, thought, action, breath, Spirit, there is a mirror. It is in this mirror that the truth of our existence, and our meaning, is reflected to us.

Relative Safety and Dynamic Stability: Awareness

The first phase of RMP is *Relative Safety and Dynamic Stability*, a term that acknowledges the reality that we are only ever as safe as we can be in an uncertain world, and that stability—the capacity to regulate and ground ourselves—is an emergent journey. This first phase is important in the beginning of our work with clients, and throughout. We cannot work with clients if they do not experience some sense of "safe enough" with us as their therapists, and with their own embodied sense of self. The therapist's ability to coregulate with a client (described as assisting clients to shift from states of fear, stress, distress, and discomfort to states of increased ease, presence, calm, and connection) promotes client *self-regulation*—their ability to connect to themselves and make any changes that support them to be more present. This can take a little time or a lot and is not possible without refining the client's awareness and attention so that they can begin to state-shift from fear to ease. In this framework, the client practices awareness by noticing internal and external cues to determine whether they are *safe as can be* or *unsafe*.

What does this look like when working with clients? I worked with a woman in her twenties, newly married, who arrived in the US as a refugee, and as part of an arranged marriage. I will call her Ana. She and her family fled their home country because they had long lived in the same town as the long-ruling dictator, who was responsible for countless disappearances, torture, and violence against his own people. She came to see me because she considered herself very over-weight, and this bothered her for health and aesthetic reasons. She wanted to lose weight so she might be healthier and move easier. Her weight contributed to a "sense of depression," and she also wondered if it might be linked to trauma, which she was learning about through classes her husband encouraged her to take so she could choose a career path.

In our initial sessions, I did not know much about her history other than that her home country was a site of long-time civil war and oppressive rule and that her weight made her uncomfortable. I asked about her history of her body and weight, and initially tried to learn a bit more about her personal development than I usually do with clients whose primary presentation is adult torture. She shared that she felt her weight issues began when she was young, and that she couldn't really think of reasons why she was the sole family member to be as heavy as she was. She did not wish to be "super thin" and was well aware of what she called the "American obsession with thin bodies." I knew from my time in the Middle East that larger, curvier, and more voluptuous bodies are celebrated, and she confirmed that. Her concern with her weight was based on a distressing inability to understand why she could not lose weight, despite healthy eating and a dedication to consistent exercise.

Ana had what I perceived as an unusual weight distribution, which she spoke freely about. Her weight was all around her middle in a shape that could, at times, literally appear like a ring. She felt both protected and smothered by it. Whereas she focused on her feelings of being smothered, I intuited that her sense of being protected was more central. My curiosity was this: What was/is she protecting herself from? Her descriptions reflected a positive and affirma-tive family experience from very early life onward. Here is an excerpt of an early conversation at a time in our work when she continuously talked about being smothered. We had worked with smothering numerous times and were in a stuck place with it. We agreed not to use the word *smothering* to see if we could learn something new.

Me: Let's forget about the history and focus on now. Before we do that, is there anything you'd like to do to get settled and be prepared for our work?

Ana: I'd like to do the feet on ground practice and some dimensional breathing. (Note: These are both structured stabilization practices most of my clients learn. We took the time to do these to prepare.)

Me: Ready?

Ana: Yes.

Me: Great. Remember anytime you want to pause, find your feet on the ground, and/or find your breath inside you, we can do that together.

(Pause.)

Me: As we talk about your weight, what do you notice in your torso? Do you have a sense of this weight?

Ana: It feels too heavy.

Me: Can you describe this heaviness?

Ana: I told you; I feel like I cannot breathe.

Me: What would it be like for you to find your breath and just focus on your breathing, and occasionally shift your attention to that heaviness? You can use the dimensional breathing practice if it helps you.

Ana: (Quiet for a while. Then:) I don't feel it. It's either too heavy or I don't feel it. I need to feel it to lose it, but every time I feel it, it just smothers me.

Me: There's that word. If you can, just feel that heaviness without being smothered.

(Pause.)

Me: Which is more bearable for you now: to feel the heaviness, or not to feel it? (Note: at this point in her work, I knew she could oscillate between both. This was not true in our earliest work.)

Ana: I don't want to feel it.

Me: OK. Let's go there.

(Pause while Ana took some time to sense and bring her awareness to her experience of not wanting to feel her weight.)

Me: Just checking in, Ana. As you are aware of not feeling your weight, can you still sense that it's part of you? Is there a way in which the physical sensation, or absence of it, is different than other areas of your body?

(Silence.)

Ana: Maybe it's the lack of feeling there that is different.

Me: OK let's focus on the lack of feeling. What do you notice?

Ana: I don't feel myself. It's as if I am here and not here.

Me: Great. That's an important observation. Let's stay with that and see which is truer now. Being here or not here.

Ana: When I am in this part of my body, I am not here.

This excerpt of our work together is an example of establishing relative safety and inviting awareness. Ana already knew the two practices we used to settle, prepare, and ground while we explored some uncomfortable sensations and feelings that had previously caused her to panic and become very distressed. Beginning with already-learned practices that clients find helpful, and at times even pleasurable, fosters a *safe as can be* therapeutic space and reminds clients like Ana of their own ability to stabilize, regulate, or balance—whatever language suits them—their own body. A primary focus of this session was increasing Ana's awareness of how she experienced the area she specified she wanted to work on—her weight.

For another client, the process of promoting *safe as can be* and enhancing her attentional capacities was very different. This client, who I will call Betty, came to me with two specific requests. One was to learn yoga so she could "relax." She was a women's rights activist from a country with a horrible history of violence against women, and she and her loving family (husband and two children) had fled when she and her husband were threatened. She self-described as anxious, and in Western diagnostic terms, met the criteria for generalized anxiety disorder and PTSD. Her second request was to learn how to be safe enough to leave her home, which she could not do. She had left her country of origin, but since her arrival to the US she had become terrified to go out, despite knowing that she was in a safer place. Each time she tried to go somewhere, she panicked and ran home. Her husband encouraged her to get help, despite therapy not being something she would have considered back home. Because of her interest in yoga, which was unavailable to her back home, she sought out a therapist who worked with movement and found me.

Our early work consisted of establishing relative safety. This was challenging, as she truly did not feel safe anywhere. I spent several sessions asking questions and offering ideas for where she might experience some relative safety. When she could not think of any, I invited her to get up and move around my office (which she felt was a comfortable place) and let me know where she was drawn to, and where she felt the most comfort. Both comfort and ease have been more accessible than safety for my clients with high levels of fear and intense mobilization or defensive reactions. She liked being near my plants, which are near a large window that looks out on a green area. She said this was where she could "breathe a little easier." Breathing easier, she became aware of more space in her chest. This awareness helped her to be able to identify the micromovements—sensations, breathing shifts, and a swift change in her feeling state—that always preceded her panicking and "losing herself" in fears that kept her at home.

Her home play was to find a similar space in her home. When she returned the following week, she had decided that a window that looked out at a large cluster of trees, with many birds, was her "easiest place." She had a large, soft lounge chair she loved, and she had moved it closer to the window so she could sit and look out. She noticed she began to feel more ease, because she was more able to track and support shifts from states of panic toward tiny physiological and emotional states of comfort and relaxation. This newfound ability was our beginning place.

Contact and Connection: Owning

The second phase is *Contact and Connection*. *Contact* describes an embodied sense of self-experience, akin to Gendlin's (1982) *felt sense*. From a conscious movement perspective, contact also reflects our ability to beam our attention on our present-moment reality; to be able to oscillate attention from internal to external in a natural rhythm; and to stay present, or associated, with what we notice. Contact facilitates connection and owning. We go beyond noticing, with a sense of greater *safe as can be*, and stay affiliated with our experience. Like the Moving Cycle, the sense of somatic contact in RMP is key to how we own our experiences. In this phase, we are simultaneously restoring our connection to ourselves, from micro neurophysiological movement to the macro perception of who we are in the world and how we relate to it. The therapist facilitates connection through the deepening of contact. *Connection* includes clients connecting to their experience and to the bond between therapist and client. Conscious movement facilitates this relationship between contact and connection through the oscillation of attention from self to other and from self to the larger context.

For my first client, Ana, this phase was particularly difficult and painful. She was aware of her tendency to either be smothered by her weight or to completely dissociate from the feeling of it. She was frustrated that she could not anchor into where or when that came from. We would make a little progress in the form of a few bits of emergent memory. She began to associate her "not being here" with the invisibility she required to survive living in a cruel dictator's hometown. She went to school with his children, so invisibility was hard work. As we danced closer to this past reality, she began to have some glimmers of how this experience morphed into either being smothered, or disappearing. She gradually described "feeling myself" a little more, although she still had a difficult time staying present for more than a few moments with either of these polarized experiences. I experienced her as having a hard time landing in how the sociopolitical context she grew up in lived in and shaped her body. While she sometimes could offer a movement to express the "unspeakable things" she felt inside, these movements lacked energy or vitality, and died out quickly.

One day, feeling frustrated with my stuckness within our stuckness, I decided to approach her about playing with a movement practice originated by Emilie Conrad, called Continuum. At that point Continuum was not a usual part of my work, but it is now central to all work that I do with trauma and the moving body. Acknowledging our stuck point, I asked her if she was willing to try something different and a little bit wild. She didn't hesitate a YES.

I explained Continuum's emphasis on respect for all movement, from the tiniest micromovement to larger more expressive movements, and how it privileged nonpatterned, free-flowing, organic movements arising from our 70–80 percent watery body. I briefly demonstrated with the Lunar Breath, an inaudible, but mighty oceanic breath that can initiate a sense of internal fluidity and often looks and feels wavelike. Emilie also posited that it was a parasympathetic breath. I invited Ana to get comfortable and gave her options of remaining in her chair or lying on the floor. She chose to lie on a yoga mat so she could relax.

I taught Ana the Lunar Breath and invited her to slowly fill her torso with it, allowing any sensations, micromovements, or larger movements to express themselves. She grew very still, so still, that I became concerned. There was no movement—just immense stillness. I breathed with her, as I had promised to do, noticing all the little ripples moving inside me, curious about what she was noticing. After about 10 minutes, I saw the tiniest ripples on the skin above her chest, over the sternum, and in her neck and throat. She slowly, s-l-o-w-l-y opened her eyes, and they were moist. She smiled the slowest growing smile I have ever seen. And then she said: "I am home. In my body." Pause. "I found my body home."

With this contact to the deeper layers of her embodied experience, and through conscious and mostly imperceptible movement, she made a powerful connection and landed in her own experience of her body. "I have been protecting myself with all these layers above this deep, quiet place. I have been afraid to come here. I think I now know how to be in my body without being so afraid."

In my Contact and Connection sessions with Betty, we explored relaxing with yoga, as she requested. These sessions consisted largely of me offering her specific sequences she could do on her own at home to support complaints such as fast breathing, not sleeping, and needing to calm down. I invited Betty to begin a daily practice of sitting in her chair, overlooking the trees and birds. As she did this, I invited her to pay attention to changes in her breath, posture, sensation, until she could become more comfortable staying with her inner landscape.

This practice enhanced her attentional capacity. When she first came to me, any sense of her inner world contributed to or amplified her panic. We connected the comfort and relaxed state she experienced sitting in her chair to the comfort and relaxed state she experienced with session-based yoga practices. This bridging of in-session and at-home experiences nourished her capacity to pay attention to her internal experience (interoception) in different environments. This in turn helped her become aware of the internal sensations and changes in her breathing that preceded her panic states.

While in session one day, the image of dawn and dusk emerged—the time when she "felt God closest to the earth." She described the skies she often saw while praying at these times. This memory became a visual memory and a cue to promote this relaxed, calm state. Like Ana, she landed in her body and contacted her innate ability to self-regulate, to be in connection with her body and, therefore, herself.

Simultaneously, Betty's home play assignments expanded. Each week, after finding comfort and relaxation in her chair, looking at the trees she loved, she would walk a little farther, staying connected to the relaxed state. When she began to feel the internal sensations that preceded her panic states, she would go back, restore, and refresh, and then resume walking. She worked her way from the door to the room, to the door to her house, to the elevator of the building, to the door to the outside, and then a quarter, half, and a full block away.

Weaving the Narrative and Meaning-Making: Acceptance and Appreciation

As Betty progressed, she began to grieve the loss of freedom she experienced back home, and the loss of home she experienced by being displaced to the United States. We began to process aspects of her traumatic loss. She and her husband were followed and threatened for many years, including threats to her children's lives. She had spent so much time in hiding, literally and figuratively, her movement repressed and oppressed, that she realized she had learned to "always be running." Through our remembering of both the threats and the fear and terror she and her family navigated, and by our weaving in of the support her husband and other human-rights defenders always offered, she recognized her current anxiety and panic states were from her conditioning to always be running. She was able to clearly express this as "all the ways they changed my movements."

The third phase, *Weaving the Narrative*, is a meaning-making phase. Meaning-making is not just cognitive; it weaves together sensation, movement, perception, emotion, cognition, Spirit, and all aspects of how we make meaning. This is the phase in which the processing of traumatic memories is held. Not all memories need to, or should be, processed. The preceding phases enable us to identify, with clients, what haunts them most and what merits deeper work. Relative safety, dynamic stability, contact, and connection are consistent threads throughout the entire restorative process, like a braid. We continue to resource and source our clients', as well as our own, resilience and strength while we work through the trauma. It is in this phase that we offer space for grieving past experiences, acknowledging the harvests, both painful and helpful. We form, reconnect to, and share our story, grieving and celebrating as we can. A braid has three strands: the third strand is the *third space*, a term my teacher Tony Lee, a Larrakia medicine person, uses to describe the unique space we cocreate when we work with another human being.

Ana and I spent many months weaving her verbal and nonverbal narratives. Our mini-Continuum exploration expanded to much longer movement inquiries. I taught her more of the sounding practices of Continuum (for example, O and E sounds made on long exhales). We often worked in her torso and spine, and then extended out to her arms and legs. It is not always possible with complex trauma to begin somatic and movement work; for Ana, it was necessary. These longer conscious movement sessions, hybridizing Continuum and dance therapy, were always accompanied by conversations about hiding. She often wept as she discovered how much of herself she kept hidden, emotionally and somatically. She recognized that she had protected herself with the ring of weight around her torso, and that acknowledging this would be essential to supplementing her hard work to lose this weight and to ease her depression. And lose weight she did. It began very slowly, and we celebrated each half pound that her scale told her she had lost. As she continued to stabilize in her shifting states, shape, and physical form, we went deeper into processing the terrifying memories of her childhood, images of horrible things that haunted her. Things she knew and even withheld from her family; things she had seen when playing in remote fields as a child or walking to and from school. She cried for the first time over many of the things she endured, and she expressed some rage at what she and her childhood friends lived through, now that she could experience a place where there wasn't as much direct threat.

Integration: Action

The final phase is Integration, which refers to the process of incorporating the work done with clients' everyday life, called Action in the Moving Cycle.

Particular to trauma, one way to conceptualize this is to place traumatic experiences in their rightful place. Many trauma models refer to *putting it in the past*, and this is true within the limits of linearity, yet our lives are neither singular nor linear. We spiral in and out of the felt sense of experiences, between our feeling and interpersonal processing of experience. Our capacities to endure and stay present are also a spiral. It's not a window that we move up and down; it's a spiraling through the various manifestations of our humanness and embodiment while maintaining our attentional capacities. The past continues to influence us. It doesn't mean we will no longer be triggered or affected; it means we have restored our innate capacities to regulate, to ground, to remain centered and in ourselves in ways that don't undermine our living as they once did. The integration occurs on a continuum from neurophysiological to the cosmic or spiritual level, as illustrated in the continuum of human experience. We integrate all our experiences as a spiral weaving that includes ancestors and future possibilities so that the trauma we place in the past is part of what we weave right now. It's life changing, and the full embodiment of that change is integration.

For Ana, integration was steady and slow. After several months of meaning-making work, she was able to focus attention more consistently on the present. Increasingly, our sessions were filled with conversations about things she was engaged in now, or future plans. She requested to see me less frequently, as she was taking several exercise classes, swimming regularly, and working part time. Eventually, she and her husband decided to fulfill a shared dream and move to the West Coast, away from both their families of origin. This was unusual in her culture, and a powerful step into them both claiming their own design of their future. She was continuing to lose weight, and as they wanted to have a child, they both felt it would be better to be settled in their new home to do this. When Ana moved, she presented me with a lovely wrap she had made for me. The wrap draped and folded, and it moved like water when I wore it. This was intentional: she had come to associate her experience of her own body in our work as "all the ways a human being can move and be in this world. I have learned how steady my body is, always there for me, and how, like water, it can change." A year or so later, I received a note from Ana that she was pregnant, at her desired weight, and loving living near the ocean. She described a very fulfilled life, having integrated her past consciously, which helped her find the courage to take actions she had previously only dreamed of.

Betty's sessions ended more quickly. She wanted to get back to her work and find ways to support women's causes in the United States. As we worked through her longer ventures out of her apartment and into her neighborhood, she cultivated her ability to walk to a corner store and buy things she needed. We processed the loss of freedom she had internalized, and she began metabolizing these memories more quickly. It took us five months until she was able to walk to the end of her block. In the remaining three months, she began walking to stores, going into stores, and interacting with people. She also began driving and was driving herself and a new friend to dance classes. At this point, she decided she had completed therapy. It is rare to have a typical closure in therapeutic work with refugees. Betty brought her entire family to my office with a cake they had baked for me, displaying a colorful THANK YOU in sprinkles. We closed our work together with her stated commitment, in front of all of us, to "keep moving farther and farther away from my calm and relaxed place, and any time I feel afraid, to recall the prayers of dawn and dusk and retreat to my calm place, inside."

Conclusion

Healing is a restorative process that is never a straight line. It might be better conceptualized as a spiral through a continuum of embodied human experience, a weaving of past, present, and the possibility of the future, in our present-moment conscious movements—all movements, from the smallest to the grandest. For both my clients, working with conscious movement within the powerful and adaptable framework of the Moving Cycle supported them to reconnect to forgotten and repressed voices that for years had been hidden under literal somatic manifestations such as Ana's weight, and symptomatic expressions such as dissociation, anxiety, panic, and suffocation. These hidden voices slowly began to express as micromovements and micromoments that gave way to larger movements and patterns. Exploring these layers of expression helped us disrupt stuckness in movement and behavioral patterns associated with complex histories of traumatic exposure. RMP and the Moving Cycle offered these clients opportunities to reassociate with familiar, helpful, and easeful movements. We also codiscovered brand-new movements that allowed them to access newer and more emergent possibilities in their bodies via their sensations, perceptions, emotions, movements, thoughts, and actions. Ana's history of silencing and hiding was due to living in proximity to a brutal and cruel dictator and her socially unfavorable position because of her tribal affiliation and ancestry. Betty lived in a country whose rulers blatantly discriminated and persecuted against her gender. Her courageous human-rights activities amplified her exposure and her risk. Their many years of being silenced and oppressed disconnected them from who they truly were and are. Working with conscious movement in seemingly small ways birthed bolder movements that enabled Ana to redefine her body's shape and her own way of inhabiting her body. This allowed her to make decisions and take actions that she previously only dreamed of. Betty literally learned to move again, traveling to and from her new home, something she had lost the ability to do. This restored her sense of self-worth and dignity, so she reengaged with meaningful activity in her life. The Moving Cycle provided both clients a frame to explore within a *safe as can be* context and allowed them to venture into new territories of the body, opening pathways to both familiar and new experiences of their unique humanity.

References

Fogel, Alan. 2009. *The Psychophysiology of Self-Awareness: Rediscovering the Lost Art of Body Sense.* New York: W. W. Norton.

Gendlin, Eugene T. 1982. *Focusing.* New York: Bantam Books.

Herman, Judith. 2015. *Trauma and Recovery: The Aftermath of Violence from Domestic Abuse to Political Terror.* New York: Basic Books.

Hindi, Fatina S. 2011. "How Attention to Interoception Can Inform Dance/ Movement Therapy." *American Journal of Dance Therapy* 34, no. 2 (December): 129–40.

Porges, Stephen. 2011. *The Polyvagal Theory: Neurophysiological Foundations of Emotions, Attachment Communications, Self-Regulation.* New York: Norton Books.

7

Moving the Self in Dialogue

A Contextual and Fluid Process to Identity Exploration

LAIA JORBA GALDOS, LPC, PhD (she, her, hers), is a Catalan teacher, counselor, supervisor, and mentor, originally from Barcelona and currently residing in Colorado, the unceded land of the Cheyenne, Arapaho, and Ute tribes, among others. She holds counseling specialties in Body Psychotherapy and Dance/Movement Therapy. Her clinical interests include working with trauma in the individual and collective bodies, as well as exploring the embodied experience of migration. She has taught at different universities and lectures nationally and internationally.

In all people I see myself, none more and not one a barleycorn less,
And the good or bad I say of myself I say of them.
And I know I am solid and sound,
To me the converging objects of the universe perpetually flow,
All are written to me, and I must get what the writing means.
And I know I am deathless.
I know this orbit of mine cannot be swept by a carpenter's compass
I know I shall not pass like a child's carlacue cut with a burnt stick at night.

—WALT WHITMAN, *LEAVES OF GRASS*

Introduction

I am. . . . I'm alive and in motion. I am a grandchild, the child of my parents, a sister, a partner, and a friend. I am the dream of my ancestors, and the wisdom of those that came before me. I am the whisper of my mother in a hurry, and the playfulness and curiosity of my father. I am the surprise of spiritual openings in the midst of kindness, service, and urgency. I am the fire of fighters that preceded me and the wind of goddesses and witches. I am the vessel of trauma and pain, and the promise of a kinder tomorrow. I am your witness and your reflection, and the outcome of our intermingling together . . . When I look in the mirror now, who do I really see?

When I try to describe who I am, the answer varies depending on the person in front of me and the context of our conversation. The answer also shifts moment to moment as we speak; I come up with new realizations about myself through the effort of putting my experiences into a coherent narrative and by the questions and feedback from the person I am with.

At times, like in the opening paragraph, I have defined myself through roles and relationships to others, such as being a child of my mother, a sister, or a partner. My identity can include my profession, which is often associated with my social value. If I use social categories to identify myself, such as gender, race, or ethnicity, even at an unconscious level I feel a pull and push dance between what is externally projected on me through the gaze of the person I am talking to, and my own internal sense of identity around those categories; what others project onto me as a female-identified body or an androgynous body (depending on the clothing of the day) will be in tension with my internal sense of gender and how I am reacting to the gendered remarks of another.

Other times, when asked about who I am, I reflect on my own personal characteristics; I'm determined, sensitive, and moved by service. Yet, even if some of these attributes were born with me, I did not receive them passively; they were either accentuated, supported, or muted by people around me. Other non-inherited qualities, like my focus on service, were and are shaped through interacting with situations and people that influenced my behavior, thoughts, and emotional world, which in turn have led me to serve others. Interestingly enough, I have an internal sense of the continuity of these attributes, as if I have always been the same person, dismissing how often I am editing this narrative for the sake of knowing who I am.

In other situations, I am driven by others to think about where I come from, my ancestors, and my lineage. How far back should I trace those origins? My answer could wind all the way back to the formation of nations in Europe, which gave gradual rise to the construction of my Catalan culture, or just to the immediate cultural formation of my parents and grandparents.

From any of these viewpoints, it is difficult to defend the idea of identity as something sturdy or permanent, being confronted by its constant movement and change. This lack of solidity becomes problematic in moments of increased uncertainty, such as our emergence from the COVID pandemic. Ideas of progress that were mainstream a few decades ago are being contested by the Right and Left; social justice approaches are being challenged to incorporate more ecological and sustainable ways of thinking; liberal and capitalistic markets are failing to deliver promised equilibrium; extremism in politics holds onto the past while it dismantles foundations of democratic processes; scientific gains are clashing with partial solutions and uncoordinated efforts; and we lack a consensual story that can give us hope for a better world and motivation for living (Eisenstein 2013). Social, political, professional, and familial spaces are increasingly becoming arenas of opposing identities that, instead of embracing movement and change to creatively manage our differences, foster a longing for fixed identities in an attempt to avoid uncertainty.

Interrupting these dynamics requires us to embrace movement and change, bear the unknown, and let go of old ideas of who we have been or who others are; it also requires us to take the risk of being impacted by others without worrying about being inconsistent. I am advocating for a framework of exploration and embodiment of identities that is both fluid and solid, a movement practice that calls for the wisdom of body-identity to adjust and adapt creatively to these challenges.

This chapter envisions identity as a process; it envisions this process as developing fluidly in different contexts, which in turn could help us better adjust to increasingly shifting environments. The chapter first reviews two of the foundations of Western identity development theory, namely autonomy and continuity. Then the chapter explores non-Western ideas that support a more relational and ecological identity development. In exploring these foundations, I use *identity* to refer mostly to social locations of the person and the concept of *self* to refer to our sense of "who I am and what I am." The final part of the chapter applies these concepts to a process-oriented exploration of identity through the lens of the Moving Cycle. The Moving Cycle is a therapeutic framework that facilitates ongoing and ever-changing processes, threading together internal and external experiences in a temporary but stable composition of the self that holds both fluidity and integrity. Although I use my work with therapy clients to illustrate the process of identity inquiry and formation, similar explorations can be applied in educational spaces, mindfulness practices, and creative endeavors.

The Myth of Autonomy: Envisioning the Self in Systems

One of the cornerstones of identity formation theories in Western societies is conceptualizing our self as an autonomous entity that forms separately from the groups we belong to, from one another, and from nature. Some trace the first chronicled step toward "individual separation" to the Greek philosopher Plato (Csaki n.d.), but it was not until Christian thinking matured in the Middle Ages that this philosophical thread, the specialness of the individual over collectives and nature, took root enough to support ideas of individuality. These roots unfold fully from modern political philosophers, who conceived of the individual as the ultimate unit of society, displacing the tribe and the family as the foundations of social organization (Siedentop 2014).

The rise of these theories informed the development of modern liberalism, founded in the moral equality of every individual and the legal imperative to protect individual privacy and property rights. This paradigm enticed many to the promise of the liberation of the individual, but it simultaneously created the seeds of isolation and loneliness, where we gain a sense of autonomy and uniqueness but are also expected to be self-sufficient at all times. Our tendency to feel pressured to resolve moments of distress in loneliness and place the responsibility of life's failures solely on ourselves can cause a constant uncertainty that explains many of the mental health struggles of the clients and students with whom I interact daily.

This undercurrent of separate selves is palpable in mainstream identity and development theories in the West. Even though current formulations of these theories highlight the impact of the environment on us, the fundamental belief that individuals exist independently, as agents needing to forge a path forward toward self-growth and individuation, still pervades. Take, for instance, Erikson, one of the West's most classic and influential developmental psychologists. He placed the interactions between the individual and the cultural environment at the center of this theory (Erikson 1968). Erikson defined the ultimate stage of identity formation as the outcome of a "crisis"; a crisis that involves a clash between personal and environmental forces that influence each other, but that also preexist without one another. This perspective continues to reinforce what I call the *autonomy myth*—a final stage of my self-development that is solid and ongoing across different situations.

The notion of disconnected parts within a system that will influence each other but are essentially separate doesn't hold water in fields such as biology, ecology, or quantum physics, though these fields have yet to prove strong enough to counterbalance the weight and inertia of individualistic narratives in the West. But they do steer us toward a completely different way to conceptualize the self. One of these threads is the idea of dependent origination, which lies at the foundation of many Buddhist teachings that conceive of the world as woven of interconnected threads. In it, we only exist in relation to everything else; in other words, our being is *interbeing* (Nhat Hanh 1991, 2017). We can also trace back the tenets of interconnectedness to many ancient and native cultures that have historically envisioned the self as co-belonging and coexisting. This is reflected, for instance, in the North American native nations greeting "all my relations" (*Mitákuye Oyás'iŋ*, in Lakota language), which refers to our interdependence with everything and everyone around us—nature and animal world, past and future generations—a system of oneness governed by principles of unity and radical equality. We are all a continuation of something and a result of something else, not in a linear trajectory but in a fluid dance with everyone else around us. I am possible because of the confluence of many forces around me.

Since the moment of conception, the infant develops in a cultural environment that not only interacts with the infant but that also conditions their senses and perceptions, shapes their brain structures, and builds the substrate for relational interactions. Pregnancy itself "cannot be studied outside societal influences," Bertau points out (2012, 68). The external expectations of rearing a child affect the way we orient and care for our babies and for ourselves, which in turn influences our developing infant. In addition, the rhythms of our movement and our verbal and nonverbal intonations are somatically and sensorially orienting our infant to their culture in an early synchronization of physiology and culture (Bertau 2012). As infants, all the stimuli that we receive through our bodily senses are integrated and interpreted, but most importantly, they shape our brain differently depending on what is needed in any situation. This includes visual depth, the acuteness of color perception, sound orientation, the importance of different objects (individualistic cultures) or holistic background orientation (collectivistic environments), to name a few (Miyamoto, Nisbett, and Masuda 2006). In a truly cocreative process, external information creates internal representations of the world around us, which become the lenses through which we see the world. As Fogel put it, "Cognition and perception are not mirrors of reality, but relational processes" (1993, 4). We are born with somatic and neurological structures of possibilities, but we cannot come to be whole without the environment (Harris et al. 2015). We can see this interdependence when we interact with others, in the process of relating to each other—from early bodily touch between caregivers and their infants to the exchange of ideas between two adults—that our identities are discovered, formed, and transformed. It is the questions that you pose to me that allow me to reflect on who I am, and in my response to you, I am also shaping and influencing your understanding of yourself. Without this dialogue we would not know ourselves. In a dynamic open system (Fogel 1993), we are never fully defined but forming dynamically through the process of relating.

The Continuity of the Self:
Fixed versus Fluid Narratives

The second cornerstone of individualism is the idea of *self-continuity*. The idea that we are always the same is defined as our sense of the connection between our past, present, and future, and a retrospective and prospective capacity to make associations (Sedikides, Hong, and Wildschut 2023). The process of building our biography involves stitching together specific experiences to give ourself the illusion of congruency over time. Although this story may feel solid, we are constantly adding new information and editing out incongruencies that do not align with our present idea of self. Hence, despite their fluid character, identities often feel and are experienced as if they are stable.

This natural tendency to think of our identities as objective and permanent is made worse in moments of increased anxiety, as we can see in both progressive and conservative sides of the political spectrum. On one hand, some of us with marginalized identities resort to arguments of identity differences as a way to defend our group rights and advance political causes. On the other hand, many of us with privileged identities hold onto conservatist ideas of identity fueled by the fear of being pushed off the pedestal of privilege. Additionally, we can also see some forms of essentialism in how we pursue ancestral identities through DNA analysis and historical reconstructions of family lines. This seems to be specifically unique to the US, where many Black communities have lost the continuity of their lineage due to slavery's practices of separation and silencing; but also in many white Americans who are disconnected from their cultural origins and traditions. The traumatic interruption of what would have naturally been the fluid transmission of lived identities often leaves us with a grasping for an unknown distant cultural heritage.

In the need to be seen and known, in an attempt to find a sense of belonging, and in the process of defending the fundamental rights of the self, we often default toward self-continuity, essentializing something that is mutable and fluid, and we end up holding onto self-images too tightly. Essentialism, in a way, is connected to the need to clarify identity, but often it is held in rigid juxtaposition to others, fueling prejudices, stereotypes, and the perpetuation of oppression (Bastian and Haslam 2006; Morton, Hornsey and Postmes 2009). We cannot ignore the role of self-continuity in the well-being of the individual and collectives, but these identities are more adaptive if held in softness (Sani, Bowe, and Herrera 2008; Sedikides, Hong, and Wildschut 2023; Zou et al. 2018). For instance, we can conceptualize gradual and progressive changes to our sense of self, which has both elements of permanence (we can relate to who we were a few months or years ago) and malleability (but maybe not relate as much to who we were several years back).

From another angle, self-continuity is not always a positive attribute, specifically when we hold a negative concept of ourself that is perceived as a permanent trait (Sedikides, Hong, and Wildschut 2023). In these instances, these beliefs of who we are become a roadblock for personal transformation; for instance, believing that I have always lacked motivation, or have addictive tendencies, without leveling this narrative with other counterbalancing facts reduces my own likelihood of change. Additionally, in times of major life ruptures, such as during migration or the loss of a job, ideas of who we are based on our past experiences may not be adaptive to new realities and needs (Izadifar 2022). These outdated self-concepts can become the fuel for unresolved grief and emotional and cognitive rigidity.

The concepts of identity and the self can be difficult to work with due to their shifting nature, which is also dependent on context. Holding on to individualistic ideas of the self as separate and ubiquitous is proving to be nonadaptive to a rapidly changing world, while also feeding mental health struggles of separateness and loneliness. We have much to gain by seeing identity as a process—a practice of conscious movement. This is what I intend to look at now, focusing specifically on applying these lenses and the Moving Cycle to identity exploration.

Searching for the Self in Therapy: The Moving Cycle Approach

As Christine Caldwell has defined in the introduction to this book, the unifying principle of life, and how the self relates to life, is movement. The Moving Cycle framework allows therapists to use this process of inquiry in counseling and bridges therapeutic explorations to the outside world in a more embodied and conscious way. The Moving Cycle is a therapeutic lens, an intervention tool, an ethical endeavor, and a radical action project, providing a guideline for clients to come to terms with shifting identities and to engage with the world and its challenges adaptively. The Moving Cycle offers us the opportunity to pay attention to and participate mindfully in forming and redefining these identities as an open system in perpetual motion, but also an empowered embodiment of identities.

Because clients bring many inquiries about self and identity to therapy, I have opted to provide different examples and presentations to illustrate these explorations. The disadvantage of this approach is that I will not be able to detail the interventions and therapeutic tools for each of the examples and phases of therapy. The advantage is that multiple illustrations as variations of the same theme will give you a sense of how to apply creative possibilities to different projects of identity exploration both in therapy and in other fields. I do think that for the purpose of this chapter, breadth is better than depth. Here are some of the general examples that I refer to throughout: a) a client who feels a sense of estrangement from their relatives as a result of polarization around political positions and party lines; b) a Black client who only knows their ancestry lines up to their grandmother; c) a client who emigrated to the US for political reasons, who experiences relative safety as well as loss from leaving behind what was nurturing and known; d) a mestizo client who has never felt any belonging to a specific community; e) a very exhausted gender fluid client who is working at a nonprofit for the advancement of gender-affirming rights and care; and f) an adolescent who does not feel at home in her own skin, trying to impress her peers, and feeling the need to repress parts of herself to be accepted.

In what follows, I review the four stages of the Moving Cycle as I apply them to the exploration of these identities and the self in therapy:

1. *Awareness* of the shifting and contextual self in dialogue

2. *Owning* the experience of interrelational being

3. *Appreciation* and integration of the new capacity of being

4. *Action* feedback loop: how to be in an interrelational world

Awareness of the Shifting and Contextual Self in Dialogue

We cannot move with clarity if we do not first know where we stand. When distress around identities is present in therapy, clients tend to be at two different points on the spectrum of identity: either they do not know who they are (which often presents as depression and anxiety) or they are trying to hold tight to identities that feel threatened in some way (which normally shows up as pain, exhaustion, and anger). Any kind of action from these positions is bound to be unclear and reactive, and as a consequence, can potentially lead them to feeling more separated and isolated.

The therapist must first increase the client's clarity by bringing mindful attention to their internal processes during the Awareness Phase. With those who are at a loss for who they are, we might begin with something as simple as *noticing*—getting familiar with the experience of being "at a loss." I might guide the client to attend to this experience mindfully and gently, holding back judgment and observing internal sensations, emotions, and beliefs with a descriptive stance.

I might then guide the client to explore more consciously the potential anchors of the self underlying that fog, offering the simple and open prompt, "I am," and encouraging the client to "listen" or observe the emerging internal impacts. I would ask the client to allow the prompt to land inside and to notice microresponses that they can verbalize using descriptive words. The purpose is not to find an answer to the prompt yet, but to notice its impact, sense the body's response to the inquiry, and witness the somatic experience that emerges. As the client slows down, keeps repeating the inquiry "I am," and lets the body move in response, associations in the form of emotions, images, memories, and sensations may arise. I encourage this bottom-up approach, helping to hold back narratives and explanations in favor of what is emerging in the present moment.

If the client begins on the opposite pole, with a rigid sense of their identities, I might still orient them to explore these identities with the same process of embodied mindfulness and a descriptive stance, attending to their somatic experience of these identities. Here, the client starts with a complete statement as a prompt—"I am _____ (fill in the blank)" (for example, "I am a mother" or "I am Black")—and opens up to the deep listening of the somatic experience. In the process of moving these identities, some associations with images, emotions, and memories may arise. I help the client first acknowledge these associations and then let them go to see what comes up next. In the process of observing the fluid nature of these experiences, the client gradually holds to these identities less rigidly.

Identities exist in a social web of relationships. Therefore, I make sure to contextualize awareness practices by placing the client in different relational scenarios. I might first support the client in imagining themselves in a specific cultural or environmental setting and then begin the same open practice of mindful awareness to the inquiry "I am" or "I am _____ (fill in the blank)." For instance, the activist client presented earlier explored their internal experience of gender identity, imagining themselves in different types of communities or social scenarios: at a wedding with mostly heterosexual couples; in a drag party; in a demonstration for abortion rights; in their childhood neighborhood in Oklahoma. In each of these scenarios, the prompt "I am nonbinary" elicited different angles and explorations of the somatic experience of that contextualized identity. With the mestizo client, I helped contextualize the inquiry sequentially in each of his two families of origin and helped open a mindful awareness of what movement arose when he was primed with different elements of his heritage.

For the purpose of exploring self-continuity, I would bring the client's attention to their chronological story. Here, the prompt could be something like "When did you first learn this way of being in the world?" but instead of a narration, the client continues to observe somatic responses and arising associations. This may lead the client to body memory associations of how these identities formed, which further supports them in softening their hold on some of those identities by identifying their social origin. If exploring self-discontinuity, the inquiry "I am" or "I am___ (fill in the blank)" is complemented by this prompt later in the session: "Back then I was" Or "Back then I was this kind of_____ (fill in the blank)." This prompt again facilitates an increased perception of progressive shifts simultaneously holding elements of change and continuity.

In exploring self-continuity it can also be important to evoke the lineage of the client's ancestors. Inviting prior generations into the room through imagery, and supporting the client to bring awareness to their internal experience as they relate to their ancestors is a powerful experience of inquiry that brings bodily sensations, movement impulses, and a breadth of emotions. Many clients have a sense of disconnect from their ancestry line, like the mestizo who never knew the tribes he came from because of the practices of silencing those traditions by the white part of his family. Even though he did not know and could not trace the names of these ancestors and their specific stories, he experienced body feelings, sensations, and transmissions at the preconscious and collective level through nonverbal cues. In cases like these, I physically place the client in different locations in the room that represent generations of ancestors. I invite the client to be in that space while holding the awareness of these generations and opening themselves to emerging bodily experiences. Just physically holding a space with awareness allows sensory states and bodily movements to surface that were previously unknown, often accompanied by emotions, yet rarely associated with memories. Through this process, the client starts to awaken the thread of intergenerational being, metabolizing old suffering, and connecting themselves to the embodied experiences of intergenerational resiliency.

The sense of continuity of the self not only relates to ancestors but also to the generations of tomorrow. Embracing this perspective increases the sense of responsibility, but also reduces the urgency of having to take action alone. With the activist client working at the nonprofit for gender rights, it seemed especially important to connect with the resiliency of the origins of the movement—of all prior generations who were able to plant seeds for more inclusive rights—but also to connect with future generations who will continue the fight when the client is gone. By helping the client contextualize rights advocacy and embody this historical perspective, I worked to lessen their sense of urgency and increase their capacity to focus on their experience of being in the present. This allowed them to clarify what actions to take and when, increasing the sustainability of these actions in this lifetime and reducing their burnout.

Finally, part of this process of contextualized awareness is helping the client bring attention to the eyes of the external witness. For the adolescent client, this meant helping her to increase awareness of the impact of her peers, the internal sensations that the peers triggered in her, and the consequent impulses she had to hide or suppress parts of the self, while simultaneously feeling the longing to connect. I facilitated the client not only to pay attention to her own internal experience, but also to oscillate out and investigate her own impact on others. The process helped to increase awareness of the interrelational feedback loop of actions and responses between herself and others. The focus was not yet on making decisions or clarifying actions but increasing somatic consciousness and literacy of the interconnectedness between all things.

The focus of the Awareness Phase is on sharpening the client's perception and mindfulness of their present-moment experience of identities. The client awakens to what feels alive and present and also has access to parts of the self that may have been hidden or lost. This process also helps with the awareness of what parts of the self are stable across context and time; it becomes the first step in the consolidation of self-continuity but also helps identify and understand how the self is socially shaped and transformed by everything around it, which also helps in identifying discontinuities of the self. Additionally, the process of paying attention and bringing awareness increases the client's capacity to tolerate intense states, which in itself starts regulating those states. Here lies the first paradox: paying attention to what emerges in the present moment starts the process of transformation. This naturally leads to the Owning Phase.

Owning the Experience of Interrelational Being

Following the organicity of the Awareness Phase, change starts to occur; when change is mindfully facilitated, the client can participate in the wisdom of their inner capacity for self-actualization. They shed stuck forms of hurt, and new forms of emergent presence develop. When the client trusts the organicity of their body, my task is to provide them structure and encouragement so they can move and metabolize stuck emotions and to support the client as they organize the movement into a new way of being.

When clients explore identities in the Owning Phase, a common theme is the emergence of intense waves of grief of lineages that have been lost, but also other strong emotions such as anger, shame, or fear of losing who they are. As I work to create a space for the client to process these emotions, I coach the client in observing and being in the emotional experience, supported by the triangle of sensing, movement, and breathing. Little by little, this facilitates the sequencing and metabolizing of affect. I can also coach the movement by asking the client, "How does the grief/anger want to move your body?" and I can support the client in listening to their body's narrative of the emotions as they unfold. I can even mirror or accompany the client with similar movements, almost as if I am saying without words, "This is OK" (giving permission) or "I can handle this" (being the external container of the process).

It might also be important and powerful to place this emotional processing in context; for instance, the Black client moved their grief in the presence of imagined ancestors who can receive this grief and externally regulate it, activating a collective sense of holding the pain. For the activist client, it felt important to situate their pain and their determination to continue the fight within a community of like-minded individuals who could witness the movement of these emotions.

Another common occurrence when the client is exploring identities in a chronological and contextual way is that collective resources emerge for the client and they reclaim parts of those identities that feel congruent to their self. For instance, the mestizo client explored the prompt "I am_____," which brought forward his mother's and father's respective families of origin, opened up the identification of resources tied to specific environments, and brought a breadth of possibilities for the client's regulation. In this case, I helped the client identify what felt resourcing and what did not in each cultural context. After identifying these resources, such as specific songs or the smell of food, I supported the client in embodying them through a practice of noticing the impact on the client's lived experience, letting that impact grow and be felt internally, and then expanding it with movement to the whole body. The result was a unique reclamation of hybrid identities (Jorba Galdos and Warren 2022) crystallized in new meaning-making and embodied beliefs: "I am a mestizo, and this is what that means to me today in this time and space." The client furthered the embodiment of this experience by moving in response to the new meaning-making, from the first gesture to a full sequence of movements generalized to the whole body. He started with a tentative sense of groundedness and lifted his head, a clear body marker from one side of his racial upbringing, while having some movement in the hips from his other racial identity. He then played with this polarity for a while, increasing his awareness of body-centered racial cues as anchors, but also playing with the relationship between solid ground and fluid movement. This helped him to notice how the different parts of his body moved in a more integrated sequence as he walked around the room, finding a body narrative that reflected the particular experience of his mestizo identity.

Transitions between identities and contexts are another relevant theme when exploring embodied identities. Supporting the client to move between two culturally different contexts can help them organize their body in a fluid manner that supports a more coherent choreography of the self (Jorba Galdos and Warren 2022). Let's look at the female-identified client relocating from Afghanistan to Colorado for political reasons. First, the client somatically explored her experience of being a woman back in Kandahar; second, she repeated this body inquiry of her gender identity and expression in Denver; and finally, she engaged in consciously moving back and forth between those two cultural spaces that had been placed on two opposite sides of the room. The client was increasingly aware of the continuous shift of her bodily organization, attending to the costs and tensions she experienced in both locations, but also of elements of a strength that she could reclaim as the underlying force supporting her migration journey. In the choreography of moving back and forth between the two countries, the client was able to come up with a movement sequence that was less effortful and more resourceful. She was also able to enrich this movement with associated cultural images, key memories in the formation of those identities, and emerging emotions that she was able to move and process for the first time.

Finally, another common theme in the Owning Phase is the process of identity discernment. Any live system is protected by permeable boundaries that allow nutrients in and push toxins out. In our alive identity system, discernment becomes a critical capacity; it helps us consciously claim the parts of our identity that feel good and keep out projected identities that feel toxic. The process of discernment in the therapy room helps us embody softer and gentler boundaries that are solid but feel less effortful and exhausting. For instance, the client with relatives at the other end of the political spectrum practiced delineating physical boundaries with their hands, which helped them to feel an embodied sense of limits that was more grounded and less explosive. The boundary for the client contained internal messages that said, "This is me," and "It is OK to be me," and external messages that said, "This is not me," and "It is OK to be you." Part of the practice for the client was to remain open to dialogue with their relatives, while also speaking to what felt internally congruent.

Appreciation and Integration
of the New Capacity of Being

As the exploration and processing of the Owning Phase settle, the client is able to appreciate the difference of this new state. The Appreciation Phase is focused on nurturing something that is emerging and on increasing the possibility of embodying this outside the therapy room. In my work I help the client to create ease and comfort in embodying this new experience, savoring it, and enjoying a more resourced and congruent state, letting it organically expand throughout their being (somatically, emotionally, and cognitively) to make it more familiar and fuller. The adolescent client felt prouder of her values and less shy or worried about rejection as she held healthier boundaries that helped her discern what friends to invest in and how to voice her opinions and values. The immigrant client brought a sense of knowing her origins and was able to move in the world with the support of her ancestors, while simultaneously embracing the possibility of more freedom in her new neighborhood. The mestizo client was able to embody a hybrid sense of identity that feels congruent wherever he is, dismantling the prior sense of never being enough.

This new state is not a unitary fusion of prior fragmented parts, but a temporary hybrid identity that serves as a container of the many selves within each of us. Even more important than this state are the capacities emerging from the identity exploration process. These include the capacity to remain open to an abundance of inputs, the possibility of organizing movement within to prevent freezing, and the trust in shifting between states with more presence and ease. Helping clients embody this *state* of being and, even more importantly, the *capacity* to explore these states, supports the client distancing from a sense of fixed identity that can feel too rigid at times. Appreciation supports finding a version of ourselves that is solid, while it is still open and in dialogue.

Action Feedback Loop:
How to Be in an Interrelational World

With this increased sense of capacity and clarity, action unfolds as a logical and organic next step. When the client knows in an embodied manner their location in the place of things, it is clearer what to stand up for, what actions they need to take, and how to take them and engage with others in the world. Again, the orientation is not only about the *what* but also about the *process of engaging*.

In therapy, we explore the Action Phase by helping the client imagine their new identities in different situations so they notice not only how they can continue nurturing, embodying, and being in those states but also explore the impact of that way of being in their relationships. I work to help the client to visualize how they move, respond, and stand in relation to others with a sense of integrity. The Black client chose appropriate responses in front of microaggressions while assessing for safety; the client with an estranged family chose to move beyond confrontation and submission in a family celebration; the mestizo client reclaimed with empowerment and clarity his hybrid identity in different contexts in a way that highlighted the strength and creativity of new fusions; the adolescent client impacted and inspired other teens to reclaim their authenticity. By visualizing these different scenarios and somatically rehearsing how to respond, I try to help the client bridge the learning in therapy to future encounters outside in the world.

Embracing an open system in the Action Phase also means listening to internal and external inputs regarding when to take action and when to rest, knowing when to push forward or take a break, how to pick "battles," and how and when to choose play. The Action Phase helps clients listen and attune to the dialogue between doing and non-doing, action and rest, tension and release. In the case of the gender rights activist, it is a process of ongoing inquiry to allow for rest and action in a way that is less reactive to a sense of urgency and more responsive to integrity of the self, which in turn has a ripple effect on other people around them, creating more sustainability for the gender affirming rights movement overall.

Final Thoughts

This chapter has reviewed the shortcomings of theories of the self and identity formation rooted in individualism, including the increasing difficulty of responding to current societal challenges and the mental health corollaries of isolation and fear. With the inspiration of frameworks of interrelational developmental theories and interbeing philosophies, I have advocated for an idea of the self as an open system embedded in contexts and in fluid motion. This perspective connects to Conscious Moving and specifically to the Moving Cycle framework to support clients' explorations of identities in therapy. Within this contour, clients move through a process of somatic awareness, processing and claiming their own temporary sense of self, appreciating the emerging hybrid forms of identity, and clarifying their actions in the world. This specific embodiment of identities provides both the stability and flexibility needed to respond to challenges with clarity and creativity.

In the future it will also be paramount to apply this lens not only to the individual but also to the identities of groups and collectives. I believe that an open system perspective applied to identity group formation and transformation can integrate the diversity within groups while maintaining cultural practices important for collective well-being. It will also support intercultural dialogues by allowing the cocreation of new ways of being together.

References

Bastian, Brock, and Nick Haslam. 2006. "Psychological Essentialism and Stereotype Endorsement." *Journal of Experimental Social Psychology* 42, no. 2 (March): 228–35. https://doi.org/10.1016/j.jesp.2005.03.003.

Bertau, Marie-Cécile. 2012. "Developmental Origins of the Dialogical Self: Early Childhood Years." In *Handbook of Dialogical Self Theory*, edited by Hubert J. M. Hermans and Thorsten Gieser, 64–81. New York: Cambridge University Press.

Csaki, Steve B. n.d. "The Native Self versus the Myth of the Autonomous Being." Southeastern Oklahoma State University. Accessed September 10, 2023. www.se.edu/native-american/wp-content/uploads/sites/49/2019/09/A-NAS -2017-Proceedings-Csaki.pdf.

Eisenstein, Charles. 2013. *The More Beautiful World Our Hearts Know Is Possible*. Berkeley, CA: North Atlantic Books.

Erikson, Eric H. 1968. *Identity: Youth and Crisis*. New York: W. W. Norton and Company.

Fogel, Alan. 1993. *Developing through Relationships*. Chicago: University of Chicago Press.

Harris, Laurence R., Michael J. Carnevale, Sarah D'Amour, Lindsey E. Fraser, Vanessa Harrar, Adria E. N. Hoover, Charles Mander, and Lisa M. Pritchett. 2015. "How Our Body Influences Our Perception of the World." *Frontier in Psychology* 6 (June 12): 819. https://doi.org/10.3389/fpsyg.2015.00819.

Izadifar, Morteza. 2022. "The Neurobiological Basis of the Conundrum of Self-Continuity: A Hypothesis." *Frontiers in Psychology* 13: 740542. https://doi .org/10.3389/fpsyg.2022.740542.

Jorba Galdos, Laia, and Marcia Warren. 2022. "The Body as Cultural Home: Exploring, Embodying, and Navigating the Complexities of Multiple Identities," *Body, Movement and Dance in Psychotherapy* 17, no. 1: 81–97, https: //doi.org/10.1080/17432979.2021.1996460.

Miyamoto, Yuri, Richard E. Nisbett, and Takahiko Masuda. 2006. "Culture and the Physical Environment: Holistic versus Analytic Perceptual Affordances." *Psychological Science* 17, no. 2 (February): 113–19. https://doi.org/10.1111 /j.1467-9280.2006.01673.x.

Morton, Thomas A., Matthew J. Hornsey, and Tom Postmes. 2009. "Shifting Ground: The Variable Use of Essentialism in Contexts of Inclusion and Exclusion." *British Journal of Social Psychology* 48, no. 1 (March): 35–59. https://doi.org/10.1348/014466607X270287.

Nhat Hanh, Thich. 1991. *Old Path White Clouds: Walking in the Footsteps of the Buddha*. Berkeley, CA: Parallax Press.

———. 2017. *The Art of Living: Peace and Freedom in the Here and Now*. New York: Harper Collins.

Sani, Fabio, Mhairi Bowe, and Marina Herrera. 2008. "Perceived Collective Continuity and Social Well-Being: Exploring the Connections." *European Journal of Social Psychology* 38, no. 2: 365–74. https://doi.org/10.1002/ejsp.461.

Sedikides, Constantine, Emily K. Hong, and Tim Wildschut. 2023. "Self-Continuity." *Annual Review of Psychology* 74, no. 1 (January): 333–61. https://doi.org/10.1146/annurev-psych-032420-032236.

Siedentop, Larry. 2014. *Inventing the Individual: The Origins of Western Liberalism*. Cambridge, MA: Belknap Press.

Zou, Xi, Tim Wildschut, Dan Cable, and Constantine Sedikides. 2018. "Nostalgia for Host Culture Facilitates Repatriation Success: The Role of Self-Continuity." *Self and Identity* 17, no. 3: 327–42. https://doi.org/10.1080/15298868.2017.1378123.

8
Revisioning Addiction through Conscious Moving

RACHELLE JANSSEN is a dance/movement therapist who lives in a small town in the most southern province of the Netherlands, Limburg. After completing her bachelor's degree in Dance/Movement Therapy, she started her own practice working with great passion and pleasure with people who find it difficult to "be at home in their bodies." Rachelle has been active in addiction care since 2013. While she was employed by both large and smaller institutes, such as Vincent van Gogh and Connection, she worked with groups and provided one-on-one sessions as well as outpatient treatment. Over the last ten years, her experience within this field of work has moved her toward a different view on addiction. Rachelle has since integrated the Moving Cycle in her sessions and inspires people to move in a way in which they feel like they're truly living.

Introduction

In this Chapter I explore addiction from a viewpoint developed in Christine's first book, *Getting Our Bodies Back*, in which she writes that addiction goes beyond the stuff of drunks and druggies; it is simply a very human movement, a consistent habit of withdrawing from ourselves (Caldwell 1996).

At the same time, it is an automatic reaching for something that is not ourselves. Through conscious movement and "inhabiting from within," we can get a sense of learning to choose what we want to be devoted to in our lives, breaking free from snoozing through life by getting in touch with our bodies. Throughout the chapter I suggest videos of various practices that may assist you in exploring this topic. These videos can be found on the book's website, www.consciousmoving.com.

About Feeling Amazed and Getting in Touch

In 2016 I read Christine's book, *Getting Our Bodies Back*. It moved me! At that point I had worked for several years in addiction care for different organizations in the Netherlands. I worked with groups and provided one-on-one sessions in clinical treatment as well as outpatient treatment. This book just hit home in so many ways. Starting my own Moving Cycle experiences in 2017 felt like coming home again and again, and I began integrating it into my daily sessions at work.

I had begun working in the addictions field in 2013 and was surprised to find it just clicked with me. It was as if many of my own character traits were being recognized, even though I was the therapist. Ten years on in this field, I can say that I don't differ that much from the people I treat for addictions. When I began working with clients experiencing addictions, I saw that I could connect with them in the sessions in a more personal way than I was used to. I heard so many stories from my clients—intense, emotionally moving stories in which I recognized parts of myself, such as the tendency to flee, being very sensitive, feeling like I'm different, and the need to keep feeling that way. Feeling lonely a lot. Not feeling heard and seen. Holding on to anger inside.

We all seemed to have a desire and ability to be creative and share as well as connect deeply, but we are held back by this core pattern of not feeling good enough. The most important thing I came to realize was that we were all having trouble being at home in our bodies. We try to flee from our bodies and direct experiences by keeping our minds occupied and our words constant. I noticed that we all have similar ways to leave our bodies and lessen what we are feeling and, at the same time, we have really specific/individual means of leaving our direct experiences. For example, the way we try to leave our bodies when we feel sad or experience grief can become a movement of our right foot rubbing the floor, a small touch under the nose, increasing pressure in holding our hands, a biting of the lips, or a specific way of avoiding eye contact or placing our gaze onto an object in front of us. Over the years I've seen so many movements that showed me where and when people were leaving their bodies.

Yet what amazed me is how my clients let me in when I saw myself in them. I would just sit next to them and share this space where they could feel their feelings, step by step. I came to see that they would allow me to call them out on their avoidances and at the same time, by being a mirror and letting them get in touch with the emotions they tried to run from, I could connect with them as someone who also shared their struggles to feel and be present in their bodies. They gave me permission to be direct, to confront and challenge them, and I now know it is because I felt a connection with their stories and their movement in my own experience. Although I wasn't the one suffering from drug or alcohol abuse, we connected on an emotional level. They felt I understood because I used to move in the same way as they did, away from my body.

I suggest looking at the video called "Inhabit the Practice" from the website that speaks to this issue.

Snoozing through Life

Nowadays, it feels like we can snooze through life in so many ways. And it also feels like we can leave our bodies in so many more ways! As I noted before, addiction is so much more than the stuff of drunks and druggies. We hold on to things that dampen our feelings, whether it is nail-biting, obsessively browsing dating apps, overthinking, social media scrolling, overworking, snoozing in the morning, binge-watching, and so on. We aim for quick fixes on the inside by focusing on or controlling something on the outside. Because we do not deal with the actual problem and stay focused on this quick fix, we move in the same patterns over and over, not oscillating between comfort and being outside of our comfort zone. Staying in this comfort zone seems to have a habitual, snoozing kind of movement in itself. We snooze.

Let's get a closer look at snoozing and what it means to snooze. On a literal level, when we talk about snoozing in the morning, right after waking up, we might say it feels pleasurable to fall back to sleep. However, snoozing tends to interrupt the waking of the brain and can leave you foggy and groggy for hours. Snoozing can feel great in many ways: you can snooze your emails, snooze notifications on your phone, or just have an actual snooze. When we snooze, we are not really here, experiencing life. Snoozing appears to happen when we don't want to deal with life as it is in that present moment. When we don't want to deal with emotions because they bother us, like grief or fear, for example; we try to keep it outside and by doing so, we hold back the energy flow of these emotions. On the other hand, we are trying to keep other emotions close because we like (for example) love and happiness. Here we are also pushing back this energy flow by holding on to these emotions. In both cases, we hold movement back.

I resonate with Brené Brown when she says, "We live in a culture of people who don't do discomfort. We choose fun, fast, and easy and choose comfort over the courage of feeling our emotions." For examples of these ideas, you can search for her on YouTube, where she has several videos that help us understand how to be with our feelings.

After working in addiction care, I recognized something similar that moved me beyond this field of work and led me toward questions I think many people can relate to:

- ▶ Why do we leave and abandon our bodies?
- ▶ Why do we snooze so much instead of truly living?
- ▶ And more important: How can we come back home and enjoy life to the fullest?

Bodylessness as the Root Issue

The abandonment of our body forms the root of all addiction. We withdraw our awareness from our bodies and perform habitual behaviors when under stress. Christine talks about this in her book *Getting Our Bodies Back* (1996) and explains that addiction involves leaving our bodies in a way that takes away self-awareness so that we can flee from intolerable experiences. This abandonment can show up in many ways. These habits of leaving the body are often socially acceptable. Perhaps it happens in front of the TV, with food or a couple of glasses of wine, or while scrolling online; we lose our awareness of self—our spirit.

My most recent experience in being confronted with this abandonment was at the airport, while I was waiting for a flight. I noticed so many people were looking at and scrolling on their phones, not being aware of their bodies. At the same time, I was walking around the waiting area and I noticed so many feelings I felt while looking at the world I was actually in: I saw a dad walking around with his one-year-old. I saw friends at the table sharing drinks, laughing, talking expressively with their hands and bodies. I saw a guy pushing his mother around in a wheel-chair, taking care of her. I witnessed all these people, all their stories of the present moment, and let it move my emotions. It moved me toward this question: When am I really here, in the present moment, in this world that I am looking at?

Let's dive deeper into this by looking at two of the fundamental principles of Conscious Moving. First let's discuss Principle 4: Movement is phenomenological. What we do when we distract ourselves with mindless activities is that we abandon our direct experiences. We are not relating to our body and our immediate experiences—we are relating to a screen, for instance. When we stay within our direct experiences and move with and through and from them, learning, healing, and creativity awaken.

Staying in the present moment and connecting with our direct experiences can be harder than we think. Let me give you an example from the Moving Cycle (MC) experience of a client I worked with in addiction care. We started this MC from a memory he recalled of his mother. It was a memory in which he spoke the words "I don't know who she is." At that moment the Moving Cycle began. I asked him to close his eyes and stay with the words and the feeling that came up in his body. A lot of micromovements were visible around his mouth. He was rubbing his hands together. His head moved backward in a small, sudden way.

As we continued, I saw how the movement around his mouth changed into small movements at the jaw. He suddenly mentioned the memory was gone. He noticed he was searching for something to get angry about, yet feelings of sadness were emerging from underneath that anger. As he allowed himself to feel and move with the sadness, staying in the direct experience and the physical free association, he stopped looking for things outside himself to feed his anger, such as people talking outside of the room or the air conditioning fan. The movement habit in his jaw indicated the point where he typically checked out of his body. As the sessions progressed, this client stopped doing drugs. He now faces the problems that the drugs were masking and acknowledges his addiction to anger as well.

We have multiple things we can do to get away from or lessen the intensity of these intolerable feelings that hurt so much. Addict or not, we tend to move in the same way when we are facing feelings that we can't bear to feel at that moment. Take a look at the figure of the mobility gradient in Appendix A; you can see that addictive processes tend to move the person toward the more stereotyped movement end of the continuum. When we reclaim the phenomenological experiences of our bodies, addictions can be treated.

Second, let's take a closer look at the third principle of CM, "The movement of attention structures and determines experiences." We all need attention, especially as children. Being witnessed helps us get our needs met, especially our need to know who we are, what we feel, and what we want. When we don't receive sufficient high-quality attention, we tend to bury intolerable feelings of shame and worthlessness and distract ourselves from those inner feelings by attending to addictive processes. The Awareness Phase of the Moving Cycle (or Conscious Moving in a nontherapeutic context) breaks the cycle of attentional wounding and allows us to pay high-quality attention to our direct experiences.

Let's look at high-quality attention through a recent experience of mine. Several years ago, as I was engaging with different Moving Cycle practices, I noticed this feeling of not being able to be in my own body/experience feeling. I grew up with loving parents, which I am super grateful for, but they couldn't provide me with the high-quality attention around my emotions that I needed. A little while ago, after visiting my parents, I came home not feeling heard and seen in my emotions. I shared this with my boyfriend and explained what I was feeling: I felt not worthy, left alone, and not able to be myself. After I shared this, he asked me if there were any moments that I felt otherwise in the presence of my parents. His question gave me the feeling that I couldn't feel what I was feeling, which is something I recognize from childhood. I shared this with my boyfriend the moment I became aware of it. He asked if he could give me a hug.

And here's the thing! I noticed so clearly how I was still trying to run from this—that I wasn't allowed to feel what I was feeling, that it was wrong for me to feel this way—because in my mind, I could hear the words coming up over and over: "I am not here, I am not here, I am not here." It was a mind-blowing experience for me, as if many Moving Cycles had come together. It seemed to be coming into my direct awareness at that exact moment. I felt where I left my body by being aware of the body tension that got stronger in the hug that my boyfriend and I shared and in my own body posture that slightly moved away from my boyfriend's body. At the same time, I could feel the need to discharge the feeling through my thought pattern by hearing these words in my head. It was such a deep, intense, and beautiful experience!

If you hold back on the emotions—if you don't allow yourself to go all the way through them—you can never get to being detached, you're too busy being afraid. You're afraid of the pain, you're afraid of the grief. You're afraid of the vulnerability that loving entails.

—MITCH ALBOM, *TUESDAYS WITH MORRIE*

I think working in addiction care—but also in my own practice of working with clients who have core beliefs around not being seen, not being heard, and not being worthy or lovable—has shown me how important it is to work with high-quality attention and to be a witness that spots thought patterns and emotional patterns embedded in micromovements that then can bring my clients back into their direct experiences. Within addiction care, within my practice, and in my own life, I notice that all feelings need to be heard, seen, and held, especially the ones we are trying to run from. When we let ourselves be with the discomfort of a difficult emotion, we develop a higher tolerance for staying in direct experiences and working with them to solve problems.

The Importance of the Therapeutic Relationship

When I help clients get back in touch with their bodies, I notice certain things are important in order to stay in direct experience. Clients reported that where I was in the space around them mattered (this is called Facing/Spacing/Pacing in the Moving Cycle); it made a difference if I was standing or sitting next to them when they entered difficult emotions or experiences and whether I was facing them directly when we both reflected on behavior patterns they were avoiding. They needed someone to be at the same level.

Being at the same level can mean many things. Let me start with an example of a client I met for the first time in the group session I was leading. We were exploring the mind versus the body and talking about the voice inside your head. One client made a statement about his inner voice saying that he and the other people in the room were junkies. He talked about himself from a place of disgust, hatred, and shame. I called him out on the way he was talking to himself and asked if he really wanted to talk to himself that way. I asked him how that made him feel.

After that, we started an exercise of feeling our bodies in the room and walking up to a wall with eyes closed. I already saw what was happening—he walked with tension in his jaw toward the wall and bumped into it with his leg. I noticed anger in his face and body and when I asked what was going on, he yelled at me.

I confronted him with what I saw and drew a boundary right there. I explained that he could be angry and could express his anger also, but in no way was he going to put that on me, because he was projecting it! I asked him to see if he recognized this behavior and explained that this was a safe space to work through it, if he wanted to. Before we moved toward the end of the session, I explained that this kind of behavior could keep people at a distance and give him a sense of power. But if he did this in the outside world, people would move away from him. Now he had the chance to get closer to himself and others if he wanted to.

At the end of the session, I asked him to stay. I sat down next to him and asked if he could understand what I was reflecting. I made sure he knew I was there for him, that it was not going to be easy, and that he could choose something else besides anger. His head hung and he started crying. This is the same man I mentioned earlier that I started working with one-on-one; he became aware that his addiction to anger was as a way to distract himself from what was really going on.

As the therapist, I can be the one to challenge what is going on, especially when the client tries to withhold, withdraw, or project. This is something that is really important for me to address when I'm trying to move toward a co-committed relationship instead of a codependent relationship with my clients. In their book *Conscious Loving: The Journey to Co-commitment* (1990), Gay and Kathlyn Hendricks explain what a co-committed relationship entails and why it is so important: "A co-committed relationship is one in which two or more people support each other in being whole, complete individuals. It's about being alive to the full range of your feelings, speaking the truth at the deepest level of which you are capable, and learning to keep agreements." For me, this is also true in a client-therapist relationship. I can step into the direct experience of relating as a way to get to unacknowledged feelings. Clients tell me that this relational contact is so important to them, that it puts me on their level. They share that they don't see me as an authority figure, which helps them keep the agreement of telling the truth instead of projecting anger. They feel authenticity when I confront them when they exhibit judgmental behavior toward others or themselves and when I shared what I am feeling from my own experience. All together this gives them a sense of security and safety so they can be vulnerable as well.

Being at the same level makes room for us to enter the four phases of the Moving Cycle, and as a therapist, I give them the space and reflection to enter this sequence safely so that they can

- ▶ be honest about the movement that is going on and reflect on it (awareness);

- ▶ confront the pattern and take ownership of the behavior and feelings (owning);

- ▶ give themselves space to be as they are and move with the pattern, making it into a learning experience (appreciation); and

- ▶ engage in learning experiences that involve pressure and pleasure and that awaken the desire to bring the practice into daily life (action).

In my sessions, this moved me toward providing a practice in which they could work on this at home (you can see a video of this practice, called "Co-committed Relationships with Our Bodies," on the Conscious Moving website). What would happen if we invested in feeling all our feelings, telling the truth about them, and keeping our agreements with ourselves?*

Taking In and Letting Out

When we focus on bodyfulness, conscious movement and inhabiting from within, we move closer to who we were, who we are, and who we will be. This closeness toward ourselves causes us to suffer less, feel more pleasure, and experience fewer challenges in life, as expressed by this poem:

We chain ourselves to free ourselves
We lose ourselves to find ourselves
We hurt ourselves to heal ourselves

---

* These three actions—feeling, telling, and keeping—were mentioned originally in the Hendricks's *Conscious Loving* book.

Aren't you meant to fly?
Sing your song and touch the sky.
Or do you want to wait until you die?

—*The Wanderer, "Aren't You Meant to Fly?"*

Fight, flight, freeze, and faint are defense strategies that take over our system when we are in danger. But because we can't always flee or freeze like a deer does when it is scared, we withdraw into ourselves. We close in and put up the walls. When we close in to protect ourselves from possible hurt or past hurt, we protect that part that feels like it needs protection. This doesn't fix the problem. By doing this, we are locking the pain inside and it will only get worse.

My experience is that if you want to grow, you have to stop protecting these parts within yourself. When we look back in this chapter to my own encounter with not being able to stay with direct experience, it shows how I tried to keep it at bay by repeating the words "I am not here." When I would stop at this point and not practice Conscious Moving, my emotional patterns would get reactivated continuously. Conscious Moving allows us to let go of the past and focus on what we can do currently to have a better future.

If we want to move in the direction of truly living, this is where our work comes in. Different experiences take place in our bodies. When we become more bodyful, we can begin to experience our interbeing on a more immediately useful level. Christine talks about this in her book *Bodyfulness* (2018). What would happen if we practiced more deliberately, choosing what we take in and releasing what we no longer need in our lives and bodies? Truly living means experiencing the moment that is passing through you and then experiencing the next moment, and then the next. If you could live in that state, you would be a fully aware being. You might want to check out the practice called "Taking In and Letting Out" in the book's website as an illustration of this idea.

Coming Back Home

So far, we have looked at the habitual movements we all make in which we leave our bodies, what it can feel like to snooze, when we can snooze in our lives, why we snooze, and how important it is to practice bodyfulness and work from and within a co-committed relationship.

Now let's talk about leaving our comfort zone. I already mentioned this briefly in the beginning of this chapter; that "snoozing through life" seems to have a connection with not leaving our comfort zone.

Owning our story can be hard but not nearly as difficult as spending our lives run-
ning from it. Embracing our vulnerabilities is risky but not nearly as dangerous as
giving up on love and belonging and joy—the experiences that make us the most
vulnerable. Only when we are brave enough to explore the darkness will we dis-
cover the infinite power of our light.

—BRENÉ BROWN, "DO NOT NEGOTIATE WHO YOU ARE"

Again, within addiction care, within my practice, and in my own life I notice one thing that makes so much difference! I see people change, grow, and get in touch with themselves. They move forward into creativity, play, joy, and love. I have so many stories to share about where people did the most daring thing: whether it was letting themselves feel the deepest pain they tried to run from all their lives or taking ownership of their own behavior they felt ashamed about; they literally and figuratively looked in the mirror and felt the absence of love toward their bodies and themselves. So many brave people moved my heart and soul, and I feel the deepest respect for them. I feel so grateful when I get to be part of these people's stories for a little while and I see them getting their bodies back, and as a result, getting the love back in their lives.

There's a smile on my face when I think about all the times that these clients left their comfort zones, showed courage, and started embracing something that I call *contrast*. It led them to what was already within them—their creativity, for example. I got to be the one who saw them get back in touch with their passions, like the spoken word, playing the guitar, painting, or dancing.

For me embracing *contrast* is about getting in the habit of accepting all experiences and all emotions in life. For me, this habit is about working to get in a different relationship with change, to stop numbing and start to feel again. It is a journey that has moved me in so many ways; it is a feeling of coming back home, again and again.

For me, coming back home and enjoying life to the fullest is about leaving my comfort zone, whatever that may look like. There's this song from Matt Simons called "Catch & Release" in which he sings about going to a place where no one knows him; he doesn't find it lonely; he calls it a necessary thing. This song reminds me of the time I went traveling through New Zealand by myself. Way out of my comfort zone, I can say I truly experienced contrast after contrast and found out what I am made of. Most of the people that I work with are scared of spending time alone. When I enter this fear with them, I recognize that it is because we are afraid of what we might feel.

What our comfort zone looks like and what it means to move outside of it may be different for different people. I hope you feel inspired and brave to choose to act and move outside of your comfort zone. May it bring you closer to experiencing the feeling of coming back home.

If you would like to see a video of me "Owning My Story," check it out by following the link under my name in the Chapter Contributors tab on the Conscious Moving website, www.consciousmoving.com.

Over the years my own experiences moved me toward making some choreography about my journey: from snoozing, to embracing my feelings and owning my story, to stepping into my light and sharing this co-commitment relationship with others. Feel free to check out these experiences, also under my name in the Chapter Contributors tab:

▶ "We don't know that we're living": https://vimeo.com/792645276?share =copy

▶ "Come back home": https://youtu.be/y_NHHqElW00?feature=shared

▶ "I'm gonna make it": www.youtube.com/watch?v=quhAgSnQkR0

And check out the video on the book's website for a Conscious Moving home practice called "For Practice at Home: Conscious Moving." Enjoy!

References

Brown, Brené. "Do Not Negotiate Who You Are." www.youtube.com/watch ?v=EI89XK2L6I4.

Caldwell, Christine. 1996. *Getting Our Bodies Back.* Boulder, CO: Shambhala Publications.

———. 2018. *Bodyfulness: Somatic Practices for Presence, Empowerment, and Waking Up in This Life.* Boulder, CO: Shambhala Publications.

Hendricks, Gay, and Kathlyn Hendricks. 1990. *Conscious Loving: The Journey to Co-commitment.* New York: Bantam Books.

9
Conscious Moving in the Service of Learning

JOANA DEBELT is an art therapist and researcher in special education who has been playing with different forms of movement and dance since she was four years old. She joined the Conscious Moving community in 2014. In her current research, she focuses on the body as a source of knowledge and communication.

Learning is a place where paradise can be created. The classroom, with all its limitations, remains a location of possibility. In that field of possibility, we have the opportunity to labor for freedom, to demand of ourselves and our comrades, an openness of mind and heart that allows us to face reality even as we collectively imagine ways to move beyond boundaries, to transgress. This is education as the practice of freedom.

—BELL HOOKS, *TEACHING TO TRANSGRESS*

Because we move our bodies, we can feel and communicate, move and touch ourselves and others, think, understand, and influence things by creating and destroying them (Bakker 2018; Koch 2011). Embodiment approaches prove that the body plays a central role in processing emotional, cognitive, and social stimuli. They show that learning tools and knowledge transfer are situated within the felt experience of the moving body. Through the movement of the body, we explore the world around us, realize our dreams, and live our realities. In a life-long process, we learn. This means that we, throughout our lives, in a self-motivated and ongoing way, strive for knowledge.

Since 2014, I have been learning Conscious Moving from and with Christine Caldwell and her movers and have found it a great approach for personal growth. My passion for researching the body and movement was ignited when I was four years old. I saw the local ballet class perform and decided that I wanted to join them. Even though officially I was not allowed to start before the age of five, I insisted. After days of me crying, begging, and dancing at home, my mum convinced the ballet teacher that I could come for a test lecture. I have been dancing and inquiring into my movement and the body ever since. Over the years, in my practice as a special educator and researcher, working with a diversity of people in different contexts, I see others' and my progress through my understanding of the body as a resource. The body as a source of knowledge and communication in everyday interactions has emerged as the focus of my interest. Like Conscious Moving, special education embraces a holistic view of situations. Both disciplines are aware of the central role the body actually plays in everyday life and how little it is still taken into account and considered a resource. Even educational literature emphasizes that more consideration must be given to the body and movement in the learning processes of all people throughout life (Goddard Blythe 2017; Kontra, Goldin-Meadow, and Beilock 2012).

Conscious Moving in educational contexts means working in detail with our ability to pay high-quality attention, as well as our openness to new information and involving the body in learning. In this chapter, I focus on how learning can occur in an embodied and experiential way. We look at curiosity, creativity, and caring for the learning bodies as tools that make learning possible. And we find out what using those tools can mean for learning processes in everyday life. This chapter also looks at how the learning body can be integrated into classrooms and other pedagogical contexts.

Curiosity

The embodiment of our social world plays a role in learning processes. When we look at learning processes through a Conscious Moving lens, we need to be aware that every body brings their own world experience, history, and cultural language into a room. And by language, I mean spoken, but also body language that is always present. It is an embodied knowledge we carry that can be limiting and enriching, that has specific individual aspects, some that we share with people in our social categories (Thielen 2021). This means that we as teachers need to practice awareness about social constructions of identity, like embodied theories about the world and social ideologies (Coffey 2021; Siebers 2013). Let us look at how women are seen to move by society in some parts of the world. For example, we have a certain picture in our heads of how girls throw a ball. This form of embodiment is not caused by physical differences, but by the representation of femininity in this society and the women acting according to this definition. Such embodied social theories and constructs of the body in the social world exist about gender, (dis)abilities, nationalities, cultures, sexual orientations, and jobs (Caldwell and Leighton 2018; Shilling 2008). They can restrict the movements of people who are assigned a certain category—by excluding them from certain areas, for example.

In a Conscious Moving context, we discuss and curiously question these categories society dictates by moving through these pictures of body identity. We do so by moving through the phases of Conscious Movement as described in Chapters 2 to 5 of this book. In a research seminar where we inquired about gender, Christine invited the participants to imagine a spectrum of gender categories in the room. We stood in a circle and everyone was to picture their spectrum of gender categories as an invisible line. The exercise was to move back and forth on this line and play with the categories of femininity and masculinity. This exercise brought up a diversity of emotions and memories of situations in which we had behaved according to or in opposition to those social categories and expectations. It also caused interactions between the participants in the group because individual lines crossed each other. With this exercise, we queered the lived experiences of our bodies in this world by interrogating body and gender norms in, as Johnson puts it, "ways that offer the potential for disrupting implicit assumptions about what bodies are—as well as how they should look and behave—while simultaneously anchoring our bodily expressions in subjective sensory data" (Johnson 2018, 106).

After the movement exercise, we sat and discussed our experiences. We found that society expects individuals to turn their gender identity into something permanent so we can be categorized. And that it can feel empowering for individuals to be able to live in a society where they can freely move on the spectrum every day. And that it can also feel empowering for individuals to find a point on the spectrum where they feel at home. After our discussion, we took time to move individually again, to digest this experience, and to write down thoughts and insights. By consciously cycling through these different steps of the exercise, we listened to the stories our bodies had to tell on an equal basis as we listened to our oral language, moving away from language hierarchies. We applied a quality of care that allowed us to take time on both an individual and group level. This is what I mean when I say "knowledge transfer" and the learning tools for it are situated within the felt experience of the moving body. Conscious Moving in the service of learning is to keep ourselves educated about these social ideologies—to stay curious about what can and wants to be in this moment. This allows us to be aware of social categories, to critically reflect on them, to dare to play with them, and to meet learners where they are with the stories their bodily voices tell.

Transferring this kind of Conscious Moving into other pedagogical contexts means meeting our learners at eye-level, appreciating them for who they are, and offering spaces where they can explore and grow. For example, in a kindergarten, as teachers, we can invite children to read books together in which they can see themselves represented. These might be books that show a diversity of bodies or family types. We can then ask the children questions about how they can relate the story to their daily lives. In this way, we can learn with and about each other.

Conscious Moving teaches us to stay curious about all forms of expression, every kind of language our bodies use to communicate. The visualization of embodied diversity and knowledge in pedagogical contexts includes *translanguaging*. As a holistic way of understanding how language is used, translanguaging embraces multimodal multilingual practices as natural and desirable (Holcomb 2023). In other words, it is a perspective that appreciates the individual use of linguistic as well as semiotic resources in the process of meaning-making. Translanguaging further describes, understands, and evaluates this experience. Scholars understand translanguaging as containing cognitive and also sociopolitical aspects that explain why language is used in certain ways by individuals and groups. García et al. write about translanguaging in American schools:

> *Translanguaging in the context of the U.S. educational system entails divorcing the expectation that everyone should think and produce language in the same ways as monolinguals and their standard registers. (2021)*

Translanguaging enables our learners to connect what they already know to new information without our direct influence. Our communication in pedagogical contexts can be enhanced when we recognize and acknowledge the cultural and linguistic elements our learners embody.

Let's come back to the example of learners in a kindergarten context. We could offer material in the languages the children speak at home and adapt learning situations individually. We could read a book in a coteaching team with the group. For example, one of us pedagogues would tell the story in German sign language and the other would tell it in German, using signs. We would ask questions to the group while reading together and the children would reply using their language resources. In this example, the teachers would repeat the answer for everyone in German sign language and German. In a school context, even a monolingual teacher who works with multilingual learners can use translanguaging by learning from their learners and their community, and with the help of tools such as digital resources to support the learners. Conscious Moving in pedagogical contexts enables us to understand the diversity of bodies that come with a diversity of languages, and the fact that not everybody learns in the same way. Opening up for curiosity like this allows us to provide spaces and facilitate classes where the learners themselves can create in their own way and show their facets. Making a quick decision about a particular learner in our head leads to the opposite: we get stuck in the habits of how we move through educational situations with this learner and everything we experience together will just be proof of who we already know both of us are. This leaves no room for growth.

The triangle of breathing, moving/expressing, and sensing we know from Conscious Moving enables us as teachers to become aware of those rigid images and to guide learners and ourselves through a learning process with curiosity. It also bears an immense potential for creativity. Breathing can, for example, be the first type of language we choose to step into communicational exchange with a learner. In educational or caring situations with people who don't communicate through vocal language, we can sit down next to them and imitate their rhythm of breathing and making sounds. Doing something together connects us, and it can calm down and also activate feelings of excitement. It can help spread a feeling of safety in a classroom and it can create curiosity for more contact and language exchange. Moving our bodies consciously supports us in reaching out and shaping a common ground of awareness and allows us to create a space for learning and exploration.

Creativity

The movement of our bodies has a powerful effect on our processes of learning and on how we explore and experience the world throughout our lives. However, "action experience is ubiquitous, and its influence may therefore be easy to overlook" (Kontra, Goldin-Meadow, and Beilock 2012, 738). In many ways what happens in therapy and creative processes is a type of learning—experiential learning—and this ability to learn can be effectively enhanced and applied in classrooms. I understand the term *experiential learning* to be learning by doing, and experiential experiences are a powerful tool for learning. As teachers, we are facilitators who structure lessons in a way that our learners can make hands-on, meaningful, and deep on-going experiences. We then reflect on these together and support our learners to look for ways to link what they learned to everyday life (Kolb 2015). This interplay of trying out, listening, taking in, discussing, moving through, reflecting, going back to the group to be inquisitive, questioning and celebrating processes and learnings, and finally digesting, resembles the process we go through in Conscious Moving.

Experiential learning theory understands learning to be a process cycling through four steps that we can relate to the four phases of Conscious Moving: The first step is taking part in a concrete experience that we can relate to the Awareness phase in Conscious Moving. The second step is reflective observation, where learners share what they observed; the teacher can support them through questions like "Did you notice this?" as we do in the Owning Phase of Conscious Moving. We appreciate the richness of the process itself and in this way, learning is embodied. This next step is abstract conceptualization, where the teacher guides the learners through questions on how to apply what they learned to their daily lives. Like in the Appreciation Phase in Conscious Moving, the learner reflects on what they learned in the first two steps of this cycle. Finally, the process can move on to active experimentation. Here, teachers reflect with their group of learners on questions like "Why did this happen?" "Why is this important?" and "Where can it be of use?" With this feedback, they can integrate the learned into everyday life, like in the Appreciation Phase in the cycle of Conscious Moving. This last step is also about playing and being creative with what they learned. It supports learners to find a conscious ending to the learning experience. In Chapters 2 to 5 of this book, Christine describes practical examples of how each of these phases can be cycled in educational settings. They vividly show how we educate conscious movers by crafting practices that can be embedded in daily life.

The Conscious Moving principle of oscillation can be supportive when we want to apply experiential learning. To cycle our attention between relational closeness and separation helps our teaching bodies to remember that they have an impact on how we teach and how and what learners learn from us. Also, when we move our attention to a learner, we touch them by looking at them or by physically touching them, and this starts a movement on the in- and/or outside of the learner. bell hooks explains it like this:

> We must return ourselves to a state of embodiment in order to deconstruct the way power has been traditionally orchestrated in the classroom, denying subjectivity to some groups and according it to others. By recognizing subjectivity and the limits of identity, we disrupt that objectification that is so necessary in a culture of domination. (1994, 139)

Welcoming the awareness of the previously mentioned subjective and collective embodied knowledge and body narratives into the context of learning means we teachers need to pay attention to that and to how our movement influences the movement of our learners. These interactions with others and how they exist differently through their senses impact the individual embodied experiences and can lead to both taking on new paths and transgressing (Adams Lyngbäck 2016). So, tuning into our own bodies in pedagogical contexts to see what we bring to the classroom, how we are doing in the situation, and where our personal boundaries are is as necessary as focusing on who we are teaching and what resources they come with. Education is optimized when the learner is present, focused, stable, and caring. As teachers, we know that these qualities are strongly influenced by the atmosphere we create in the classroom, as well as by the emotional regulation of each learner and ourselves.

This brings us to the relational work between teacher and learner. The philosophy of experiential education, one aspect of which is experiential learning, focuses on the exchanges between teacher and learner and interweaves this process with direct experiences with the content of the class and the learning environment. Together, the learner and teacher engage in focused reflection "to increase knowledge, develop skills, clarify values, and develop people's capacity to contribute to their communities" (Association for Experiential Education 2023). In this understanding of education, as in the Conscious Moving sessions, the roles of teacher and learner move toward each other, and the teacher becomes an active learner as well.

Both the teacher and the learner create the foundation to make learning possible by paying high-quality attention and taking active responsibility for creating a learning community. In the 90s bell hooks already pointed out that this kind of attention is necessary for the relational work teachers do to create a community where learning is possible and meaningful. She explains that knowing learners' names and meeting with each learner in the class for quality time—for example, scheduling lunches together—contribute to building a learning community and even prevent problems from arising (1994). This underlines that in educational contexts, we can make use of Conscious Moving by paying attention to the learners' micromovements. We can show, with our body and voice, that we are there for the learners, to listen to them, and also we can react to their bodily voices to help them feel seen and heard. By reacting to the tiniest movements and expressions, we can respond to the diversity of learners and their ways of using language and communicating, meeting them consciously. hooks calls this kind of high-quality attention *engaged pedagogy*. As a form of progressive and holistic education, engaged pedagogy expects the teacher to constantly be creative to be able to relate to the individual. At the same time, it asks for constructive feedback from the learners, encouraging them to critique and make suggestions. For instance, say that a learner in our reading group likes to be supported to feel their bodily boundaries in learning situations. It helps them to focus. We could offer to roll the learner up in a blanket, I call it a "blanket sausage," so they could follow the story with the group.

Here again, we can see how Conscious Moving happens in learning processes because with it, involved individuals flexibly and spontaneously react to each other. They create a deep process together, which can be challenging and surprising for both of them at times. Conscious Moving also encourages them to cultivate creative curiosity for what happens in the classroom and carry what they learned on to their daily lives. The teacher creatively constructs inclusive classroom practices and spaces that make "the democratic ideal of education for everyone" possible (hooks 1994, 189). In this way, teachers and learners can tune in to the feeling that they are moving bodies on the moving body of this earth (Caldwell and Leighton 2018, 60).

Caring for the Learning Bodies

For me, working in education brought with it the challenge of remembering to take care of my own body and to move; to stay playful and take time to creatively express myself as well as rest. I sometimes engage so intensely in my role as a listener that I neglect myself and get distracted. In other words, I step out of the Conscious Moving triangle of work, play, and rest because I think that I don't have time for all of them. But actually, engaged pedagogy requires me as a teacher to stay self-actualized because this promotes my well-being. Only when I am doing well can I teach others in the empowering way this approach affords. Here *self-actualization* means keeping this triangle of working, playing, and resting in balance, being aware that none of them works well if we ignore one of the others. If we lack time for playing, we don't allow ourselves to be creative; we risk losing the feelings of being in the moment and believing "I can do this." This can have a negative impact on the quality of our teaching and on learning processes in the classroom. If we don't rest, we will have trouble integrating our experience into the multiple senses of ourselves. Keeping the balance of the triangle means practicing bodyfulness through moving consciously and staying "awake to and reflective of . . . our body identity" (Caldwell and Leighton 2018, 40). Then we can embody and live what we teach the learners.

Approaching pedagogy by moving consciously is to apply a holistic perspective. Information emerges from bodies, and working holistically means teachers do the same as they expect from their learners: To come to the classroom "being wholly present in mind, body, and spirit" (hooks 1994, 21), to share their experience about how they live in this world. In the context of dance therapy, this way of moving through the classroom is called *authentic movement*. In educational contexts, teachers who come to the classroom as their whole beings meet learners with a will and a desire to listen and answer to their unique beings. When we risk being this vulnerable in front of each other, the classroom can be a space for empowerment and growth on both sides. This contrasts with the picture of the infallible teacher who knows everything, is the authority, and asks the questions in a classroom where performance and pressure are dominant.

Another aspect that comes up when we consciously move in pedagogical contexts is the importance of the community. The group seems to play a major role in the individual learning process. In Conscious Moving classes we experience this when the facilitator functions as a witness in the mover's process, and also in the reflective talk between them or in the group afterward. Experiencing this high-quality attention as an individual in a group opens up the room for learning from the diversity of the group members. An implicit theme that learning, growing, and understanding are possible and meaningful in this space because we are so different and can therefore relate to each other or contrast with each other begins to operate. Everybody's presence is valued, and what they contribute to the dynamic learning community are resources. The classroom is a democratic, communal place where students create collective effort by being present, responsible, and caring for each other. When teachers and learners meet in this engaged way on the common ground of lifelong learning, thus growing and nurturing the learning community, the excitement that enables them "to feel the joy of learning" is generated (hooks 1994, 204).

Maybe the book that the group in our example reads together is Tyler Feder's *Bodies Are Cool* (2021), which celebrates the diversity of bodies in this world. We could continue the process together and decide to draw bodies we have met in our daily lives or our own bodies. As teachers we would, in constant exchange with the learners, guide and structure the process of drawing. With the group we could follow the book for inspiration on how to start. The process might go like this: "Right, it starts with the diversity of body sizes and body parts. Then it shows what shapes bodies can have and their colors," and so on. We could start a discussion about the words the learning community uses for body parts or shapes; we could learn them in each other's language and define a vocabulary we want to use in our learning community. Having all of us who are learning together reflect on this diversity of bodies and words and visualize them makes us feel seen and encourages us to be ourselves. This is what we take with us to our everyday lives, and it affects the way we encounter other bodies moving in this world.

Conclusion

Conscious Moving in educational contexts means taking the diversity of all present bodies with their languages into account and supporting us all in learning with and from each other to grow into a bodyful community. This engaged pedagogy asks us as teachers to come to the classroom as our whole selves and to be open to meeting the learners as themselves. It acknowledges that we both are in our unique processes of learning about ourselves and the world in a flexible and creative way. Conscious Moving in the service of learning lets us stay curious to ask each other every day who we are, what we bring to the classroom, and what this means for our learning community, and it naturally lets us carry what we learned out into the world of our daily lives.

References

Adams Lyngbäck, Liz. 2016. *Experiences, Networks and Uncertainty: Parenting a Child Who Uses a Cochlear Implant* [Dissertation]. Stockholm, Sweden: Stockholm University.

Association for Experiential Education. 2023. "What Is Experiential Education?" Accessed September 12, 2023. www.aee.org.

Bakker, Marta. 2018. "How Hands Shape the Mind. The P400 as an Index of Manual Actions and Gesture Perception." *Digital Comprehensive Summaries of Uppsala Dissertations from the Faculty of Social Sciences.* Uppsala, Sweden: Uppsala University.

Caldwell, Christine, and Lucia Bennett Leighton (Eds.). 2018. *Oppression and the Body: Roots, Resistance, and Resolutions.* Berkeley, CA: North Atlantic Books.

Coffey, Julia. 2021. *Everyday Embodiment: Rethinking Youth Body Image.* New York: Palgrave Macmillan. https://doi.org/10.1007/978-3-030-70159-8.

Feder, Tyler. 2021. *Bodies Are Cool.* New York: Rocky Pond Books.

García, Ofelia, Nelson Flores, Kate Seltzer, Li Wei, Ricardo Otheguy, and Jonathan Rosa. 2021. "Rejecting Abyssal Thinking in the Language and Education of Racialized Bilinguals: A Manifesto." *Critical Inquiry in Language Studies* 18 (3): 203–28.

Goddard Blythe, Sally. 2017. *Attention, Balance and Coordination: The A.B.C. of Learning Success,* 2nd ed. Hoboken, NJ: John Wiley and Sons Ltd.

Holcomb, Leala. 2023. "Writing Development and Translanguaging in Signing Bilingual Deaf Children of Deaf Parents." *Languages* 8(1): 37. https://doi.org/10.3390/languages8010037.

hooks, bell. 1994. *Teaching to Transgress: Education as the Practice of Freedom.* New York: Routledge Taylor and Francis Group.

Johnson, Rae. 2018. "Queering/Querying the Body: Sensation and Curiosity in Disrupting Body Norms." In *Oppression and the Body: Roots, Resistance, and Resolutions,* edited by Christine Caldwell and Lucia Bennett Leighton. Berkeley, CA: North Atlantic Books.

Koch, Sabine C. 2011. *Embodiment: Der Einfluss von Eigenbewegung auf Affekt, Einstellung und Kognition. Empirische Grundlagaen und klinische Anwendungen* (2). Berlin: Logos Verlag.

Kolb, David A. 2015. *Experiential Learning: Experience as the Source of Learning and Development,* 2nd ed. New York: Pearson.

Kontra, Carly, Susan Goldin-Meadow, and Sian L. Beilock. 2012. "Embodied Learning Across the Life Span." *Topics in Cognitive Science* 4, no.4 (October): 731–39. https://doi.org/10.1111/j.1756-8765.2012.01221.x.

Shilling, Chris. 2008. "Introduction." In *Changing Bodies: Habit, Crisis and Creativity,* 1–7. [Online] SAGE Publications Ltd. https://doi.org/10.4135/9781446212295.

Siebers, Tobin. 2013. "Disability and the Theory of Complex Embodiment—For Identity Politics in a New Register." In *The Disability Studies Reader,* edited by Lennard J. Davis, 272–91. New York: Routledge.

Thielen, Diana. 2021. *Me, My Body and . . . Movement Activism.* www.movementactivism.com/post/2019/06/30/me-my-body-and.

10

Conscious Moving as a Means of Working with Desire Differences in Intimate Partnership

MELISSA WALKER, LPC, CST, R-DMT is a licensed professional counselor, dance/movement therapist, and AASECT Certified Sex Therapist who specializes in intimacy and relationship therapy. Melissa applies Conscious Moving practices in her work with couples to support their creation of inspiring and loving intimate connection. Her book, *Whole-Body Sex: Somatic Sex Therapy and the Lost Language of the Erotic Body*, was published in January 2021.

Introduction

At some point in every intimate relationship a desire difference will surface. You look at your intimate partner and realize that you feel some distance or disconnection from them. You feel the need to guard your heart in some way, or you find yourself seeking ways to open your partner's heart and interest toward you. Perhaps you haven't been "clicking" lately and you haven't been sexually intimate for far too long. Perhaps you've been affectionate during this time and perhaps you haven't. But you know that something is not lining up, and you are having difficulty finding the words for it.

Desire difference or *desire discrepancy* is when intimate partners find that they are interested in sexual intimacy at different levels of frequency, and intensity, or they are interested in different types of sexual activities. The desire difference may present as partners having the most interest or energy for sexual connection at different times of the day, the week, or in different settings. They may discover that they define sex itself differently or that they want to initiate and transition into or out of sexual intimacy differently. Desire difference may also be an indication of miscommunication, a misperception of body expression, or something challenging that is happening in the relationship dynamic that will benefit from the couple's attention and tending.

Desire difference is also an indication that the intimate partners are experiencing different desire styles. Perhaps one person experiences a more *spontaneous* desire style (quick to access sexual arousal) more often while the other has a more *responsive* desire style (sexual arousal arises in response to connection and touch), or they don't experience sexual desire at all (*asexual*). Desire styles can change over the life span, so it is unsurprising that intimate partners will at some point experience a mismatch.

Intimate partners can enter into this phase for short or extended periods of time, and it has the potential to evoke feelings of being unsure, unmet, and unseen. It is important to note that desire difference itself is not a problem— it's actually quite normal and common. It's our socialized tendency to interpret this as a problem that intensifies our disheartened confusion about the situation. Many of us have not been taught the relationship skills to navigate differences in how relational intimacy is experienced and expressed.

Fundamentally, desire difference is an indication of the normal variation of personal differences and changing life conditions that arise day to day, and more broadly, across the span of a relationship. A life transition, the impact of stress, different nervous system organization due to different life experiences, or the impact of illness, surgery, or pregnancy can all set the stage for a desire difference and, when it is paired with misunderstanding, it can initiate a challenging period of feeling disconnected in an intimate relationship.

No matter the reason for the desire difference, this challenge can be an opportunity for intimate partners to create a safe-enough space to learn more about themselves and each other and to cocreate sexual intimacy that prioritizes pleasure, connection, and continued learning. This chapter is an exploration in how the practice of Conscious Moving can support intimate partners to turn this common challenging experience into an invitation for their intimate dynamic to grow and evolve with them. In this chapter I introduce the body-based practice of Erotic Bodyfulness along with a shared movement practice that frames the relationship between challenge and mastery states and how to engage in effective relational expression.

How Socialization Frames Desire Difference as a Source of Conflict

Unfortunately, many people are exposed to a sociocultural environment that portrays a desire difference as something detrimental to the relationship that must be reconciled quickly or it is a harbinger of the end of a relationship, rather than a normal occurrence that can be navigated with relational skills and education about intimacy.

While the dialogue is beginning to shift to a more holistic understanding of sex/ual/ity,* sexual function, and intimacy, many misinformed and unrealistic beliefs are still in place. It is important to understand how social location impacts perceptions about what a desire difference means. For example, the sociocultural environment can put expectations on roles in sexual intimacy based on gender norms that then contribute to unhelpful and inaccurate sexual schemas (a collection of beliefs that form a cognitive map that influences assumptions and behavior). These schemas put undue pressure and expectations on women, on men, and on gender nonconforming people to perform in certain ways or expect certain behavior from an intimate partner. They also can create real difficulty and discomfort in both dating and long-term relationships. While gender differences do exist, sociocultural norms oversimplify these differences, exclude personal context, and generally put them in a contentious light. This is often the root of performance anxiety, sexual dissatisfaction, and even body boundary violations.

The sociocultural environment also perpetuates misunderstandings about the connection between arousal anatomy and different nervous system states. The nervous system has two general strategies when it comes to relating with others: the *social engagement system (SES)* is the active relationship strategy that we have access to when we feel safe enough and energized enough to interact with others, whereas the *social inhibition system (SIS)* is a state of activation or recovery-seeking when we are too stressed, exhausted, or feeling unsafe to directly interact effectively with others (Porges 2011). When an intimate partner is in their *social engagement system*, arousal anatomy is more likely to respond with the excitement of desire and sexual arousal. But when an intimate partner is in their *social inhibition system*, arousal anatomy is much less likely to respond (and will have great difficulty responding) with sexual interest or indicators of arousal.

Although desire difference can be interpreted as a "problem," I like to reframe it as a challenge to be met with curiosity and nonjudgment—an opportunity to

---

* Sex Educator Richelle Frabotta uses this spelling of sex/ual/ity to help clarify the layers inherent in, and often misconstrued through, the use of this word. This way of writing sex/ual/ity defines it as: sex, as in the behaviors and physical expressions of sex; sexual, as in things that have a sexual energy or connotation to them; and sexuality, which is the general expression of the creative, generative energy of the body through movement, gender, intimate relationship structure, and so on (Wadley 2019).

deepen and expand knowledge about intimate connection—and any frustration a couple feels can be the fuel to empower their dedication to learning. With accurate information and diligent self-inquiry, different desire styles or different nervous system states begin to make actionable sense, arousal can be modulated and channeled consensually, and the sexual repertoire can be expanded with embodied consent to encompass the desires and boundaries of the intimate partners. When it is reframed as a meaningful challenge, the intimate partners can unravel the inaccurate sexual schemas they have absorbed from their social environment to create personally relevant and informed schemas that serve to support their unique dynamic. This is worthy personal work.

Looking at Desire Difference through a Body-Centered Lens

When we look at how this shows up in body organization or somatic architecture,* these inaccurate and minimizing sexual schemas create a body-mind organization that intensifies incongruence between what is felt in the body and what is cognitively understood and physically or verbally expressed. It can narrow the repertoire of expression, create an insecure attachment with and mistrust of one's own body, increase nervous system dysregulation with difficult or unwieldy emotions like fear and frustration, interrupt the ability to oscillate attention, and create difficulty, dislodging attention from rigid or hypervigilant thinking.

When I sit with couples who are in this dynamic, I notice more rigidity in their bodies, and it takes more time and effort to get them to turn their attention inward to notice what they are feeling in the present moment. They are emotionally overwhelmed and are hesitant to let down their guard and be transparent in front of their partner. When my clients get to this point, they are carrying the belief that to be vulnerable and expressive of their deeper selves with each other is emotionally risky.

Within intimate relationships, the repetition of this dynamic impedes whole-brain functioning and the ability to offer compassionate validation to the desire and boundaries of both the self and a partner. Intimate partners find that they minimize their expression and exploration and have difficulty with relational

---

* *Somatic architecture* is the interior anatomic structure—the unique organization and responsiveness of muscles, connective tissues, bones, interoceptive and exteroceptive senses—that is formed as the growing body interacts with the social and the natural and human-impacted environment. Somatic architecture impacts how one perceives and responds to experiences (Keleman 1985).

self-advocacy, which is the skill of requesting a need or desire from a partner while being open to modulating a request based on what the partner is feeling in the moment.

When we look more closely at the body-mind organization of desire difference, we see that these intimate partners are demonstrating a mismatch in somatosensory experience and movement expression. This mismatch of nervous system state, body rhythm, pace, and lack of resonance in their connection creates a pre-effort dynamic. *Pre-effort* is what dance therapists define as hesitant, uncertain, and poorly coordinated movement expression where someone is learning something new or defending against something uncomfortable. Western culture in particular values confidence and directness—qualities that dance therapists define as more full-body "effort" expressions where movement and spatial intent are coordinated and masterful in their engagement—which can make the pre-effort dynamic that much more uncomfortable and confusing.

When intimate partners are caught in the pre-effort dynamic of desire difference, it may be that both people are in a pre-effort state, one person could be in pre-effort and the other in a full-effort state, or both could be in full effort, yet opposed states. No matter the combination of the type of expression, it is the *mismatch* between the partners that defines the difference and therefore the potential misunderstanding and difficulty. For example, one partner may be in full effort and ready for high-energy or passionate intimacy in the moment, while the other partner is stressed, in pre-effort, and needs a bridge into intimacy to relax their body to be receptive to pleasure. The higher-energy partner may feel rejected, and the stressed partner may feel misunderstood.

When this mismatch is paired with misunderstanding and hurt feelings, a desire difference can activate body armor—the defensive strategy of somatic architecture that organizes breath, posture, muscles, attention, and movement of the body into a form that serves to disconnect from difficulty or defend the more tender parts of self. Body armor is formed from a confluence of early attachment or relationship wounds and basic nervous system reactions. The nervous system is experience-dependent, which means that our early experiences impact the way that our brain and the complex network of nerves that make up the nervous system read and react to our environment. The body learns to respond to the emotional and relational movement patterns of human dynamics in ways that get the best results when trying to get our needs met within a family. Once body armor is formed, it becomes automatic in reaction and activates during moments of stress before our cognitive mind realizes what's happening. Therefore, how our family expresses love and affection, how they manage conflict and difficult feelings, and how they deal with celebration or stress, all impact how our nervous system responds.

Additionally, the pace and tone of speech (called *paraverbal qualities*) are another indicator that body armor has activated within the pre-effort dynamic of desire difference. When partners are communicating verbally about their intimate dynamic, body armor causes the qualities of voice to change. Breath will be shallower and restricted, voice tone will often be higher-pitched and louder in volume, and the pace of speech will be quick and choppy. This voice quality indicates that the individual is having difficulty listening to their bodies to detect what they want or do not want. If they do have a sense of what they want, they may not be able to find the words for it or it may be communicated in a tight, frustrated tone. It may be easier for them to just say what they don't want or avoid the topic. The overall feeling for the couple is that they are no longer in the present moment with each other—they are replaying a very old tape that was formed earlier in their lives.

This is where desire difference also opens intimate partners up to projecting assumptions or interpretations on each other without checking in to see if their assumption is correct. Notice if the absolutes of *always* or *never* are being used. These words indicate that perspective and nuance have left the building. When desire difference is present between intimate partners, body armor is activated, communication is tense, and you know that your present relationship dynamic is activating old hurts and disappointments. This also makes it more difficult to navigate the challenge of wanting intimacy to be different than what your partner seems to want. When body armor, tense communication, and old hurts are present, people can feel personally rejected, deeply misunderstood, or they may feel like an object to their partner. Over time, sexual intimacy wanes until much of their intimate or affectionate contact becomes strained or absent.

Yet, the present moment provides an opportunity to rewrite how the mind-body understands and reacts to relationship dynamics. Fortunately, our nervous system continues to be experience-dependent throughout our life span and can therefore learn new and more satisfying ways of relating to others when the whole body and present-moment attention is engaged through Conscious Moving.

A Challenge Becomes a Meaningful Opportunity

The presence of a desire difference is an invitation for the intimate partners to intentionally enter into the pre-effort space as a team within an environment that prioritizes curiosity and validation to put the learning mind-body back to work as they navigate into a new place of resonance together. It is an opportunity to practice the relational skills that, over time, make the sexual dynamic personally meaningful and relevant to the context and life stage of the couple.

The pre-effort dynamic created by desire difference is an opportunity to slow down and learn more about yourself and your partner, to cultivate emotional intimacy and rewire outdated habits, to encourage congruent and genuine expression. This opportunity is most effective when Conscious Moving is incorporated into the work for a whole-body learning process that engages the deepest areas of the brain and nervous system as well as the newer brain structures for lasting and intentional change.

By engaging a bodyful connection with the sexual self through present-moment awareness and phenomenological inquiry, individuals are invited to learn what their experience-dependent nervous system has absorbed from their culturally embedded social location. By exploring how the sociocultural environment and early messages made the meaning of sexual intimacy for them, the intimate partners get to dismantle this belief system and learn to discern between what is actually true and what is not true for them and the dynamic of their relationship.

The Process: Awareness and Ownership of Self with Erotic Bodyfulness

Sexual schemas have somatic architecture through body posture, expressive movement, pacing, breath quality, and body-to-body patterns of relating. A Conscious Moving practice allows intimate partners to learn how their sexual schemas are playing out between them through a desire difference by setting the absorbing content and situational details aside in order to focus on the unfolding somatic story. This process allows the partners to uncover resilience and connection from their present-moment experience as they shift from externally defined meaning to the personal and relationally defined meaningfulness of sexual intimacy. As a somatic creative process, Conscious Moving provides a structure to identify the limiting or incongruent beliefs around sexual intimacy and the corresponding limiting somatic experience and expression. This method then guides the couple through a process of change that supports the discovery of what I call their *embodied somatic resonance.*

This method begins with the awareness and explorative practice of *Erotic Bodyfulness* (Walker 2021), a body-based mindfulness and Conscious Moving practice that incorporates orienting toward pleasure and connection into Caldwell's concept of *Bodyfulness* (2018). I invite my clients into a phenomenological inquiry that serves as a useful interface between inner somatosensory experience and outer expression that opens the door to present-moment awareness of the interoceptive and exteroceptive senses, the internal network of sensing nerves that allow us to detect how we feel in terms of sensation, movement impulses, and emotion. The interoceptive senses tell us details of our internal world, like if we are hungry, comfortable or uncomfortable, or if we are experiencing pain or pleasure. The exteroceptive senses tell us what we are experiencing in the environment, which then activates the movement impulses of the somatic nervous system—the network of muscles, tendons, and connective tissues—which is expressed through movement and breath quality. This is the process that awakens the deeper structures of the nervous system to rewrite ineffective and unsatisfying patterns of relating.

When my clients sit in my office and describe their frustration about how they are not synching up in their sexual intimacy, I invite them to notice how their body feels and how their body organizes into posture and movement as they describe their experience. We begin to explore what their body is saying in the moment and, because I value my client's understanding of the process, I describe to them the practice of Erotic Bodyfulness, which contains eight overlapping stages:

- ▶ *Identify anchor*: This is the beginning of the practice as I invite my clients to identify something that is grounding to them. This could be breath, their feet on the floor, the texture of the pillow on their lap, or a pleasing piece of artwork on the wall. This is what they can return to if they begin to feel spacey or uncomfortable.

- ▶ *Intentional breath*: This stage is where clients invite three full in-breaths and three long out-breaths to increase circulation throughout the body and awaken their somatosensory experience.

- ▶ *Awareness from the whole body*: At this point, I guide my clients to notice what their body is beginning to say to them through sensation and quality of micromovements, settling into the places where the somatic architecture feels meaningful.

- ▶ *Oscillate attention*: It is normal to begin to have thoughts or memories connected to the felt sensations, what they mean or why they are happening, and I encourage clients to notice their thoughts and oscillate back to the sensations themselves to study the texture, temperature, and movement qualities that they notice. Dislodging attention from meaning-making at this point begins to unravel the automatic thoughts that are tied to old assumptions.

- ▶ *Notice sensation with description and nonjudgement*: This is where I invite my clients to describe what they notice in their body as descriptively and nonjudgmentally as possible while validating the feelings that arise.

- ▶ *Notice movement impulse from sensation*: Sensations also have a movement quality. Tension pulls from the inside or compresses from the outside. Bubbles or shakiness have a pace and rising or dissipating quality to them. Warmth has a spreading or opening quality to it. This stage encourages noticing how the body is already moving and expressing itself from the inside-out.

- ▶ *Invite movement from impulse*: While clients are continuing to oscillate attention toward the origin point of the sensation, I invite my clients to slowly sequence movement from the sensation to the endpoints of the body (hands, feet, crown of the head, pelvic floor). What is automatic and internal becomes intentional and informs expression through action.

- ▶ *Follow pleasure and yield*: Once the movement has been expressed with clarity, I invite clients back into stillness to notice their somatic landscape. I encourage them to ask the questions "Do I feel the same or different? What is here now?" Often, intentional or conscious movement expression evokes a feeling of relief, of movement of stuck energy, of warmth, and even pleasure. At this point, I invite my clients to yield or soften into their bodies to encourage appreciation of how they are able to access resilience and vital energy in the face of difficulty.

The purpose of this practice is to increase awareness of one's embodied experience and to put a gap—a few breaths, a few moments—between noticing the impulse and slowly sequencing the impulse into action. This gap is intended to provide an empowered sense of ownership of one's dynamic somatic self and opens the crossroad between habitual movement expression and the potential of more congruent movement expression; to ask "What expression does this impulse usually lead to?" versus "What is the actual need or intention behind this movement impulse?"

For example, if a client is exploring how they feel hesitant to reach out to their intimate partner for touch when they feel interest, the slowness in following the movement impulse can reveal the tension in the chest and retraction in the shoulder muscles. The individual can then identify the tension and retraction as elements of body armor protecting them from the possibility of not being met in their interest or desire. They may have a memory from their younger years of reaching out for touch and being pushed away. By acknowledging that their body is holding this memory, inviting a full breath around the tension, and reconnecting with the grounding anchor, the individual has the opportunity to validate and follow the impulse with consent to reach out for a partner with more full-effort expression. In receiving this type of touch, their partner will most likely have a more relaxed response and a desire to lean toward them.

Notice how the slowness and intentionality of this moving practice provide the space to interrupt the habitual pattern that corresponds with the minimizing sexual schema in order to follow what truly wants to be expressed, as well as how to express it in a more relational and connective way. This is an opportunity to develop a securely attached relationship to one's own body, desires, and boundaries and to practice the rhythm of secure attachment with a partner.

Erotic Bodyfulness practice also builds embodied consent into the new relational pattern. I define *embodied consent* as an awake and alive relationship with the desires and boundaries of your body. This is where you source your "yes," your "no," and your "let's slow down so we can feel the level and direction of interest." In relationships, this also supports listening to and honoring the desires and boundaries of another in a way that does not negate your own experience but modulates your interactions. This is a core component to effectively navigate desire difference because it generates a mindset that the goal of sexual intimacy is for mutual pleasure and connection, and awareness is necessary to navigate the pre-effort dynamic. When mutuality is the goal, the space is made for curiosity, compassion, and attunement. With this new realization and the corresponding somatic choreography, intimate partners have the opportunity for a more congruent and satisfying way of interacting as well as uncovering the true needs and desires of sexual intimacy.

The Process Continued:
Cocreating a New Dynamic

As the intimate partners become familiar with the Erotic Bodyfulness practice, we shift into the Erotic Mapping process where they start by exploring two different sexuality schemas: the challenge schema that is superimposed onto the desire difference and the resource schema that offers a new pathway of resilience and connectivity.

I always begin Erotic Mapping by identifying the embodiment of resource— as I like to say, "resource early, resource often." The intimate partners are invited to consider what they love to do, an activity or a place where they feel at ease, excited, or confident in their bodies. This activity can be something sexual or nonsexual (like hiking, dancing, or gardening) since the vital energy of the body is present whenever embodied in an activity or creativity. As the couple visualizes this activity or place, they begin the Erotic Bodyfulness practice with full-body breaths, descriptive and nonjudgmental awareness of sensations and inner movement, awareness and intentional exploration of movement impulse as they clarify expression and then yield into the body as they appreciate the pleasurable and relaxed potential that their body can access.

The intimate partners then have the chance to share their movements with each other, to mirror their partner's movement, and to explore how their movement expression can synch up or complement each other in a resourcing and inspiring way. As they witness their partner's expression of what feels good to them, partners can learn the pacing, movement qualities, and rhythm that bridge their partner into a state of receptivity for connection and pleasure. I find that couples are often surprised by what they discover—they often recognize that they had been misreading their partner's somatic cues when their internal assumption prevented present-moment awareness. As they practice offering and receiving positive physical and verbal reflection with each other, they can even move into offering and receiving bodyful touch (nonsexual touch within the session) to learn how to initiate contact with each other that is consensual and enjoyable. This becomes the anchor to return to when a challenge is activated between them.

Once the partners have found their combined resource movement, we shift into exploring the challenging dynamic that the desire difference has activated. The challenge schema usually begins with something like "I should/shouldn't" or "my partner should/shouldn't" and, through Erotic Bodyfulness practice, the partners explore how this statement impacts their somatic architecture. As the couple begins the full-body breaths and activates awareness of the somatosensory body, most often we find qualities of pre-effort expression in the challenge realm. For example, people often experience a tightening quality in their muscles, movement is more abrupt or protective, and breathing is shallow or restricted. As they begin to describe their somatosensory experience, they often find that describing with nonjudgment is a difficult task. I encourage them to take their time here, to describe challenging sensations with a compassionate witness perspective. And when they notice and then follow the movement impulse, it often sequences into completion of a protective movement that they previously have not fully let themselves follow. When the intimate partners witness each other in their challenge movement, I encourage them to breathe into their back body to support them as they offer "Thank you for sharing your movement" instead of mirroring. It is a way to honor that their partner's challenge is their own and they can make space for each other's humanness.

Because we resource early and often, I invite the couple to again find their full breath, shake off the challenge movement, and shift back into their combined resource movement. Once a challenge schema has been explored, it can take a bit of time to oscillate back into the present moment and return to the full breath and easefulness of movement that are characteristic of the resource schema. I encourage them to really take their time here, to not rush into just being "okay." This is an opportunity to write a new and fully satisfying nervous system pathway toward their full-effort embodied self. This is the creation of their *resource bridge*, the breath and movement sequence that helps them identify when they are in challenge and shift nervous system states into their resourced somatic expression.

As they engage the resource bridge and return to their own easeful and confident movement, engaging in the rhythm of secure attachment with their own body as they validate and support themselves, then they can sequence their movement into connection with each other. The partners get to learn their individual processes to regulate their nervous systems and reconnect with themselves, and then learn how to reconnect and coregulate with each other, taking actionable steps to cocreate their inspiring resourced dynamic together in the present moment.

Once intimate partners find the resource bridge that allows them to shift out of challenge and attune with each other in their physical intimacy, they are encouraged to repeat this bridge and to incorporate it into daily life. This sequence of movements that help them return to connection with themselves and each other is the key to living in a sexual schema that is true to who they are as individuals and as ever-evolving intimate companions.

Visioning into the Future, Together

Ultimately, a desire difference is a mismatch of states in the intimate partners that activates misunderstandings and dysregulation in their relationship. Conscious Moving practices allow couples to rewire their body-to-body connection to create a new quality of being with themselves and with each other. By practicing conscious movement together, they can unravel the unhelpful sexual schemas and cocreate a more actionable and meaningful dynamic together that makes space for their humanness. They can now navigate any desire differences as a normal part of intimacy within a committed relationship.

References

Caldwell, Christine. 2018. *Bodyfulness: Somatic Practices for Presence, Empowerment, and Waking Up in This Life.* Boulder, CO: Shambhala Publications.

Keleman, Stanley. 1985. *Emotional Anatomy: The Structure of Experience.* Berkeley: Center Press.

Porges, Stephen W. 2011. *The Polyvagal Theory: Neurophysiological Foundations of Emotions, Attachment, Communication, and Self-Regulation.* New York: W. W. Norton and Company.

Wadley, James C. 2019. *Handbook of Sexuality Leadership: Inspiring Community Engagement, Social Empowerment, and Transformational Influence.* New York: Routledge.

Walker, Melissa. 2021. *Whole-Body Sex: Somatic Sex Therapy and the Lost Language of the Erotic Body.* New York: Routledge.

11

Conscious Moving: Support for Art-Based Expeditions into the Realm of Grief Work

GRETL BAUER, Diploma in Social Pedagogy, is a dance therapist, teaching therapist, and supervisor in the BTD (a German dance therapy organization), certified Qigong teacher, and Moving Cycle trainer. Bauer is also a freelancer in performative music and theatre projects. Bauer has studied Dance/Movement Therapy since 1989 and worked as a D/M- and play therapist in day treatment and residential psychiatric settings with adults, children, and adolescents from 1991 until her retirement in 2020. Bauer has also been the builder and leader of a sociocultural seminar house in the northern German countryside since 1988.

By shedding light on the usual, the practice of Action Theater disturbs the status quo, reinventing the improviser, moment to moment. Scar tissue from the years of repeating ways of being—perceiving, interpreting, inhabiting our bodies, responding to the changing world—becomes loosened, relaxed, released, and replaced by conscious embodied experience.

—RUTH ZAPORAH, FROM *ACTION THEATER*

All the videos mentioned in this chapter can be accessed via the book's website: www.consciousmoving.com.

Introduction

From the perspective of art-making, fundamental aspects of Conscious Moving offer us an opening to develop and build on our resources, encompassing a broad continuum of creative potential. This creative potential can then explore a wide spectrum between heavy burden and the lightness of joy.

Grounded in basic Conscious Moving (CM) principles, especially the themes of attending to nonjudgmental awareness and experimenting with bodily felt change agents, Conscious Moving meets with art-making in my studio, where a mutually informed dialogue with materials, music, and movement occurs. A full cycle through all four phases of CM unfolds, inviting integration, transformation, and empowering results.

In this chapter, I introduce the CM practice known as *Pressure, Pleasure, Inquiry* as a means of illustrating how a specific CM practice can hold and inform art-making. I use my own experiences of working with grief and experiencing the challenges of the COVID pandemic to demonstrate the power of art-making within the framework of moving consciously through the four phases that this form uses.

Grief Work

In a general description, *grief work* is the process of coping with a significant loss. Since its introduction by psychiatrist and researcher Erich Lindemann in 1944, the theory of grief work has spread widely from psychological research into practical bereavement support offered by therapists, professional mourning companions, and funeral homes. In the 70s, Elisabeth Kübler-Ross's work and her description of the five stages of grief—denial, anger, bargaining, depression, and acceptance—were intensely discussed in Germany. Further research since then has led to an understanding of grief work as a psychological process of coping with significant loss, not solely for the mourning of death, and for processing loss experiences in any life-altering changes (Hamilton 2016).

My own search and struggle to cope with difficult life-altering changes challenged me with these questions:

▶ How is it possible to confront the seemingly unacceptable without getting emotionally or mentally overwhelmed?

▶ Can the emotional experience of grief and pain be transformed into something different?

▶ Can I allow transformation within myself during the process?

Making Art as a Form of Grief Work That Responds to the Political Situation

I vividly remember how the path of exploration I reflect on here got started; it was 2017, with my response to the 2016 presidential election in the US. In my first reaction to the outcome, I balled up my airplane socks (which I now found useless) for the trash bin. Surprisingly, those transatlantic travel sock veterans would not go down silently! While I twisted them, they turned into Very Angry Bird puppets that had things to say concerning the sorrow I and many of my friends here in Germany and in the US felt.

Rather than speaking to this grief, the bird puppets had to sing, to rejoin with my dearest musical teacher Rhiannon. Rhiannon's voice and her singing were with me still, and I chose one piece from her CD *Flight: Rhiannon's Interactive Guide to Vocal Improvisation* as inspiration for my "Very Angry Birds' Song" (Rhiannon et al. 2001).

Very Angry Birds

(For more information about Rhiannon's works as a singer, teacher, and artist in deep awareness of a world of crisis, see Rhiannon [2013].)

The "Very Angry Birds' Song" called in more "birds" to be puzzled together from waste materials and developed into an improvisational in-house performance (for a video of this performance, visit this book's website at www.consciousmoving .com). This improvisation speaks to Christine Caldwell's mobility gradient, where spontaneous and emerging movements are located on a human movement continuum and valued as a source of change. As Rhiannon herself puts it:

> *Improvisation teaches us to look at our options, to keep listening for grace and when we hear it, we've got to move and we've got to move now. The time for action is swift to arrive and just as swift to disappear. Moment to moment is all there is: following one breath, one note, one idea at a time . . . There are always options.* (2013, 13)

This early work of mine, combining music with puppets and movement (trying to "wing" it as much as I could with my frozen left shoulder), laid the groundwork for my artwork in the following years. Still, in 2017, I was not yet consciously aware of how deeply the ordeals of this grief-improvisation-to-form piece were rooted in what can be described as the Pressure, Pleasure, Inquiry (PPI) practice, a practice I was familiar with due to my first Moving Cycle training with Christine in 2006. (See Christine's description of PPI later in this chapter.)

Making Art as a Form of Grief Work: Navigating the COVID Pandemic

Up to the present, and especially during the years of and aftermath of the COVID pandemic, with all of its contact restraints, health issues, and painful losses at all levels of life, the first flock of puppets mentioned earlier kept calling in all sorts of companions—fellow traveler puppets and musical instruments made out of recycled materials (in addition to "real" instruments)—who informed me of pathways through difficult territory. The shear mass of information about the pandemic—its spread and evolving nature; the discussions by experts and everybody concerned about dos or don'ts, doubts and perspectives—left me (and I suspect, you) with the feeling that we weren't in control of the situation and that we were again losing, losing people, interaction, community, a sense of safety, and a sense of connection to each other.

Not knowing what to do is a delicate challenge for a seasoned neurotic like me. It delivers pure pressure to do something, at least, in order to make a change. In a childlike regression to magic, I started to "ban" the virus and its mutations by knotting various materials into structures similar to the graphic images of virus forms shown on TV. The material I was working with was my collection of fruit and vegetable nets from the supermarket, the only public place I visited for a long period of time. I started decorating these forms so they became a COVID-fighting witch.

Apparently, this magical attempt didn't do much to tame COVID, yet collecting, knotting, and sewing by hand helped me on a bodily level to calm down emotionally and physically. Perhaps other knitting, sewing, and crocheting people know these effects well.

COVID-fighting witch

Navigating Grief and Loss Via Conscious Moving

From a Conscious Moving perspective, this work can be described as starting out from an Awareness Phase: I was facing what was there, and how my own senses, bodily reactions, emotions, and thoughts were being affected, and then I resonated with these experiences. Moving on to an Owning Phase, I trusted the impulse for change, whether it came from *pressure* (like fear, sorrow, bodily pains), or *pleasure* (like playfully knotting, sewing, putting together), or from *inquiry*, like asking "What wants to happen next?"

As Christine notes in her description later in the chapter, Pressure, Pleasure, Inquiry (PPI) practices can appear in different orders, and they can intertwine. They can unfold in all four phases of the CM framework. They can also develop in a practice called *meandering*—moving just for the sake of feeling alive. I move freely and without any plan in my studio space because it feels essential for me, either when I move silently or when I experiment with musical rhythms and phrases. By beginning with meandering and combining this practice with the PPI practice as a kind of dancing of my present experiences (both personal and as a witness), I was led into an Owning Phase of songwriting and toward adding visuals for the song videos.

This work was then followed by an Appreciation Phase, in which I tied themes and findings up into a form, and an Action Phase, in which I worked to bridge the pandemic-related social distancing we had to observe for so long with a longing to connect with others. I began sending these videos as life-signal greetings to a network of friends. (Please see links to these song videos on this book's website.)

At this point, it feels important for me to emphasize that this artwork would not have been possible without the generous support of my housemates, a family of artists who helped put together these productions. I'm deeply grateful.

Don't Panic in Lockdown!
When Pandemic Rules Set In

In March 2020, COVID gained momentum here in Germany. My housemates and I experimented with gloves and self-made masks, and after a few weeks of lockdown, we thought that everything would be under control. Flour, rice, oil, and toilet paper surely would be available again, and my puppet Francoise and I would go out and party! We rehearsed for this glorious moment in the kitchen.

Francoise and her song were created during a theater project in the early 2000s. At this moment in 2020, during the soon-to-be-lifted lockdown, I remembered that she was hopefully still surviving in her storage box. She must have learned everything about being caged, *n'est-ce pas*? I identified with her easily. It felt right to free her for this moment; to playfully translate the weird mixture of French and German words of her song into movement—*Laissez Le Bon Temps Rouler*—and to record this on video.

Gretl and Francoise

(See the "Bon Temps" song video link on the book's website.)

Our network of friends, responding to our "Bon Temps" video, repeatedly said, "It must be so much fun to make these things!" Hearing this, I noticed a freeze reaction in my body, and when I worked with this emotional reaction, it became more clear. My impetus to make art is far from fun. It comes from a place of discomfort, dissent, distortion, and distress. It attempts to avoid even more difficult states such as dissociation, or getting stuck.

The question then became one of finding a way to further be with my grief reactions to lockdown in a way that processed all these emotions. What felt important was "taking refuge in the present moment" (Nhat Hanh 1998), breathing consciously (Caldwell 2018), and allowing the process of dialoguing with the art materials and music compositions to be experimental—to try different experiments in order to fail and then try again, uncovering different outcomes as a result. I wanted to find a place of flow (Csikszentmihalyi 1990) rather than turmoil. Exploring and processing this experience reminded me strongly of the specific practice named Pressure, Pleasure, Inquiry (PPI), developed by Christine. I decided to add the PPI practice into my art-making in deliberate ways.

FROM CHRISTINE: PRESSURE, PLEASURE, AND INQUIRY: A PRACTICE OF CHANGE

One of the most compelling questions in the fields of psychotherapy and social systems theory has to do with the nature of change. Whether it's changing our minds, our hearts, or our habits, we all struggle with when, how, and whether or not to go a different route. We strive to be in control of change, wanting to be change agents rather than be at the mercy of what other people or systems want us to do. Why do we want (or not want) to change, where does change come from, and how do we accomplish it? One way we can begin to sort out these questions is to see change as complex and often involving conflicting forces. We carry within us both urges to change and urges to stay stable and the same.

Neither staying the same nor being different is problematic; neither are they virtues. They both represent choices to be made in current circumstances, choices that hopefully enhance survival, integrity, and well-being. The trick is to know how to choose correctly. Psychotherapy is in the business of change, due to the assumption that people come into therapy because staying the same is causing them to suffer. If a therapy client's problems could have been solved by staying the same, then all would be well. The business of any therapy is to help clients to experiment with and practice change in a safe environment and lessen both their fears and habits of not changing when change is called for.

Emerging research in the field of aging is pointing to *novelty* as one of the most reliable protections against the loss of cognitive and physical functioning. Changing ourselves by learning and doing new things, especially physical activities, is our best way to stay sharp. It is thought that the reason novelty is so potent a protector of the brain is because newness tends to sharpen and focus our attention. How do we support clients, regardless of the issues they come in with, to value their attentional skills, and learn to work with them proactively? What follows looks at three embodied sources for change and will suggest ways in which we can identify these sources and tailor our clinical work to deliberately include them.

To begin, here are a few orienting details:

▶ The dictionary definition of *change*: to cause to become different; alter, transform; to pass from one phase to another; absence of monotony; new or fresh.

▶ Change is inevitable and can be experienced as positive, neutral, or negative. "Change-resistant" clients have typically experienced mostly negative changes.

▶ We often form compelling beliefs about where change comes from—from the inside out or the outside in. We can alter ourselves from inner motivations, such as deciding to quit smoking, or change can come to us from external circumstances, such as losing a loved one unexpectedly.

► Change can also be *top-down* or *bottom-up*. Top-down uses cognitive and mental processes to alter our actions. If we change our thinking or beliefs, if we understand ourselves more deeply, we can influence our behavior. Bottom-up, on the other hand, arises from the body, and holds to the idea that we have to shift our physical state and our behavior as a way to turn things around. Behaviorally, we learn to calm ourselves, count to ten before speaking, breathe deeply, not reach for the drink, and learn to make better eye contact, for instance. Ideally, we have access to both these directions of change.

► Another dimension of change has to do with whether or not we have initiated it. We can consciously initiate change in our lives, and this usually leads to greater levels of satisfaction and feelings of self-agency. Or change can happen to us, often in a shocking manner. A spouse dies, we lose our job, or fire destroys our home. Unexpected positive change can also happen to us, like winning a prize. The key ingredient is that we are not in charge of the change—we may feel lucky or unlucky, but we do not feel powerful.

► Change in psychotherapy typically organizes around being our own change agent; we dig down into what we really want, identify the obstacles to achieving our goals, and strategize about how we can increase motivation and decrease resistance. Drug therapies such as antidepressants assume that we are not currently capable of changing on our own. We need the drug to change our brains for us.

THREE TYPES OF CHANGE: PRESSURE, PLEASURE, AND INQUIRY

This section describes the details of the three types of change, and how they work.

Pressure: One way that change occurs is when the way we've always done something no longer gets it done, or the price of staying the same is greater than the benefit. Evolution is the most widely known explanation for this kind of change; it states that species change over time because of pressure to do so from shifts in environmental conditions. If your predator gets faster, your species needs to grow longer legs and bigger lungs. This is our gift from Darwin.

The key concept here is being pushed into change. We alter how we operate in reaction to feeling pressured or forced to do so—being kicked out of our comfort zone. This pressure, often from the outside, pushes us out of our old habits by causing pain and suffering, even death, if we stay the same. It might look like a client coming into therapy because her life is falling apart and she can no longer stand it. It may make itself visible as you open your eyes in the emergency room after overdosing. Pressure-based change is about identifying, respecting, and addressing symptoms. It's about not wanting to hurt so much.

We all are changed in this way, even the most enlightened among us. There is no getting around painful, pressured changes, though we can certainly live in ways that minimize the struggle and suffering we experience because of them. Our loved ones die, altering our place in our world. Our bodies age and get creaky. A natural disaster occurs, and we are all thrown into something different.

The pressure symptoms can be physical, such as headaches that come on as you drive to work. They can be expressed through emotions—you feel pushed around, overwhelmed, or out of control from fear or sadness. They could be cognitive, showing up as projections or rationalizations that are off the mark. Or they could be social/relational, played out in an unhappy marriage or getting arrested for a DUI.

Pressured change usually revolves around the themes of survival, safety, and functionality. Whether or not these tend to flow from the bottom up or the top down, the therapist's job revolves around helping the client identify the pressures and listen to and honor the messages contained in their symptoms.

A pressure symptom requires some sort of self-care. One reaction is to try to get rid of a painful symptom. We may make ourselves wrong, or somebody else, we may push away whatever (we think) causes that symptom, or we may medicate ourselves out of having to listen to the symptom. So, as therapists, we educate the client about the importance of their present moment, embodied experience, even if it's painful, thus creating a culture that values the body's messages. Clients need experiences in therapy that help them to listen to and decode the body's symptom signals.

Instead of just getting rid of or getting instant relief from a symptom, we begin to listen to it. We give it our nonjudgmental attention, and we cooperate with it as a source of information about what wants to change. It involves attending in such a way that we can let the symptom speak through our bodily movements so that we decode the messages in the symptom and use these messages as levers for conscious change. In a clinical setting this looks like supporting a client to attend to a symptom, sustain attention to it, and notice what associations arise. From there, the symptom can begin to speak to the client through sensorimotor processes.

Pleasure: We can also change through pleasure. A client can come into therapy feeling OK, but want to be happier, more energized, have more fun in life. The issue is old messages that form habits that limit a pleasurable engagement in the present moment.

Both research and the field of positive psychology are demonstrating that well-being is not just about resolving suffering; it's also about welcoming *natural pleasures*—the pleasures of breathing, sensing, and moving while being in the present moment. We may just be in a habit of limiting our natural good feelings, having never been taught or exposed to the skill of it.

We are often taught by families, communities, or religions to limit pleasure. We come to believe and act in ways that justify feeling depressed or resentful just because that's how we were raised. When opportunities to laugh, dance, and enjoy ourselves come along, we can feel suspicious and anxious.

If we don't know how to feel and enjoy natural pleasures, we may be more vulnerable to *unnatural* pleasures, such as drugs, alcohol, and high-risk behaviors. In other words, we are more vulnerable to addiction as the only way to access pleasure because we cannot produce it on our own.

Working to recover the ability to welcome and enjoy natural pleasures, particularly the pleasures of the senses, can result in deep healing. Happiness is not just about the absence of suffering—it can be more about the ability to move and breathe and sense in ways that access natural pleasures.

Play, particularly physical play, is an important part of the development of pleasure-abilities. If we did not get a good amount of safe, unstructured fun as children, we are more likely to have a low limit set on natural pleasures as an adult. In adult therapy, pleasure is more complex than with children; it includes sexuality and it can also include spirituality. As therapists, we mostly focus on the ability of the body to tolerate and even welcome natural pleasures.

Working therapeutically with clients about the pleasure practice involves creating a nonjudgmental environment that encourages explorations of pleasurable engagement in the present moment, using breathing, moving, sensing, playing, and relating to others just for the pleasure of it.

Inquiry: Inquiry forms the third practice. Once we have learned to work with symptoms, pain, and suffering, as well as the ability to generate and communicate positive and playful states, then a new kind of possibility for change emerges. In inquiry, we drop our investment in whether or not an experience feels painful or pleasurable. Neither one is particularly relevant. What is relevant is that we want to keep inquiring deeply into the details of the present moment, whether or not that inquiry is painful or pleasurable. We are open to whatever arises.

In this method of inquiry, we play with *physical free association*. We transition *from moving to being moved* (a term borrowed from Authentic Movement, a dance therapy form). We wait for sensory and movement impulses without willing them. Finding a way to move without consciously willing it can be very challenging.

Often, but not always, the practice begins with slowing down or stopping the way we have been moving up until now. Most of our daily movement is will-based because we need our will to direct our actions toward various goals. By quieting our willed movements, we are in a state of bodily or movement meditation. We are inquiring. We are creating a gap between our movements where pure bodily awareness can emerge.

When deeper bodily awareness emerges, our body moves in response to it, seemingly without our direction. We are being moved by a deeper part of ourselves, and we can participate with whatever state, emotion, image, or other association that arises. It can be similar to lucid dreaming, except that the lucid dream moves the body to narrate its story. Allowing this movement to emerge and sequence helps us to discover our true (and oftentimes obscured) nature.

Once the three individual practices become more familiar as separately explored states, they will tend to weave together, so that we might go from pleasure to inquiry to pressure and back to pleasure. This is an advanced practice and should be alternated with taking time to adhere to each practice separately. At times, however, we may want to stay in one of the practices exclusively for some time, in order to more deeply experience that type of change.

THE ADVANCED PRACTICE OF CHANGE—CONSCIOUS NOVELTY

The three strategies to work with change—pressure, pleasure, and inquiry—all carry the potential for more advanced applications having to do with the concept of novelty. Novelty can be seen as a meta-process, able to be done in all three practices because of its relationship to attention. The brain automatically and reflexively orients toward stimuli that are different. New things get our attention, and being on automatic is suspended while we orient toward novelty. We can capitalize on that in therapy, as a way to help clients pay attention to things they have been neglecting and to take their attention away from things they have been conditioned to stay focused on. The advanced and meta-skill of change involves developing a much stronger capacity to be at choice about where your attention does or doesn't land and how to keep it where you want it. Novelty is the lever that makes attention easier to manage.

How do we work with novelty in the Moving Cycle? Informally, it's called *The Goofy Practice*. Formally, it entails introducing novelty into the lived experience of the body. Goofy is a dog invented by Walt Disney. He is big, completely clumsy, relentlessly cheerful, and always powerfully engaged with what is happening right now. He's not a big thinker. He doesn't plan. He moves, he feels. In American English, this dog has become so popular that we now use the word *goofy* for anyone who is being cheerfully inept, playful, and devoid of self-consciousness. In the MC we tend to use the word *goofy* because it is so much more fun, and likely more safe, to introduce novelty in a context of unselfconscious play. But goofiness isn't required—it's just another possible lever. The root skill is conscious, purposive novelty in embodied experience.

In all three practices, novelty is introduced by purposively putting the body into an odd position, one that is different than usual. It could also be odd movements. Then one notices the different sensations and associations that arise. It might look and feel like you are a pretzel. It may also just be an unfamiliar place. This lack of familiarity puts one outside the norm and these responses are clinically useful.

Another way we can introduce novelty is via relationship. Engaging in an unstructured, nonverbal interaction with another person or a group introduces novelty by not being able to predict what will happen next. It can be goofy in the sense of spontaneous playfulness, but it can also be a serious exchange between two or more people, each interaction responding to the last. This can very quickly surface associations to relational imprints.

A last way to introduce novelty is via a body-based contemplative movement practice. The idea is to commit to moving while not knowing or willing where the body will go next, and staying very conscious of that process and what it brings up. This can take practice, as it is very unfamiliar to be moved by inner forces rather than to move with purpose or ingrained habit. All of these change practices should be embarked on creatively between the therapist and client or teacher and student, and so on. Pressure, Pleasure, Inquiry, and novelty can be very different for different people, so the artist/teacher/therapist should adapt these practices to the different needs of different people. This requires that we have lots of exposure to these forms in our own body and a good sense that what works for the student/client body will likely be different.

For further elaboration, see Caldwell (2018, 178–200).

Integrating Pressure, Pleasure, Inquiry Practice into Art-Making

The Conscious Moving perspective, via three major change agents—pressure, pleasure, and inquiry—enriches my present experience. In the making of art, in the back-and-forth communication with an instrument or any material, *pressure* is mostly initial, soon to be followed by a phase of playful *pleasure*—the simple joy of unexpectedly finding out about what a material can turn into when it is literally being turned upside down or inside out, dismantled or restructured, like the plastic nets from the supermarket turning into virus models mentioned earlier. And then *inquiry*—trying out a musical phrase, a word or sentence, a sound or move, and being open to where it leads. Are mistakes tolerable (called unintentional music by Lane Arye [2002])? How about failure? What if the process gets stuck, or blocked?

As a mover, in this case, I find it rewarding to explore micromovements (Caldwell 2019). I also work with five movement interventions that Christine has developed:

- *Repeating* a movement to study it more deeply
- *Contrasting* the movement—doing the opposite of what was just done—to catch different associations
- *Intensifying* a movement so that it becomes more visible or "louder" as a way to study it
- *Generalizing* a movement—taking it into the whole body to study it
- *Specifying* a movement—putting it into some smaller, specific part of the body, like the hand, as a way to make it more tolerable

These interventions translate well into working with materials or music: intensifying a color, repeating a note or musical phrase, repeating a movement sequence, and so on. All these processes help me develop a piece—a piece of music, a dance, a sculpture—that makes my experiences coherent and my narratives sharable.

Using the PPI framework like a map of my inner landscape helps me trace where I am in my daily life. It's a rich tool for exploring which attentional muscles are active, neglected, or overworked. This translates to a social level first by generating shareable information for my dear house inmates. When I'm plagued by the poetry bug, they handle my musings gracefully and generously (a kind of household Owning Phase).

During the turmoil of the first year of the pandemic, I remember a phase of deep grief, of not knowing what to do or how to move on in the stuckness of life's circumstances as I felt and witnessed them at that time. During a walk in nature, blank-mindedly, in the wind and cold of a late autumn afternoon, I suddenly heard in my head: "Make a soup." What came out of this was the "Fall 2020—Empty Glasses' Comfort Song." The glasses came from a beer glass collection, a hobby of the former innkeeper here in the 1950s and 60s. I found them in the basement and sorted them into a sound series in different scales.

Since the fall of 2020, it took me another thirty months until I worked the musical song recording into a video, with photographs from 2020, and the image (paired with the following song) of feeling frozen, emptied out, cornered. After I completed this work, I experienced more lightness and ease, a sense of my body freeing up again; this made me realize that a cycle had been completed.

Grief work takes time and has its own rhythm, like tidal waves. From my understanding, this song video and its making is an example of the Appreciation and Action Phases. Appreciation because it tied up findings, emotions, and images into a form, and Action because it is a going out, and a daring to share (for me, revealing is the hardest part).

Beer glasses for "The Empty Glasses'
Comfort Song"

"Fall 2020—The Empty Glasses' Comfort Song"

Pick your firewood, peel a potato
Cut an onion to tears
No cry facing the frying pan, and
Everything will be fine

Uprooted yellows, reds, and whites
Wash and chop them with care
It´s been a long way to the blade,
Everything will be fine

The beauty of abundant loss
Secret in a shrine
Never mind the fading light
Everything will be fine

(October 2020)

Sharing Art-Making with Family and Friends

With the Conscious Moving framing of pressure, pleasure, and inquiry as change agents in mind, a new impulse came to me—I would ask artist friends and acquaintances questions like these: "At present, how do you start with or get into your creative work?" "Do you remember when and how you began to play your instrument, to draw, to create, to experiment with material?" "What are your ways, what is your wisdom dealing with seemingly unproductive states?" "What is your starting or most familiar point?" "Is it feeling a sort of pressure, is it a pleasure to dwell in, is it curiosity to explore and find out?"

To my surprise, everybody I asked immediately told me a lot about their creative work and ideas. I had sparkling exchanges and reflections about resourcefulness, about all sorts of changes and turns within creative processes; I found out that processes contained rewards as well as blocks and overcomings, and many said they had an ongoing dialogue with the given material and the development of themes.

The common reaction from all of the artists to my questioning seemed remarkable—everyone said they'd never been asked these questions in this way before. The exchange of experiences led to many more talks and ideas. To this day, artist friends generously gift me with inspiration and with samples of their own art for the benefit of my song projects.

The following image is one more example of my work—an object that deeply inspired me.

Sculpture for "Dance to the Glory of Life"

"Dance to the Glory of Life"

Have you been dreaming of the secret space
Way beyond the mountains of hope
Last refuge of the fool
Dancing to the glory of life

Watch him wave
Jump up and down
Watch him stumble and fall
Will he get back on his feet again
To dance to the glory of life

Did you wake up in an awkward place
Way beyond the mountains of hope
Search for a trace of the sacred fool
Dancing to the glory of life

Why not try a wave
Try to jump up and down
Dare to stumble and fall—find ways
To get back on your feet again
And dance to the glory of life

(2022)

The Awareness Phase of this song came about from a medical diagnosis I was given, with an uncertain outcome. As I transitioned into the Owning Phase, I meditated over the spiral object in the preceding photo that an old neighbor had given me many years ago as a present; he designated it precisely as a meditation object to help "go in and go out of turmoil." It's a clock spring, material he had worked with when he was jailed as a seventeen-year-old political prisoner in (then) East Germany. He'd been sentenced to twenty-five years for his attempt to flee the republic. His coprisoners, carving artists from Erzgebirge (an area world-famous for this folk art), knew how to make carving knives from metal. They taught my neighbor their art, and, by using a clock spring, he learned to creatively win back some of the life he'd been robbed of.

In my situation now as I worked with these materials, I've been asking questions about time, duration, inevitable changes, going in, going out, and about passing. In an attempt to simplify these questions while staying with the essence, I composed the song/poem "Dance to the Glory of Life." I didn't make this recording in the studio. Instead, I sang and played the song on my phone, the day before my first operation, my self-organized Action Phase. The sound quality and tone of my voice may speak for the energetic situation I was in at the time. You can find the link to this on the book's website.

Conditions, New Challenges, and Limitations: Year Three of the Pandemic

At some point during the year 2022, the counting of COVID waves came to a halt here in Germany. Attention shifted to the Russian aggression against Ukraine, with threats and terror unsaid and ongoing. In March of 2022, TV journalist Marianna Owsjannikowa dared to hold a protest board up in the midst of a Russian TV newscast, and she paid a high price—a speedy and pre-ordained trial followed by the necessity of fleeing to France. While considering her mournings and sorrows on one side, and the inspiration of her insubordination on another, I made the song/video "To Whom It May Concern." The upbeat music speaks to the quality of my felt concern, sorrow, and grief, and the struggle to cope with this situation that continues not so far from us. That's all I feel ready to say about it now. You can find the link to this on the book's website.

In my further art-making, COVID themes began to emphasize post-COVID and long-COVID diseases, as more and more people appeared to not recover fully from the infection. In the summer of 2022, I transformed my own COVID fatigue experience into the "Recovery Song" (also linked to on this book's website). I hope you can see that its wording and images reflect the Conscious Moving Phases as I've been describing them.

Until the present, my art-making practice and exchange with others have carried the burdens of the COVID pandemic. Needless to say, all artists have been and still are affected both personally and professionally. Many resources went dry. Among the resources that were not restored after the lockdown is our ability to use our house and studio as a co-creative meeting place for groups that had been happening for over thirty years. I feel so much love and gratitude for the creativity that unfolded there, alongside the grief about that time ending. Still, the house and studio are rich with materials, self-created costumes, masks, sounds, found objects, and reverberating echoes from group activities in dance and theater. Occasionally, our housemate trio still goes on the move.

Housemates "Doing the New Low Down"

"Doing the New Low Down"

Two years plus of pandemic
Keelin' over, so sick of it
Hey, ho, doin' the new low-down . . .

. . . Hopes and dreams are in Lost-And-Found
Feet, don't fail me now
Dance me to new ground . . .

(Gumboot Serenaders, snapshot from a private in-house song stage, April 2022)

Grief Work and Art in Mutual Interconnection

The therapeutic power of art rests not in its elimination of suffering but rather in its capacity to hold us in the midst of that suffering so that we can bear the chaos without denial or flight.

—S. K. LEVINE (2020)

I hope I have comprehensively described, via art-making experiences and experiments, some of the principles and tools in the Conscious Moving framework that can contribute immensely to the integration and transformation of difficult and painful life experiences. Informed CM practices such as Pressure, Pleasure, Inquiry can not only nourish the creativity required to work our way in, through, and out of challenging life situations, they can, furthermore, serve as an enrich-ing field—a groundwork even—for artistic articulation and exchange.

In the many life-threatening, worldwide challenges of our time, it seems urgent that we develop ideas to keep our nostrils above the waterline. Our body-fulness, our hope, and all of our wits are called on to preserve life on our planet. In this sense, I understand grief work to be not only for post-loss coping but also to be incorporated as a preventive and future-oriented potential for caring. For ideas in this direction, Joanna Macy's work may be a rich source:

> There are hard things to face in our world today if we want to be of use. Grat-itude, when it's real, offers no blinders. On the contrary, in the face of dev-astation and tragedy it can ground us, especially when we're scared. It can hold us steady for the work to be done. The activist's inner journey appears to me like a spiral, interconnecting four successive stages of movements that feed into each other. These four are 1) opening to gratitude, 2) owning our pain for the world, 3) seeing with new eyes, and 4) going forth. The sequence repeats itself, as the spiral circles round, but ever in new ways. The spiral is fractal in nature: it can characterize a lifetime or a project, and it can also happen in a day or several times a day. (2007, 85–86)

With this quote, I want to underline Christine Caldwell's notion about con-scious movement being like a tree with many branches. And one with widely spreading roots and seeds!

A Tiny Piece of Embodied Practice as an Endnote

For pleasure's sake, I return to the core questions at the beginning of this chapter. However, my habit is to move through my questions via art-making—in this case the following sound poem:

> Is it (and if so, in what ways)
>
> Im- Possible to confront the
> In- Acceptable,
> Trans- Form it into
> Some- Thing different, while
> Be- Ing transformed during the process?

This—admittedly unfamiliar—question format can be set into motion. When you play with its rhythm, it may invite a tap dance improvisation or a time-step routine. As such, my core question, to start into the realm of grief work, becomes firmly embodied in music. In my understanding and experience, playing a musical instrument is primarily an embodied affair as well. (I use musical notation for cooperation purposes only). Music itself holds a spatial quality for me; it takes advantage of the practical bodily motion requirements of playing the instrument.

To maintain a genuine love for my guitar, I refused guitar lessons as a child; after all, didn't I have ears to listen to how songs sounded from the radio, record, or tapes? Led by my ears, through breathing with tones and melodies, and by exploring finger patterns, I let the guitar teach me. Mentioning this background might illustrate that the exploratory character of Christine Caldwell's Conscious Moving spoke to me immediately, since I first encountered it in 2006; at that time I was working as a play and dance/movement therapist with children and adolescents.

For my improvisational kind of art-making, I understand conscious movement and other practices today to be indelible foundations in any circumstances. In times of grief and turmoil, I experience the multifaceted framework, perspectives, and elements of Conscious Moving as a supportive orientation as I navigate through the darkness of the soul.

References

Arye, Lane. 2002. *Unintentional Music: Releasing Your Deepest Creativity*. Charlottesville, VA: Hampton Roads Publishing.

Caldwell, Christine. 2018. *Bodyfulness: Somatic Practices for Presence, Empowerment, and Waking Up in This Life*. Boulder, CO: Shambhala Publications.

———. 2019. "Micromovements: Filling Out the Movement Continuum in Clinical Practice." In *The Routledge International Handbook of Embodied Perspectives in Psychotherapy: Approaches from Dance Movement and Body Psychotherapies*, edited by Helen Payne, Sabine Koch, Jennifer Tantia, and Thomas Fuchs. New York: Routledge.

Csikszentmihalyi, Mihaly. 1990. *Flow: The Psychology of Optimal Experience*. New York: Harper and Row.

Hamilton, Ian J. 2016. "Understanding Grief and Bereavement." *British Journal of General Practice* 66, no. 651 (October): 523.

Levine, S. K., cited in Newcomb, Melody M. and Isabel M. Centeno. 2020. "Research in Creative Arts Therapies: When Counseling and the Arts Meet," *Canadian Journal of Counseling and Psychotherapy* 54(3): 188–96.

Macy, Joanna. 2007. *World as Lover, World as Self: Courage for Global Justice and Ecological Renewal*. Berkeley, CA: Parallax Press.

Nhat Hanh, Thich. 1998. Personal communication during a workshop in Bremen.

Rhiannon, Joey Blake, Laurel Murphy, Linda Tillery, Jeanie Tracy, and David Worm. 2001. *Flight: Rhiannon's Interactive Guide to Vocal Improvisation* [CD]. Sounds True. www.rhiannonmusic.com.

Rhiannon. 2013. *Vocal River: The Skill and Spirit of Improvisation*. Rhiannon Music.

Zaporah, Ruth. 1995. *Action Theater*. Berkeley, CA: North Atlantic Books.

———. 2009. "Ruth Zaporah's Action Theater: The Practice." Accessed September 13, 2023. www.actiontheater.com.

Song-Videos by Gretl Bauer

You can find links to these song-videos at www.consciousmoving.com under my name in the Chapter Contributors tab.

"Very Angry Birds' Song"

"Bon Temps"

"Fall 2020—Empty Glasses' Comfort Song"

"To Whom It May Concern"

"Recovery Song"

"Dance to the Glory of Life"

"Face the Music"

"Blurry Exit Signs"

"Doing the New Low Down"

12

Conscious Moving with Groups

The Application of the Moving Cycle in the Context of Group Psychotherapy

ANTJE SCHERHOLZ works as a dance/movement therapist near Bonn, Germany. She trained in stage dance and as an actress, and works as a lecturer for dance and body language. She furthered her education as a dance therapist and Moving Cycle practitioner and has completed her MA at Alanus University. Since 2008 she has engaged in clinical work, as a depth psychology–oriented dance therapist, at the LVR-Klinikum in Düsseldorf and at the Rhein-Klinik Bad Honnef. She has increasingly focused on dance-therapeutic, attachment-oriented treatment of clients with trauma. Since 2012 she has been a deeply convinced Moving-Cycler and a lecturer at conferences and trainings for psychotherapy, dance therapy, at the University of Applied Sciences in Heidelberg, and has various publications to her name.

Introduction

In this chapter, we explore Conscious Moving in groups. I present the challenges and opportunities associated with the integration of the Moving Cycle (MC) and Conscious Moving (CM) into Dance Movement Therapy (DMT) groups and discuss how working with individuals as well as entire groups can be successful with an attitude and approach shaped by these practices. I go on to explain therapeutic principles and interventions that open up a high degree of free, creative, and conscious movement exploration in groups without overburdening the group members. This approach is based on the guiding principle that therapy should adapt to the client, not the client to therapy.

Adapting the phase concept of the MC for group therapy opens up the possibility of empowering highly stressed people in crisis situations. Moving Cycle–oriented therapy is concerned with stimulating a path to self-embodiment and bodyfulness (Caldwell 2018). Through conscious movement, mindfully facilitated by the therapist, clients gain access to stored memories in order to process traumatic experiences or shed imposed attitudes, actions, or emotions. The conscious sequencing of buried movement patterns can serve their integration to achieve a coherent self.

Ultimately, the challenge in applying the MC to the group is to adapt it in such a way that it does justice to each participant and prevents harmful emotion and memory overload. It is important to use the MC in a way that enables attention to bodily resources so that self-regulation can be achieved within a relational process. The majority of my clients tell me that in my group they have gained or rediscovered access to their body and to self-determined processes of stabilization and development, including moments of healing.

I have continuously developed, adapted, and refined the DMT group concept presented here over a period of more than ten years. This was done in the context of my work first in psychiatry and later in psychosomatic medicine. Based on my many years of experience with DMT group therapy in a trauma-therapy unit of a psychosomatic clinic, I include the applicability of this group concept for people suffering from complex PTSD and clients with a high degree of instability.

As well, I have folded into my work my studies of helplessness and its effects on regulating action, the self, relationships, and self-efficacy, as well as Bartenieff's body organization (Bender 2010; Koch and Bender 2007). Also, I've woven in aspects of attachment research and infant research. The result is an attachment-oriented, creative arts–inspired, conscious movement–oriented dance therapeutic approach (Scherholz 2017; 2021). All of these backgrounds have influenced and colored the development of this MC-centered group therapy approach, in addition to my origins in artistic dance.

The development of this group therapeutic approach would not have been possible without lively encounters with my patients, who participated and still participate in my groups with the entire spectrum of psychiatric and psychosomatic illnesses. Their feedback and reflections have been and continue to be instrumental.

Basic Qualities/Characteristics of the Therapeutic Attitude for Integrating the Moving Cycle in Groups

I would like to emphasize the following characteristics of therapeutic attitude and presence for group work as they provide a solid foundation for the challenge of being able to openly, empathically, and appreciatively encounter not just one person, but many people, with different characteristics and life stories:

▶ As therapists, we must be willing to personally explore the principles and contents of the MC and CM, in addition to intellectual learning. By intertwining intellectual and experiential body knowledge, we can become confident of and connected to our sense of therapeutic resonance and action, which has been shown to bring about enhanced therapeutic effectiveness. Our effectiveness as therapists also hinges on our self-reflection through movement and intellectual study (Geuter 2019).

▶ We can treat the client as an equal in a person-to-person encounter. This therapeutic stance is characterized by recognizing the client's expertise with their own experience (body authority). They are invited to actively participate, set priorities, and exert influence. As therapists we should demonstrate authenticity as well as genuine compassion, acceptance, and empathy (Yalom 2021).

▶ We can maintain a therapeutic attitude of learning together during the therapeutic process while simultaneously oscillating our attention to being aware of our role as organizing, holding, steering, and keeping track. This oscillating attention can result in a therapeutic attitude of patience, trust, and confidence that each person can find their own way of healing if they are given a safe, appreciative, and respectful social space (Scherholz 2021).

▶ As therapists, we can be willing to be surprised again and again by the individual developmental paths of our clients without losing sight of the big picture. This is based on a benevolent, open, descriptive, noninterpretive view of group movement processes as well as the movement processes of each individual.

▶ We support the idea that the social space of the group is a valuable location for personal maturation and growth. The group is a valuable setting for exploring social relationships. No other therapeutic setting offers such a variety and diversity of interpersonal encounters. This includes our willingness as therapists to take on a more indirect mediating function as well as an ordering, regulating, and clarifying function within the group dynamics (Yalom 2021).

Reasons for a Group Moving Cycle

I would now like to turn to the motivations for adapting the Moving Cycle and Conscious Moving to group therapy. In clinics for psychosomatics, psychiatry, or rehabilitation here in Germany, there is a focus on group therapy. If the therapeutic potential of the MC and CM is to be used in a clinical setting here, the principles and tools of the MC and CM need to be adapted for work with groups. Another argument for using MC and CM in groups is the nature of humans to be socially oriented beings. From an evolutionary perspective, we evolved as members of social groups.

The complexity of interpersonal encounters and relational experiences that take place in an MC-oriented therapy group cannot be provided in individual therapy. A group offers a more diverse spectrum of relationship levels. Relationship encounters may be reminiscent of the parent/authority relationship, sibling relationships, and relationship episodes in various peer groups. Due to the presence of many interaction partners, group therapy opens up a variety of possibilities to reenact and heal old relationship wounds. Participants also encounter a wide range of possibilities to heal myriad other ongoing relationships.

The therapeutic value of the MC group becomes clear when we consider the focus of the MC and CM on healing internalized, maladaptive patterns of being in relationship that are often only revealed through movement. A primary task in MC groups is to provide a safe, trusting, and respectful framework for the multiple possibilities of exploring movement experiences that call up and work with old relational imprints.

Geuter (2019) emphasizes the need for "symmetry on the level of respect" in the therapeutic relationship. Our task in the group is to create a framework for possible conflict resolution, to invite constructive-critical reflection, and to ensure that the social rules of interaction continue to apply. A characteristic of the MC group is that it methodically integrates both the movement-centered relational dialogues between group members and the relational dialogues between us as therapists and the group members, considering them equally important. The interactive, relational orientation of body-centered therapy requires a different form of therapeutic support than in verbally oriented group therapy. On the one hand, I can be actively involved in group events by moving with everyone; on the other, a duet can develop for a moment between myself and a client. Similarly, communicative duets can develop between clients, or small groups can be formed. The most important task here is to create a framework for respectful, appreciative interaction and assure that the social framework will be adhered to.

In this way, an interpersonal space is created that reflects a multitude of possibilities for encounters and relationships that echo in everyday life. Some relationships can be symmetrical, where clients share similar concerns and similar stress. Then there is the more asymmetrical relationship with me as the therapist, which is ideally characterized by positive authority and responsibility for the therapeutic process on my part, while for the client it is characterized by hope and the desire for support.

The group is also an excellent social space for vicariously experiencing and developing self-efficacy through interpersonal learning. Self-efficacy can arise from witnessing the developmental steps or movement processes of fellow group members who share their themes. Clients are often encouraged by such a shared experience to take such a step on their own and try to do something similar in the next meeting.

In addition to the shared experience of movement, verbal reflection in the community also strengthens the experience of not being alone with one's thoughts, views, or problems. For example, a participant reports an experience of body shame because of her movement being seen by others. Then an exchange is initiated in which the members realize that almost all of them have similar experiences of shame. Surprisingly, it becomes clear to all that none of the participants are looking at each other in a judgmental way. The relief of the individuals when they recognize themselves in others can be considerable. Often, this is the first step to feeling and experiencing oneself as part of a social community. For groups, this has a strong cohesive effect. For individuals, the moment boosts self-esteem and corrects internalized models of shame.

The moment of challenge, action, and exploration can have a circular effect in group therapy. A group member can find that change is possible and that it can be embedded in a social framework. Each member's experience reveals that this does not necessarily lead to social exclusion, burdening, excessive demands, or harming from others. They may try something similar, or they may feel a sense of hope that this possibility is available to them. The final aspect of the circular effect occurs when the co-experiencers reflect on their nascent hope. A client who has dared to try something might receive positive, reinforcing feedback. The genuineness of this social resonance is trusted and believed much more at the group level than when it comes from me as the therapist.

For me, this means promoting such moments of experience in the group by creating a space in which important relationship moments can arise between the participants. This also includes a willingness on my part not to be the central person in the group. My role as the MC group therapist is to create conditions in which different types of relationship can be experimented with. My therapeutic task is to strengthen the community of the group, to welcome diversity, to enable individual recognition, to stimulate nonverbal and verbal exchange, and to convey and promote the social value of individuality within community.

Four Levels of Consciousness and Perception: The Path to Self-Embodiment and Conscious Moving in the Group

In the clinical-inpatient context, groups are mostly heterogeneous. There may be a mixture of psychopathologies and different levels of functioning. Even in groups with a single diagnostic focus, the stability level and compensation strategies of each client can be different. The varieties of survival strategies that they have acquired in dealing with their bodily experiences are varied. In such groups, many participants are initially overwhelmed by their sensing and moving body. At the same time, the majority of clients express the desire to encounter their body again, to accept it as a part of themselves, and to be with it, even when they feel dissociated from it. The MC, with its phase-oriented sequence of practices, offers approaches to meet this challenge in group psychotherapy. The guiding principle of orienting toward strengthening resources should be emphasized here, as well as functionalizing attention (Caldwell 2016, 2017).

In therapeutic work with my clients, especially with severely traumatized people, I have established a way of working with bodily experience and movement as well as oscillating out to the surrounding world, by using different levels. I like to call them the *Four Levels of Consciousness and Perception of the Moving Cycle*. In all my groups, access to these different levels has proven successful, whether in the day-clinic setting, with clients who possess a fairly well-developed level of introspection, or in the inpatient setting, with clients in acute crisis or with severe dysfunctional patterns.

The First Level: Real Perception in the Here and Now

The intention of this level is to acknowledge the social space of the group as well as the physical space. The focus is on arriving in the here and now, acknowledging present reality, and establishing the group as a familiar, safe, and influenceable entity. It is this active exploration of the surrounding world that lays the foundation for mastery of shifts in perspective.

These are the important components of this MC level, enriched by therapeutic interventions:

- ▶ As a group we continuously use the therapeutic triangle (breathing, moving/expressing, feeling/sensing).

- ▶ We move away from interpretation and toward descriptive reflection.

- ▶ We work on the integration of sensory modalities, such as crossing the room at different speeds, looking at it from different perspectives, listening to sounds, or touching objects or surfaces.

- ▶ We begin to recognize our attentional patterns via focusing attention on the here and now as well as exploring the oscillation of attention.

- ▶ We establish awareness of our own movement and embodiment. This might involve deliberately changing position, self-touching, eye movements, or listening to sounds. The movement focus is initially on practical movement and action without symbolic charge, such as consciously walking from point A to B, picking something up and putting it down, sitting down and standing up. Symbolism emerges of its own accord when we have the psychological constitution to deal with it.

- ▶ By working first with exteroception, we can transition to interoception, such as from "Where am I in the room right now?" to "I feel myself breathing."

Patients in acute crises or those with chronically elevated stress levels are typically not in the here and now. Their experience is characterized by a continuous mixing of the present moment with the past. Emotions tend to be colored by buried memories, and the only external stimuli they recognize are ones that show similarities with past moments of stress. They can be alert to certain stimuli in the external space, yet their senses are not open to receive stimuli from elsewhere. This is especially pronounced in people with unresolved trauma who have little or no physical resonance with the conditions in the here and now. Instead, the client is emotionally, cognitively, and physically occupied with past situations that they cannot influence. The result is an increasing sense of inability to act and feelings of helplessness or powerlessness.

At this first level, all phases of the MC turn to the experience of the present moment. When the patient can tolerate this present moment, an embodied reconquest of reality can be strengthened. This in turn is an indispensable basis for allowing new experiences. The group can become a therapeutic space in which spontaneous interaction and action are allowed to occur, and the focus of attention can expand from "space" to "me and space."

The Second Level: Embodied Experience in the Here and Now

The starting point of this level is the expanded focus from "space" to "me and space," accompanied by a deeper exploration of influence. A conscious focus emerges on self-moving, and on the client's embodied presence as it takes place in and affects space. Creative impulses and curiosity become visible. Here the client begins actively testing their exploring and experiencing skills, skills that enable self-regulation and conscious moving. This opens up an embodied access to the self without the danger of an emotional overload. My task as the therapist is to provide the framework for this process and to support it. This is where the therapeutic triangle, the practice of attentional oscillation, the techniques of entering and relieving, and creative curiosity come into play.

Here are the important contents of this level:

▶ We deepen the practice of description instead of interpretation.

▶ We deepen the integration of sensory modalities. This includes consciously oscillating between the different senses, and including various materials that invite sensory-inspired movement.

▶ We expand the practice of the oscillation of attention by confronting internalized attentional patterns, such as the oscillation between "close to the body" and "far from the body."

▶ We consciously practice skills that open up self-regulation and self-efficacy by deepening exploration of our patterns, strengths, and weaknesses in the use of breathing, moving, and sensing.

▶ We also practice entering and relieving—oscillating between going into a challenging symptom and resting away from it.

▶ We work on developing inner permission for curiosity and creative exploration.

▶ We pay conscious attention to self-movement, self-embodiment, and bodily authority.

▶ We pay conscious attention to interoception so that oscillating between exteroception, interoception, and proprioception begins to become more vivid.

At this point associations may appear, but they are checked against the real, surrounding moment. The client's own bodily space can relate to the social and physical space. Body boundaries can be established so that interoception can occur without being overwhelming. The client's attention can oscillate between themselves and others in the space. They can also distinguish between their own bodily space and the external space. The foundation is laid for orientation within oneself so that the joy of experimentation and curiosity can gradually grow.

The Third Level:
Self-Embodiment and Movement Exploration

The starting point of this level is the expansion of the focus to "my inner space in the outer space." With the third level of the MC, the client begins to turn their attention to their own movement impulses. It is a welcoming of the whole self, of self-movement and bodily presence, accompanied by emotional and sensory experiences. At this point, the active inquiry into micromovements and spontaneous movement impulses begins. Emerging associations can be given space. Positive interest and curiosity are the impetus to accept challenging situations. Trial and error and exploration can loosen the client's original preoccupation with stress and the joy of novelty can be won. The experience now oscillates between the here and now and the timeless nature of inner experience and sensation. The focus is on exploring and experiencing the inner potential of movement impulses and becoming aware of the effect of following these impulses. Buried memories lose their threatening nature as the movement impulses are experienced as enriching. The client can discover authorship of their own movement narrative. Imposed movement patterns can be identified and examined. Affect overload and excessive demands can be prevented through intermittent emergence into the here and now. Oscillation techniques are expanded, attention to learned self-regulation skills is offered, and the Pressure, Pleasure, Inquiry practice is introduced.

Here are the important therapeutic components of this MC level:

▶ As a group, we maintain the practice of description rather than interpretation.

▶ We deepen sensory integration. This includes consciously oscillating between each sense and consciously focusing on the kinesthetic sense.

▶ We deepen the practice of oscillating attention by oscillating between breathing, feeling, movement, and associations in the context of conscious movement.

▶ We replace mindfulness with bodyfulness (Caldwell 2018).

▶ We use skills that open up self-regulation and self-efficacy, such as holding the therapeutic triangle, using entering and relieving, following curiosity and creative exploration, and exploring the Pressure, Pleasure, Inquiry practice further.

▶ We discover that micromovements exist and begin to explore them.

▶ We pay attention to movement impulses and form them into movement sequences.

▶ We encourage each other to oscillate between proprioception, interoception, and exteroception, as this serves as the physiological basis for self-embodiment (Fogel 2013).

In this third level of the Moving Cycle, body boundaries can be established so that interoception can be involved without flooding. Clients can oscillate their attention between themselves and others in the space and distinguish between inside and outside. This is the basis for the last step, which does not reach a new level but represents a swinging between the other levels.

The Fourth Level:
The Oscillating Moving Cycle of Conscious Moving

This fourth level of the Moving Cycle integrates all three previous levels and oscillates between them in a descending and ascending process. The different phases from Awareness to Owning, Appreciation, and Action can sometimes take place on the first, second, or third level. Oscillating between the levels of awareness and perception described here ensures that one remains within one's *window of tolerance* as described by Ogden, Minton, and Pain (2010) and Siegel (2015). This means that one's arousal level oscillates within a safe, intermediate range. Securing the window of tolerance is essential for self-regulation, sustainable learning, development, and healing. In therapeutic processes, it allows the client to exit internalized helplessness or powerlessness and move in the direction of agency, self-efficacy, and self-regulation. In the practice of MC group therapy, the emergence of curious interest, creative play, and joyful exploration, even humor, always indicates that the client is increasingly widening their window of tolerance and entering self-regulatory processes. An important task for me as the therapist is to support this on a psychophysiological level. An offer of movement and expression in connection with breathing as well as feeling/sensing (the therapeutic triangle) forms a good basis here.

In this fourth, oscillating level, movement, experience, association, introspection, and reflection meet. Clients who are in an exploratory process of movement begin to deal with their stress signals in a constructive way. They begin to oscillate between levels in order to get out of overload dynamics early; the practice of entering and relieving favors this. My embodied, empathic, therapeutic accompaniment includes offering small verbal or nonverbal hints, depending on the situation.

The levels of awareness and perception described here, which lead to the genesis of a swinging, oscillating Moving Cycle (MC), indicates a connection to the four phases of Conscious Moving. The first stage is specifically related to the Awareness Phase, the second to Owning, the third to Appreciation, and the oscillating MC is Conscious Moving in Action. Establishing the MC across the four levels of awareness and perception presented here enables an approach to self-regulation in a group. The body can be discovered as a helpful resource, and control from the mind can shift to bodyfulness. Movement can be integrated as a form of sensation and can connect with our attention.

The Multiple, Circulating Processes of Conscious Moving in the Group

Once an orientation within oneself and the space has been established through the earlier levels, many different processes of Conscious Moving can begin to circulate in the group. The group "body" also oscillates, sometimes requiring more dwelling in awareness, turning to ownership, appreciation, or action, depending on where the group is as a social body.

In order for the group to move forward, conflicts always require shared attention and embodied processing. For example, a group therapy session may be devoted to strength and grounding in order to create a basis for an active dealing with a group conflict (Awareness). When the group must actively and controversially come into contact with a conflict (Owning), a very valuable moment of shared appreciation can arise for having clarified this challenging situation in such a respectful and relieving way (Appreciation). This usually results in a much more colorful, unadulterated togetherness and an earlier addressing of the social irritation (Action). When the community's common Moving Cycle is attended to and managed, the group's growth process can go hand in hand with the individual's growth process.

In addition to this group-specific cycle, each person in each group session has theme-specific individual cycles, as well as an MC that encompasses the entire therapeutic process during treatment. It is important for me, as a therapist, to encourage and guide this process so that the client can implement what they have learned into everyday life. If the individual Moving Cycles of the participants can be observed and dealt with successfully, the growth process of the group can be linked to individual growth processes.

The most important foundation for a body-psychotherapeutic approach in Moving Cycle groups is the creation and maintenance of high-quality attention on the part of the therapist. Cultivating open and descriptive attention is a prerequisite for me to be able to perceive both the individual client and the group as a whole. It allows for a simultaneous therapeutic response to the group dynamics as well as to the intrapsychic dynamics of each individual. My attention should oscillate between my senses, as well as from the inside to the outside and from panoramic to narrow, as I capture the whole body of the group and the individuals, as well as small details in the movement of each. At the same time, I embody a steady, casual attention that captures the individual's holistic state, emerging associations, movements, breath flow, sensations, and feelings. For example, if I respond to a sudden constriction of someone's breath or to a certain form of tension in their body, a moving resonance to this can show up in the group. My embodied attunement to the group—and the resulting nonverbal perception of individual group members—is a valuable diagnostic instrument. At the same time, it promotes the self-regulatory processes of the clients through a form of casual coregulation.

A special feature of any group situation is that one person may need more therapeutic support than others. This means that I might stay with the individual group member, intervening in a targeted way or calmly accompanying the process from the side. At the same time, I follow what is happening in the room and accompany it casually. Clients reflect on this form of attention to the individual within the group as opening, deeply relieving, and healing. Clients mention three elements that trigger this healing effect: First is the realization that others in the group do not suffer from my attention being paid to one individual. Second, clients can see that they are still important as part of the group and that they are seen even when someone else needs support. And third, they realize that I offer accompaniment and attention to anyone in the group during high emotional stress.

Another addition to this idea can be an embodied, attachment-oriented, stance that empathically perceives and accompanies different persons at the same time, which has been called *inter-bodily resonance* (Fuchs 2014). This can take the form of my mirroring a group member's movement, my coregulation with clients in the form of a sound, conscious breathing, poetic language, or my paraverbal resonance. For example, I may pick up that one client's foot is stomping in a slightly modified way while confirming another client's tentative finger movement with a "Yeah, the fingers too." Here, nonverbal communication, with its attuned, embodied togetherness, is a true treasure that allows for my accompaniment of both the individual and the whole group.

A last basic element is the attentive perception of the flow of movement in the participants. A stagnation of the flow of movement always indicates inner prohibitions and insecurity. This is often associated with an emerging helplessness and inability to act, as well as increased tension and constricted breathing (Scherholz 2011). Therapeutically, this can be countered in the form of attachment and the coregulatory use of tension-relieving movements.

Basic Interventions for Conscious Moving in a Group Setting

Finally, I would like to summarize some of the interventions that have proven to be foundational to this approach:

▸ **Maintaining the Therapeutic Triangle:** In the very first group session, I introduce clients to the oscillation between breathing, moving/ expressing, and sensing/feeling. In every movement exploration I touch this triangle constantly, verbally or paraverbally (breathing), as well as through deliberate interventions.

▸ **Proprioception, Interoception, and Exteroception:** From the first group session onward, clients are working with proprioception, interoception, and exteroception. These three basic types of sensations are fundamental for entering into embodiment. My groups always begin with stretching, extension, weight shifting, and similar movements, which address these sensory types and stimulate the therapeutic triangle.

▸ **Cultivating Creative Curiosity:** The cultivation of creative curiosity as an effective factor for development and growth is crucial. Often this is stimulated by a playful group moment or intervention that includes humor and laughter. In addition, my attitude of positive interest and curiosity about people, the individual creative process, and the surprises that a group situation can hold situates me as a positive role model.

▸ **Psycho-education, or Educating the Patient about Therapeutic Principles:** This could be explaining body-centered processing or certain ideas in the MC and CM in the service of generating security, transparency, and empowerment. Psycho-educational interventions always arise as a therapeutic response to the group's questions and need for orientation.

▸ **Verbal Accompaniment in the MC Group:** Since I work with several patients at the same time, I need a strong vocal presence. Verbal interventions always emerge from the individual's own embodied experience and are expressed in an embodied way. This means that interventions I use, such as cues to repeat, to intensify, to generalize, to specify, or to contrast, are generally spoken into the space. This can take the form of general phrases, such as "Yes, exactly . . . the movement can also repeat . . .," or "Mmm . . . what if the movement becomes smaller . . .," or "Oh, the fingers . . . maybe there's something to discover there," that draw attention to micromovements. Relevant here is that my therapeutic suggestions are meant as suggestions and not commands.

- ▶ **Conscious Eye Opening and Closing:** Another peculiarity in the group is that clients often keep their eyes open because closing their eyes feels too unsettling. In group therapy keeping eyes open does not exclude deep Conscious Moving processes. Closing or opening the eyes is also a movement we consciously practice and explore.

- ▶ **My Spatial Presence in the Group:** At the first two MC levels, I am very likely to be spatially involved in the group action; at the second/third, and third/fourth levels, I am more likely to be at a spatial distance. When a client needs more direct guidance, I am likely to be spatially at their side. When many individual conscious movement processes are taking place at the same time, I tend to meander from one client to another, offering brief accompaniment or support.

All in all, it becomes clear that in Moving Cycle groups I as the therapist am constantly oscillating on all levels. The therapist is a true *oscillation athlete*.

Conclusion

I would like to close with the words of a client, told to me during our conversation at the end of his treatment:

> *Dance therapy was a special place for me. I carry with me the new experience that I am seen, even if I am not in the foreground—and I didn't want to be, because I didn't actually want to be there. And then I realized that I was still important—and that the brief moments of their attention were not too much for me.*
>
> *After some time, I knew that you were noticing me, and you were okay with me being there, without me having to give anything in return. After a while, I was able to be more relaxed with myself and not be so pressured with myself. I even had some really quiet moments with myself. In the past I could not handle attention at all and always ran away or jumped into a role. But this time I found my place and could even enjoy it and enjoy my movements. The*

beautiful thing is that the shame and fear that always had been there when I get attention became less—and I could show myself more and more—and then I could also enjoy encounters with the others that I could end myself. That is also a new experience. I noticed that I started to deal differently with the people on the ward and I also notice that I show myself differently to my wife. I carry this deep experience of Dance/Movement Therapy within me and it makes me really hopeful and joyful. I am deeply grateful about it.

References

Bender, Susanne. 2010. *Bewegungsanalyse von Interaktionen[Movement Analysis of Interaction]: Internationalen Kongresses zur Bewegungsanalyse in Erziehung, Therapie und Forschung: Moving from Within*. Berlin: Logos-Verlag.

Caldwell, Christine. 2016. "The Moving Cycle: A Second Generation Dance/ Movement Therapy," *American Journal of Dance Therapy* 38, no. 2: 245–58.

———. 2017. "Conscious Movement Sequencing: The Core of the Dance Movement Psychotherapy Experience." In *Essentials of Dance Movement Psychotherapy: International Perspectives on Theory, Research, and Practice*, edited by Helen Payne, 53–65. New York: Routledge.

———. 2018. *Bodyfulness: Somatic Practices for Presence, Empowerment, and Waking Up in This Life*. Boulder, CO: Shambhala Publications.

Fogel, Alan. 2013. *Selbstwahrnehmung und Embodiment in der Körperpsychotherapie: Vom Körpergefühl zur Kognition*. Stuttgart, Germany: Schattauer.

Fuchs, Thomas. 2014. "Verkörperte Emotionen—Wie Gefühl und Leib zusammenhängen." *Psychologische Medizin* 25, no. 1: 13–20.

Geuter, Ulfried. 2019. *Praxis Körperpsychotherapie: 10 Prinzipien der Arbeit im therapeutischen Prozess: Part of the Psychotherapie: Praxis Series*. Berlin/ Heidelberg: Springer.

Koch, Sabine C., and Susanne Bender, eds. 2007. *Bewegungsanalyse: Das Vermächtnis von Laban, Bartenieff, Lamb und Kestenberg [Movement Analysis: The Legacy of Laban, Bartenieff, Lamb and Kestenberg]*. Berlin: Logos-Verlag.

Ogden, Pat, Kekuni Minton, and Clare Pain. 2010. *Trauma und Körper: Ein sensumotorisch orientierter psychotherapeutischer Ansatz*, trans. Theo Kierdorf and Hildegard Höhr. Paderborn, Nordrhein-Westfalen, Germany: Junfermann Verlag.

Scherholz, Antje. 2011. "Von der Hilflosigkeit zur Handlungsfähigkeit. Von der Bewegungslosigkeit." Presented at Bewegung kommen: Chancen in der Tanztherapie. Unveröffentlichte Abschlussarbeit der Weiterbildung zur Tanz- und Bewegungstherapeutin (BTD). Berlin.

———. 2017. "Das Dritte im Bunde: Der künstlerische Tanz- und Ausdrucksraum als Wachstumspotential und Freiraum innerhalb der therapeutischen Beziehung." In *Tagungsband KreativtherapieTage 2015: Das Dritte im Bunde. Das Potential des künstlerischen Mediums in der Kreativtherapie*, edited by LVR-Dezernat Klinikverbund and Verbund Heilpädagogischer Hilfen, 118–33. Stolberg, Nordrhein-Westfalen, Germany: Landschaftverband Rheinland.

———. 2021. "Beziehung positiv erleben—Bindungsorientierte Tanz- und Bewegungstherapie mit Kindern und Jugendlichen." In *Brennpunkte der Sportwissenschaft: v.38. Bewegungs- und Sporttherapie bei psychischen Erkrankungen des Kindes- und Jugendalters (2. Aufl.)*, edited by H. Deimel and T. Thimme, 227–50. Baden-Baden, Germany: Nomos Verlagsgesellschaft.

Siegel, Daniel. 2015. *Handbuch der interpersonellen Neurobiologie: Ein umfassender Leitfaden zum Verständnis der Funktion von Gehirn und Geist*, trans. Mike Kauschke. Frieburg im Breisgau, Baden-Württemberg, Germany: Arbor Verlag.

Yalom, Irvin D. 2021. *Theorie und Praxis der Gruppenpsychotherapie: Ein Lehrbuch, 14th ed. (Leben lernen: Bd. 66.)*, trans. by Teresa Junek, Theo Kierdorf, and Gudrun Theusner-Stampa. Stuttgart, Germany: Klett-Cotta.

13

Sharing Beauty

How Conscious Moving Can Guide a Moving Cycle Session

THOMAS VON STUCKRAD graduated with a diploma in psychology in 1986 and is the cofounder of the Blaumeier (art and psychiatry) project in Bremen, specializing in experiential work with masks. Since 1991 he has been self-employed in a psychological practice for adults in Cologne, and he is qualified in behavior therapy as well as other therapeutic approaches (Gestalt, systemic therapy, Inner Relationship Focusing). He has been in ongoing training with Christine Caldwell since 1998 and is heartfully engaged in music and singing. In his latest project, Soul and Singing, he leads workshops alongside his wife, Sabine von Stuckrad.

Introduction

In the early 1990s, I decided to work as a psychotherapist. This was a major decision. I was in my mid-thirties, had completed my studies in psychology, and could refer to some clinical experience, but I got anxious when I thought about working with patients as a medical authority. The medical system seemed too strong and seductive; it would force me into a top-down mode of working, fixing problems and pathologies rather than engaging in vivid relationships.

In those days, I was supported by a strong political and social movement, which also extended into the scientific field, that held on to psychology and psychotherapy as disciplines originating in philosophy and the social sciences, rather than in medicine. In 1986 I was part of a multiprofessional team that founded a project in Bremen, Germany, called Blaumeier (which still exists), in which we treated so-called patients who had been permanently institutionalized in a long-term psychiatric hospital, giving them back their dignity by respecting them and focusing on what made them special in our eyes. With them, I practiced seeing symptoms and pathology as meaningful and informative. Behavior that was supposedly abnormal began to contribute to the so-called normal and the personal and social boundaries began to shift as well.

Back in those days, working with masks thrilled me. I conducted workshops in which we let our creativity guide us as we shaped faces out of clay, reaching far into the realms of nonnormality. We then worked these faces into masks and gave them life through our living bodies by engaging in stage play. It was (and still is) very profound to be part of this special experience in which a living body transforms into a moving sculpture and to observe how meaning extends into time and space.

From then on, I became aware of ways in which meaning can be understood through movement, how movement creates relationship, and that an understanding of the body is foundational to a deep understanding of movement. Furthermore, I concluded that I could only be a therapist if I could engage with my clients on a body-to-body level, balancing top-down with bottom-up approaches.

Knowing all this was helpful, but unfortunately knowledge was not sufficient. I needed skills. But who could teach me not only to have a body, but to engage with a body—my own body as well as the body of the other—in the professional context of a therapy session? I collected what I could from Gestalt therapy, psychodrama, neuro-linguistic programming (NLP), Ericksonian hypnotherapy, Hakomi, and body psychotherapy, until I met Christine Caldwell in 1998. She introduced me to the concept of the Moving Cycle, and I found what I was looking for. On a very practical level, Christine showed (and continues to show) us how her body engages with the body of the other when she works with clients, and she teaches these skills through basic guidelines and practice.

That was the beginning of a professional relationship that has endured into the present, ultimately leading to this chapter.

Conscious Movement and Psychotherapy Practice

Due to my mask-making background, I was delighted to engage in process work. I love theater, especially improvisation, and I believe that truth arises out of the moment and that its meaning can change from moment to moment. Unfortunately, this stood in opposition to the demands of clinical psychotherapy practice in the medical field, a context in which I had been trained to write reports, care about successful therapeutic outcomes as well as financial income, and be "normal" to the extent of keeping my composure in front of the health authorities. I did not know, for example, how I could get out of my chair and roll around on the floor during a session without appearing crazy to my clients and affronting them personally or endangering my professional reputation. From then on, I asked myself how I could integrate the setting of a Moving Cycle session into my everyday practice. Since I heard about this new book on Conscious Moving in its different fields of application, I have wanted to write about what makes the Moving Cycle so attractive as well as challenging to integrate into the clinical field.

Conscious Movement and the Moving Cycle

The Moving Cycle is designed to be an experiential process for both the mover (client) and the facilitator (therapist). Before the session starts, both parties agree on who will take on which role. The idea is to engage in a creative process of play and curiosity.

The session begins by focusing on the body. This focus is kept alive throughout the whole session in the bodies of both the mover and the facilitator. The mover is oriented toward themself with an attitude of openness to anything that wants to emerge. The facilitator is oriented toward the mover and also toward *them*self, and is open to what can be seen, heard, and otherwise sensed in their body.

This beginning on a body-to-body level sets the stage. Here words are usually an important catalyst to create understanding and establish contact. They communicate the story. The facilitator is listening. Through active listening, the words can sink into the body's awareness. This process is subtle and tender and relies on a sufficient amount of trust. On a relational level, it is often the case that—metaphorically speaking—these first bars of music provide the theme for the whole symphony.

Video Demonstrations of the Moving Cycle

To get more information and insight, I decided to document and visualize what happens in a session. I wanted to understand how the body can be read and how I could learn its language. I'd like to demonstrate this in this chapter. I invite you to come with me as a visitor by watching along with the video segments as I discuss them later in this chapter, observing certain moments from sessions I recorded in Berlin in May 2022, at a seminar on the topic "Intergenerational Issues." The emphasis here is therapeutic, although you can also see elements of contemplative practice, learning, and creativity in these sessions. The people in these videos are all advanced practitioners of the Moving Cycle, and they all know each other quite well and trust each other. Many have been working together for more than ten years.

My aim in this chapter is to demonstrate the beauty and completeness that arises in these pieces of developmental work and to underline my hypothesis that psychotherapy can be not only a method of healing, but also a piece of social art.

The title "Sharing Beauty" came to me while I was watching these films. I was surprised by the elegance of movement shown in these interactions. In my understanding, a therapy session of this kind is more like a dance and a piece of art than what in academic parlance would be called a clinical consultation.

Tips on How to Watch the Session Videos

As I said earlier, the people in this video are all advanced Moving Cycle practitioners who know and trust each other. These sessions tend to show the creative, spontaneous experimentation that comes with being a highly skilled practitioner.

This video is a record of a training session on how to use touch in Moving Cycle sessions, so you will see touch used extensively. The Moving Cycle does not require touch to be used. In some cases, touch is not possible or recommended. But because all of these participants are training in the use of touch, you will see a lot of it.

All the practitioners have signed "Touch Agreements" for the course; these are agreements that spell out their right to stop touch at any time and to direct it according to their own bodily authority. Notice the prevalence of holding—the mover allows the practitioner to hold their weight. Resting one's weight in the "holding environment" of another person's arms is thought to be directly reparative of early relational wounds.

Each segment of the video depicts a few minutes of a session that may have lasted for up to an hour. Most of them show portions from the middle part of a session, so you will see a lot of Owning and Appreciation, and not a lot of verbal processing.

The people in these sessions come from six different countries and speak different languages. Most of the sessions take place in the shared language, English, though you may hear German in a few of them. However, none of the videos require verbal language in order to be understood.

These sessions are meant to show the power of immersion in ongoing emergent movement as a way to support bodily narratives. As such, they all show us the power of an attuned relationship that evolves via spontaneous relational actions. Notice the mover waiting for movement to emerge, and note how each emergent movement is greeted and supported, without analysis or judgment.

There are several assistants in the room, along with Christine, the teacher. Christine was dealing with a persistent leg cramp during this class, and so she was moving with difficulty. The other assistants are learning to be Moving Cycle teachers and can be seen offering support for the practice sessions.

The video of these sessions can be accessed on the website for the book: www.consciousmoving.com, under my name in the Chapter Contributors tab. It is a single video that includes all the session segments in the order they will be discussed here. As you read the rest of the chapter, have this video open and watch each segment of the video as you read.

Awareness, Owning, Appreciation, Action—Stories of the Body

The following example shows how the understanding of phases can help to identify how movement unfolds and organizes itself around an issue the mover is dealing with.

The orientation in the beginning of this session, seen in the first segment of the video called "Beginning a Session," focuses on a sensation of pain in the right shoulder. The facilitator and the mover stand next to each other. They engage in a story. The mover's story is this: "I am dealing with pain. Where do I get the power to face my facilitator in this situation? Do I get what I want? Can I reject what I don't want?"

Both the mover and the facilitator use words. The main channel of communication is verbal speech and oscillation between inner and outer awareness.

See how the exchange of words regulates and stabilizes the relationship and how the stage is set.

Then in the next segment of the video, called "Body Awareness," the process evolves, and there is a shift from "talking about" an experience to "having an experience" (Owning phase) by bringing awareness into the body.

This then deepens in the segment called "Deepening Awareness" and moves toward owning in the segment called "Owning."

In the segment called "Owning through Touch," we can also observe how the mover is manifesting her bodily authority by placing the facilitator's hand precisely where it feels right.

In the context of the whole session, this phase of awareness and owning takes around 5 minutes and exhibits a relational pattern. Later in feedback, the mover called it an "Eiertanz" or "walking on eggshells" as a reference to tiptoe-ing through a complex, difficult relational situation. (Later, still in feedback, it became clear that this was an issue around trust and responsibility.)

Then we see a change in minute 15 of the session, shown in "Body-to-Body Interaction." The mover's and facilitator's bodies are closer to each other than they were before. The mover's body touches the facilitator's body.

Later in feedback, the mover said: "I could stay and hold on to myself without having to watch out for and take care of the other, and I could even allow the other to hold my weight for a while." The inner sentence here is "I am I, and you are you, and I dare to be me in front of you."

This culminates in Appreciation in minute 40 of the session, seen in "Moving into Appreciation."

The muscles of the mover's shoulder loosen, and the pain is released. The facilitator is no longer absorbed in the relational pattern. The inner voice says, "I allow myself to extend into space. I am enough on my own. I am who I am."

Note how the movement into Appreciation is organized through a shift of attention into the feet and a rhythm in the feet from right to left, awakening more movement and bringing warmth and energy into the body, as shown in "Appreciation," and culminating in "The Peak of Appreciation."

From here the Moving Cycle develops further into the Action Phase, as seen in "Beginning the Action Phase."

In "The Action Phase in Play," notice how the facilitator plays with the dis-tance between their body and the mover's to allow space.

Finally, in "Ending," this session "ends" in action by making contact with another person, bringing back external awareness while maintaining contact with internal awareness and balancing the two.

The mover's feedback at the end of the session was "I am able to want and to reach out, and I am allowed to want. I can be me, and I am allowed to be me."

Let's look at another example, starting with "The Awareness Phase":

The session begins with an awareness of the body. In this example, you will notice the different interventions being used to work with awareness. The mover is working herself into the essence of her present bodily sensation through move-ment focused on her right leg.

In "Movement and Emotion," note how emotion evolves and organizes the movement. Emotion can be empowering if movement comes with it, and emo-tion can promote movement.

In "Owning," this further develops into a sequence of highly conscious moving in the process of owning.

Then in "Appreciation," this proceeds from Owning to Appreciation through playful movement, connecting the movement of the leg to the spine and then the whole body, using a blanket for support.

How can we understand what is going on here? That question is probably not of primary importance to the ongoing process of movement. Later the mover put words to the story behind what she experienced:

> I started with the word past. I felt strong sensations in my left leg, but I started with my right leg. Associations came up, like intelligence and support. I noticed one spot where there was much more sensation. I began to be moved, inhabiting my emotions. A memory came up. I have a pair of boots that cause me physical pain. When I was having a very difficult time, I wore the boots consciously, taking a walk for an hour. I felt pain in my foot. I felt the pain in my foot more than my real-life pain in that moment.

In another example, beginning with "Awareness," the mover begins to be aware of her body and concentrates on the sensations around her eyes.

In owning those sensations, the body moves from an upright sitting position down and to the left, until it reaches the ground, as seen in "The Beginning of Owning."

Six minutes later, as seen in "Energy Work," the arms beat against and the fingers scratch along a curtain covering the wall of the studio. Energy is directed toward a boundary. Power is involved. The body wants to go forward and has to deal with a boundary.

In the next phase, shown in "Demonstrating a Push," the body pushes against the wall and the facilitator provides support at the base of the spine. It seems as if the body wants to push through this wall.

Then a shift happens as the body spins around 180 degrees in "Body Shift." A new movement appears as the body now utilizes the wall as a support. Through that support, it can position itself upside-down in "Upside-Down Body," and the mover's laugh shows that this is obviously appreciated.

Going further, in "A Full Turn of the Body," the body begins to play with this energetic movement, utilizing support from the wall and up to three facilitators until it finally makes a full turn. Then it rests. Appreciation is shown in "Appreciation," and soon afterward the face moves downward.

Then comes a break in which the body takes a rest and integrates, as seen in "Integration." Notice how the mover's eyes make contact with the facilitator, and how the mover touches her eyes differently than she did at the beginning of the session.

"Integration and Resting" shows the end of this cycle; the mover and the facilitator use words to integrate the experience. It looks as if the session will end here. But it takes another turn, on a different level of space in the room. This is typical for a Moving Cycle session. The ending of one cycle is the beginning of the next.

We now see a whole set of appreciative movements as the body plays with trusting the support it gets and with the different positions that can be experienced utilizing the support that is available. You can see this in "Appreciating Support," "Appreciating Touch," and "Appreciating Play."

This ends in playfulness and gratitude in "Appreciating the Body's Fullness."

Later I asked the mover to share the story that was taking place in her mind as her body was moving. She wrote down the following words:

In my family there is a narrative that says life has to be heavy. Everything is laborious, the world is bad, and other people want bad things to happen to us. So I have to be suspicious and [I] have to take as much control as I can over situations. I have to work out alternative plans for situations, in case something goes wrong.

Through the session, I realized that this is not my story. Life can be light, and I am allowed to take the easy way, and in that case, I am not lazy but playful, lively, and full of self-confidence. I am not alone.

How do these words relate to the movements we saw? Can we find evidence for this?

Let's jump to another example, beginning with the story that the mover put into words after the session.

I began by thinking about my grandmother and how she was isolated in East Germany [the GDR], being faithful to the socialist regime, betraying other people to the government, while all her children fled to the West.

That was the story I was told as a child, and I realized that it was just a story. In this session I could contain the story, and feel and sense her helplessness and her children's helplessness in living apart from each other, divided by the Iron Curtain.

Thanks to the facilitator's suggestion not to stop but to trust the movement and the feelings in the process of moving, I could literally move forward on the floor, beyond helplessness, through feeling and owning that helplessness, and then . . .

. . . a lot of other bodies came in and supported me. It felt like the family support I never had. I realized that I am on this earth because my grandmother was on this earth, and without her I would not be here, and I was thankful to feel this family in the present moment. I would not have been able to experience this in a personal, one-to-one session. In this Moving Cycle we created one body, one organism.

Here are the movements at the end of the session. "Appreciation" begins with Appreciation and then moves through experiencing contact with a support system of different bodies, forming a whole body of oneness and fullness.

In "Action," this ends in Action, through awareness of the external support system of a new "family in the present," reframing the "old trauma" of isolation and deprivation: Usually a session begins with words, and it often leads to a story, as seen in "Beginning a Session."

Then awareness of the body brings up sensations and/or feelings (in the example, this occurs around two minutes later), which opens the door to owning the experience and making it meaningful on a body level. This is seen in "Moving into Owning."

In "Moving into Appreciation," another session shows Appreciation (the facilitator protects the mover with a blanket). In "Action," this then proceeds into Action. A major shift happens in "Action through Space," when the mover (with a weight on her head) consciously senses the connection between her head and her feet, through her spine, and opens her eyes, concentrating and balancing her body, which later enables her to move freely through the space.

The mover describes this as follows:

The session began with strong feelings of anger. And there was a resistance to following this feeling of anger. I realized that my body was endlessly tired and exhausted. My facilitator brought to my attention that when I spoke about my father, I turned my head to the right, and when I spoke about my mother, I turned it to the left. This enabled me to make a major discovery: the freedom of choice. By moving the body from left to right, I could move forward instead of screaming out my anger and remaining victimized. By balancing and dancing from left to right, I can balance my father's world (to my right) with my mother's world (to my left) and go forward in my way. Here I am.

"Two Bodies Playing in Bodily Fullness" shows another essence of shared beauty, as described in the title of this chapter. The mover's and facilitator's bodies are involved in play, in such a way that it would be difficult and indeed pointless to decide who is in which role. This interplay shows the beauty of sharing movement: the boundaries between the mover and the facilitator become fluid, and their respective roles dissolve so that they appear as one body during a session. We might all remember moments like this from our childhood, when we played like young animals, feeling fulfilled and delighted.

Let's look at another example: "Movement and Trust." There is a special moment in which the mover sinks into Owning, trusting the process that the facilitator is navigating. Notice the eye contact.

Finally, let's take a look at one last example: "Oscillating Attention." This video shows the mover going in and out of the body, entering and leaving the inner experience at the end of a session. It depicts a process of integration, going back and forth from an inner to an outer focus of attention; it also shows the use of ventral vagus interaction through the participants' faces.

Stories and Meaning

In the practice of conscious movement, we watch carefully and train ourselves to postpone meaning, to let the body move forward in its own way. "Trust your body and where it wants to go" is a supportive reminder the facilitator often gives to the mover in the process of a session. The words that come at the end of the process, pulling together what happened, are very important—not for the sake of the words as such, but because those words are carriers of meaning, held through the presence and the experience of the living body *telling* that story. The body tells the story, and words are the signposts of that journey. To return to our music metaphor, this might be similar to the relationship between text and melody in a song. Without melody and sound, the text would appear naked, stripped of emotion and connection.

After a session is done, we rest and enjoy. A song has been created and sung; a painting has been put to paper. The end of a Moving Cycle includes the implicit knowledge that there will be another beginning. Clinically speaking, a session of this kind is not goal oriented, as is an attempt to solve a certain problem or get rid of a symptom, for example. It is essentially a dedication to staying alert and consciously sticking to what is happening with the body in a given moment, a moment in which we decide to take responsibility for what comes to our awareness.

In a workshop, we usually begin the day with a movement practice called Pressure, Pleasure, Inquiry. This is a way of training our attention. We begin by examining sensations of pressure in the body, continue with sensations of pleasure, and move on to inquiry, which means Where does my interest go? What do I get curious about? This is fundamental for the session's development. Movement is conscious as long as it is carried through awareness and curiosity, and this encourages development. In one of the earlier examples , the mover said: "This was not the end; I was not satisfied. I wanted to do another sequence of turning-around movements."

Conclusion

Psychotherapy as a whole-body experience is fun. It takes you back to the good old days of being a child: running, jumping, shouting, joking—in other words, playing. On a cognitive level, what I am sharing here is probably nothing really new to you. We all know that it is essential for us as humans to feel safe in a community of other humans, where we are accepted and welcomed as we are. In that sense, the Moving Cycle is just a label for something that arises as the most natural thing in the world when we connect to ourselves with focused attention and allow something to happen that may extend the boundaries of that which is already known and familiar to us. The body holds all sorts of possibilities and options for movement that can be expressed. In order for these to emerge, support and safety are essential. Safety and support can be provided through the presence of one or more other humans (facilitators), who offer their best attention and their willingness to be loving and helpful. In this sense, a workshop may even allow a whole group of people to move forward together, by supporting and challenging each other. This is a very familiar experience in a lot of the workshops I give and attend.

When this kind of development occurs, we experience moments of grace and beauty. I hope the video material provided here shows a few such moments. Yet *writing about* something is different than *being part of* something. My hope is that this chapter has successfully invited you to be part of the experience.

PART III
Moving Forward

14

Integrating the Living Wisdom of Others in These Fields

Introduction

Because Conscious Moving plays an important role in so many ancient and modern traditions, the purpose of this chapter is to take a glimpse at some of the ways it integrates into the work of others, professionals who currently take their work all over the world. To do this, I interviewed seven colleagues, most of whom I have known for decades and all of whom I respect deeply. The interviews took place over Zoom in late 2022 and early 2023. I asked some of the same questions of each one in an effort to get seven views on one topic, but inevitably each interview took its own path.

Each Zoom call lasted about an hour and was then transcribed. I poured over the transcripts and looked for commonalities and distinctions and different adaptations of Conscious Moving. This chapter discusses my findings and the implications for the practice of Conscious Moving. Edited versions of these transcripts can be found on the website, www.consciousmoving.com, under the Book Resources tab.

The seven movement experts come from a variety of traditions and embody a range of methods within the areas of art-making, contemplative practice, education, and healing. In many cases these areas overlap so that a person's work could be seen as both education and healing, or as art-making and contemplative practice. These seven professionals by no means represent the totality of the movement field, and it is likely that I was drawn to them because they express similar views to my own. I also asked specific questions that guided what they talked about. It would be very useful to either read the full text of these interviews first, or alongside this chapter, so that the details of each interviewee's views are appreciated. Let me briefly introduce you to these seven experts.

Who the Interviewees Are

Arawana Hayashi

Arawana's work as a choreographer, performer, and educator is deeply sourced in an awareness-based collaborative creative process. She is a cofounder of and senior faculty at the Presencing Institute where she heads the creation of Social Presencing Theater. Working with Otto Scharmer and colleagues, she brings her background in performance art and meditation to an embodied presence practice that makes visible one's relationships within a current social system and the emerging possibilities within organizations, schools, and communities. Since 1980 Arawana has taught meditation and creative process. She is the author of *Social Presencing Theater: The Art of Making a True Move*. I met Arawana many years ago while we were both teaching at Naropa University. I briefly studied her work when I took an Authentic Leadership training, within which she was teaching participants different self-exploration and relational movement practices that helped them study leadership from the perspective of their moving bodies.

Barbara Dilley

Barbara, BA, graduated from Mount Holyoke College and trained and performed dance in New York City (1960–1975) with the Merce Cunningham Dance Company, Yvonne Rainer, and the Grand Union. In 1975 she designed the Dance/Movement Studies program for Naropa University, served as president (1985–1993), and retired in 2015. Her memoir, *This Very Moment ~ Teaching Thinking Dancing*, was published by Naropa University Press in 2015. I met Barbara in 1981, as I began to teach at Naropa University. At that time she chaired the Dance/Movement Studies program, and we worked together as I developed the Dance/Movement Therapy BA program within her department. Along the way, I briefly studied her work in Contemplative Dance, and took inspiration from her about meditation and art-making.

Rae Johnson

Rae, PhD, RSW, RSMT (they/them), is a social worker, somatic movement therapist, and scholar/activist working at the intersections of embodiment and social justice. Rae's approach is informed by decades of work with homeless youth, women in addiction recovery, psychiatric survivors, and members of the queer community. Prior to their current faculty appointment in the Somatic Psychology doctoral program at the California Institute of Integral Studies, Rae served as the Cochair of the Community, Liberation, Indigenous, and Ecopsychologies program at Pacifica Graduate Institute. Rae is the author of several books, including *Embodied Social Justice* and *Embodied Activism*. Rae is one of my dearest friends as well as a colleague. I cannot say that I have ever formally studied with them, because whenever we get together we talk incessantly, often on long walks or during meals in different cities around the world. Rae's work and ideas have influenced mine in ways that are hard to calculate, but that go deep and wide.

Edan Gorlicki

Edan is the choreographer and artistic director of INTER-ACTIONS—More Than a Dance Company, based in Heidelberg, Germany. Edan works as a freelance choreographer, mentor, movement researcher, and dance-activist. In his previous life as a dancer he worked with the Batsheva Ensemble Dance Company (Israel), Inbal Pinto Dance Company (Israel), NND/Galilidance (the Netherlands), and Club Guy & Roni (the Netherlands). He was the recipient of the Dance and Theater prize of the state of Baden-Württemberg in Germany in 2017 and 2019. The philosophy of his artistic practice is based on questioning the self within its surroundings. Layered, complex, and thought provoking, his works aim to explore social, psychological, and emotional realms. Recently Edan's artistic works revolved around the theme of embodied trauma in individual, collective, and cross-generational contexts. It was in this context that I met and worked with Edan and his company, while they were in the midst of choreographing and performing a set of three pieces. I was hired by the company to help them with their experiential research into trauma, working together to allow the theme of trauma to percolate through the dancers' bodies so that the choreography would express genuine engagement with this tender subject. I was so moved by the cocreative structures of the company, and moved to tears by the public performance of the third dance in the series, that I knew I had to continue the collaboration by interviewing Edan.

Judith Aston-Linderoth

Judith is widely recognized as a pioneer in the art and science of kinetics and for her development of Aston Kinetics™. Judith recognized a new paradigm for the body as a dynamic three-dimensional model for movement and posture. Her ability to "see" the body in stillness and motion and train others to see, move, and exercise established her system of bodywork and movement training. Judith is a

former college instructor of movement, physical education, and dance for performing artists and athletes (1963–1972). She has worked in the field of psychology, assisting in identifying and processing patterns of physical and emotional
expression. In 1968 she created and taught three programs for the Rolf Institute: movement, seeing, and practitioner mechanics. Currently, Judith divides
her time between presenting and teaching bodywork, fitness, athletic performance, and movement workshops. It is hard to quantify the profound influence
that Judith has had in my life. I met her when I was a teenager, babysitting for a
friend of hers (Sophie Otis). I was so enthralled by Judith and Sophie's work in
movement education that I studied with Judith and became an Aston-Patterner
at the age of twenty-three. Though I ended up going in the direction of movement-based psychotherapy, my early years with Judith taught me foundational
principles that I carry in my body and in my work to this day.

Brian Linderoth

Brian is a graduate of the University of Colorado with a BS in Physical Education.
His dedication to physical education was seen in his passion for swimming. He
was an All-American Swimmer and a swimming coach for two master's programs. He is also an avid cyclist. He graduated from the Boulder School of Massage Therapy in 1981 and moved on to teaching massage therapy courses. He
taught at his alma mater and joined the Aston-Patterning Practitioner training
and became a member of the Aston-Patterning Faculty in 1988. Brian has been
teaching advanced Aston-Patterning for thirty-five years. His experience in his
practice of bodywork, movement coaching, and fitness offers clients and students a broad choice within his wealth of information and expertise. Judith and
Brian are married and live and teach in Tahoe, Nevada. I actually knew Brian
separately from Judith, before they ever met, both of us being Boulderites and
working in similar circles. When Brian and Judith met and married, it felt like
kismet! As I set up my interview with Judith, Brian graciously volunteered to
offer his wisdom and expertise, so we spoke together as a threesome.

Ann Weiser Cornell

Ann is an internationally known author and psychology educator who has been
working with the Focusing technique (developed by Eugene Gendlin) since 1972.
As the CEO of Focusing Resources, she has taught in twenty countries around
the world for more than thirty-five years, as well as online. She is the cocreator
(with Barbara McGavin) of Inner Relationship Focusing and Untangling. Her

books include *The Radical Acceptance of Everything* and *Focusing in Clinical Practice: The Essence of Change.* Amazingly, I have never met Ann in person, though I did briefly meet Eugene Gendlin while I was at UCLA in the mid-70s. Ann and I have presented at some of the same conferences and trainings for decades, occasionally running in similar circles and sharing students. I have admired her work for a very long time and have assigned her books in my classes. I consider Focusing to be one of the most powerful and elegant change practices in current times. While Focusing is typically not considered a movement practice, its careful tracking of and radical acceptance of the experienced body puts it in the same realms as Conscious Moving.

With the thoughts of these seven illustrious movers at hand, we can begin to see the threads that weave together a large and diverse tapestry of movement practices into a coherent body of knowledge about the moving body and how to use movement consciously for a myriad of purposes, mostly centering around art, healing, reflection, and learning.

What the Interviewees Said

Most Have Backgrounds in Both Classic, Structured Movement, and Improvisational Forms

One interesting and unexpected finding of these interviews is that almost all of the folks I talked to had a background in both highly structured, inherited movement forms and extensive experience with open and more spontaneous practices. Barbara Dilley and Edan Gorlicki engaged in early and long-term ballet training. Barbara stresses the exploration of the relationship between structured and open forms of movement. Arawana Hayashi studied bugaku, an ancient Japanese dance form that uses highly specific and prescribed motion. She noted that "true moves" in her work arise out of the relationship between "loving precision and open spaciousness." Brian Linderoth grew up in the competitive swimming and sports world, and Judith Aston-Linderoth received her master's degree in dance, after studying different forms of ancient and modern dance.

Most of these movement specialists have immersed themselves in experiencing and studying the breadth of the Mobility Gradient, from movement that must be performed in an exact and precise way all the way to unpredictable forms of action. This bodes well for being able to work with people who are stuck somewhere on the gradient and need support to open up movement experiences so that other aspects of their embodied being may be supported.

When we have access to movement that helps us connect to our various communities through our prescribed actions, we find and strengthen the bonds between us all. As well, when we deliberately and accurately inhabit a movement that has been done by others for thousands of years, we call up a sense of stability, ongoingness, and freedom that can be comforting and stabilizing, and a platform for self-study. On the other end of the continuum, when we support ourselves to move without dictates, without predictable sequences, and without plans, we create the conditions for novelty to work its way with us. Our movements inhabit a creative realm where new possibilities emerge.

Life tends to demand both these skills from us at one time or another. By having a baseline of physical prowess all along the Mobility Gradient, we prepare for life's demands within acts of daily living. Our bodies are ready for more of what comes, more of the what's next. Interestingly, the study of dance shows up among many of us (myself, Rae Johnson, Judith Aston-Linderoth, Arawana Hayashi, Barbara Dilley, Edan Gorlicki), possibly because dance can hold movement practices all along the gradient, while infusing these varied forms with artistic, educational, and therapeutic potentialities.

Movement for Movement's Sake

Many of the interviewees either mentioned or implied the idea that moving just for the sake of moving felt central to their work. This often took the form of talking about movement impulses emerging from an open and nonjudgmental invitation to see what comes up. Barbara noted that starting with relative stillness (as in sitting meditation) helped the mover recognize impulses that weren't generated by thought. She talked about the resulting movement research that became possible at that point. Rae Johnson advocated listening to movement impulses, which they defined as organic shifts in movement rooted in proprioceptive awareness, and that this awareness liberates movement. Judith and Brian noted that releasing unnecessary holding in the body allows creative impulses to emerge. Arawana spoke of "loyalty to whatever the experience is." Ann Weiser Cornell centralizes the question of "What wants to happen next?" in her work, implying an openness to allowing the experience to guide the flow of the practice, rather than a predetermined goal.

Movement impulses pretty much avoid having any kind of immediate purpose. We simply welcome what emerges from the home base of open and nonjudgmental attention, and don't try to immediately make what shows up useful or explainable. We are moving and sensing just for the sake of moving and sensing, as a celebration of moving and as a means of accessing buried, unfinished material, new information, and creative novelty.

This puts me in mind of the two basic divisions of science into *basic* and *applied*. Basic science asks open questions about the world, with no immediate sense of how the answers could be useful. Applied science asks questions about pressing issues in the world as a means of solving problems. Basic science is necessary because you never know when something might be useful later. An example might be a researcher going into a rain forest and cataloging new plant species. Later, other scientists trying to find new medicines would consult this basic research as a possible means of finding a cure for a disease. But another equally important justification for basic science is our human thirst for knowledge, and our longing for awe. Finding out, for instance, that billions of years ago stars, as they died, exploded and flung their internal elements out into space, thus seeding the universe with all the necessary components for building planets and the human bodies on at least one of them, is just plain marvelous to contemplate. We are stardust, as they say. How cool is that?

In applied science, we first identify an unknown that we want to make known for the purpose of the common good. When the COVID pandemic hit, we didn't know diddly-squat about where it came from, how it operated, or how it moved through populations. In order to limit the damage of this virus, we mobilized massive numbers of researchers to solve this problem. The results of this research helped us manage our responses toward being as effective as possible at alleviating suffering.

Several of the interviewees mentioned their work in the context of basic and applied research, though no one used those two terms specifically. In my work you can start a Conscious Moving session in one of two ways; either by opening up to what is happening right now (basic research), or by beginning with a theme or problem you want to work with (applied research). Either way, movement begins for movement's sake via the process of postponing meaning-making and pushing back against a "What do I do about it?" attitude. Edan Gorlicki spoke of dancers as researchers, and noted that when they move for moving's sake using bodily attention practices, this moving invites a "creativity window" to open; movement can "arrive," stories be told, information can be discovered. Barbara called her classrooms "creativity laboratories." Both Rae and I identify as researchers, having engaged in multiple studies involving movement that have been published and performed.

In a sense we could say that Conscious Moving is a method to help us access information, transform it into knowledge, and allow it to integrate within and among us as a generator of wisdom. With that wisdom in hand, the interviewees showed us that great good can come from moving for moving's sake.

Being in Direct Experience and Waiting for Emergent Material

Perhaps more than any other theme in these interviews, people stressed the importance of a transition from ordinary daily life to a dedicated time and space that allowed, fostered, and demanded a commitment to direct experiencing as a primary source of our knowing and our wisdom. This process of entering direct experience in an open and curious way generates bodily responses that seem to self-organize outside our normal consciousness, allowing emergent phenomena to inform and move us.

We are attentive to ongoing sensorimotor processes, curious about feelings and felt senses, taking in the atmosphere and the people around us, and leaning away from thoughts about these processes. We are inhabiting experiences from within them. Arawana spoke of a felt knowing as the basis for creativity and learning, a being open to this moment. She also stated that a "true move" emerges on its own, with no contrivance. Rae advocated a return to the senses, not to improve them but to reconnect, appreciate, and mobilize ourselves and others. Choreographer Edan noted that in a given moment something new can occur via a bodily embracing of everything that comes.

Perhaps this idea is best expressed via the Focusing work of Eugene Gendlin that Ann Weiser Cornell continues and enhances. Gendlin was the originator of the term the *felt sense* and asserted it was the linchpin of therapeutic change, creative growth, and learning. In a way, we could say the felt sense is the body's way of knowing something, in some cases alongside our thoughts about it and in other cases in opposition to it. We get curious about our tight jaw, or our argument with a friend, and we turn our attention to our direct experience of that theme in our bodies. In her interview Ann spoke of the felt sense as forming when we pause, bring awareness, and postpone analysis or judgment. We simply experience the state as it is. When that happens, the body responds by organizing its own sensations and impulses that could be seen as our nonverbal language system. This wordless language system holds the key to unlocking what Arawana calls creative possibilities, and what Rae might call liberation. But in order to unlock these potentialities, another theme echoed by all the interviewees must be present and strong.

Letting Go of Thinking, Analysis, and Judgment

To a person, all the interviewees stated that direct experiencing *must* be accompanied by an open curiosity that pushed back against the mind's tendency toward judgment, analysis, categorization, and meaning-making. Many noted that without this skill, engaging in direct experiences could be overwhelming and unusable. Barbara asks movers to let go of constraints, criticisms, and particular storylines. Ann enjoins us to relate to our experiences with compassion and without judgment, not trying to change things but to accept them with warm compassion. Judith and Brian work by asking simple, descriptive questions about body structure and function so that clients can increase their perceptions of their unique body, and therefore problem-solve its challenges. Arawana asks us to let the mind rest and be in the background, with no opinion and no figuring out, suspending normal meaning-making. By doing so, she says, "it boycotts the habit of quickly wrapping experiences up into our conventional or psychological sense-making." Rae notes that at least some of our thinking about our bodily experiences has been colonized by oppressive systems; that we have internalized their messages in ways that forfeit our ability to know ourselves and stand up for ourselves and others.

At least two things are going on here. One is that what meanings we make of our experiences could be distorted or wrong. Our habitual way of thinking about our experiences and our world simply doesn't match the data that our bodies constantly give us. The other thing going on is that the act of meaning-making, however closely or distantly aligned it is with our direct experiences, forecloses our ability to open up to something that exists outside that explanation. We cut off novel, unexpected, or nonsensical input, to our detriment. We ignore creative input toward solutions.

All these interviewees have strategies for how to work on this human tendency to over-categorize or mis-categorize our experience. These strategies included deliberately using attention and physical presence so that a person can slow down, get quiet, adopt a listening mode, and work to identify and push back against the intrusion of thinking. Everyone noted that there is nothing wrong with thinking, but it needs to be contextualized so that it doesn't bully the direct experience. The direct experience is what creates possibilities, and thinking, when properly used, supports that creativity rather than shutting it down. This is accomplished by letting direct experiences take the driver's seat, either by going first, or by being alternated with moments of descriptive reflection.

Attention Is at the Root of All Direct Experiences

The capacity to minimize or postpone analysis, judgment, and categorization relies on the skill of what I have called *attentional athleticism*. Attention is like a muscle, and muscles need to be used in order to be fit. This is why it's called *meditation practice* or *yoga practice*—it needs ongoing, deliberate doing. The ability to hold attention on something that is happening, as well as the ability to withdraw attention from that which is no longer salient or wholesome, forms the basis of the previous skill-building themes. Edan speaks of keeping our attentive abilities open and oriented toward what is asking for attention in the body, as a precursor to dance-making. He asserts the importance of training attention directly, which dovetails with just about any contemplative tradition. He tells us that attention is a catalyst, a portal, a channel, and he uses the same metaphor as I do, that of attention being like tuning a radio to access coherent signals. "Attending consciously is the effort to be present," he notes. Ann says that careful attention allows the body's voice to become more vivid, and that careful attending creates a sense of coherence and well-being. Judith and Brian advocate listening to the body—feeling and sensing motion, stillness, pain—as this creates strategies for movement and support. Ann weighs in by stating that Focusing is the kind of attention that doesn't fixate on an emotion or idea but widens out from what you have been thinking and feeling to get a sense of the whole thing (the felt sense). Rae posits that attention supports more choices, and that we can see choices as the definition of liberation. The reason this book is called *Conscious Moving*, and not just *Moving*, lies in the fact that it's not just about moving, it's about attending while moving.

The Fluidity and Multiplicity of Identity

Somewhat due to my prompting, several of the interviewees spoke about identity and the importance of resisting the facile narrative that identity is fixed, singular, and permanent. When I asked Edan about it, he laughed and said that this might be why he likes to use fog in his performances, and by this I think he means that identity shouldn't be all sharp edges and defined shapes. We might see identity as a story we tell ourselves about who we are, and this story changes with our changing circumstances, age, ability, social connection, and group membership. Rae linked identity to body stories, saying that they help make sense of various identities we carry. "How we are in our bodies is the foundation of identity," they note. Ann put it succinctly when she said, "One's 'I's' move." She also felt that our natural state of self involved being curious, calm, and available to others. Some things can be a thread that runs through identity across a lifetime, much like the premise in Buddhism that we all possess an inherent goodness.

Conscious Moving, in whatever form of it we practice, enriches identity formation and dissolution by providing us with a home base of sensations, feelings, and actions that can be touched into and used as the "here I am, right now" infrastructure of an ongoing and changeable sense of self. In this way, our sense of self not only contributes to our stability and coherency, but it can also plant our feet on the ground of equity, justice, and inclusion. On the side of dissolving a fixed sense of self, we can play with identities as a generative project.

Tolerating Uncomfortability

"You show up whether you feel like it or not," says Barbara Dilley. Several interviewees spontaneously opined our Vygotsky maxim that learning takes place in a mild state of discomfort, and that the skill of being tolerant of discomfort carries important benefits. Arawana put it gracefully when she said that simply being friends with discomfort generates well-being. Ann asks her clients to stay with difficulty as a curious observer, because it holds the answer to stuckness. Some pains are too much to bear and need friends and family to help us hold and care for the suffering we feel. It's fine to take pain relievers during certain specific experiences of suffering. Our felt sense of things knows best when to exit a symptom and when to lean into it. But leaning into symptoms and difficulties can be a gold mine of solutions to problems because the discomfort is a voice that needs to be heard and taken seriously. It encases body stories that put us on the path to liberation, to well-being, and to a creative life.

Social and Environmental Embeddedness

Understanding and including the external environment into our definition of body, of movement, of self, and of experience break down the arbitrary and un-useful idea that we are separate and independent from it. The outside and inside of the body are matters of degree, not differences in kind. Environment is everywhere and all environmental locations nest within each other and exist interdependently in what Thich Nhat Hanh called *interbeing*. We inter-are with everything. There is no sharp distinction between the inside of my body and what seems to lie outside of it. Edan's fog during performances wafts into this location as well. Edan wants dancers to use movement as a tool to communicate something valuable to the community as audience. Even though there are different locations called *stage* and *audience*, Edan talks about these as simply different gazes into the same experience. The art of dance, as with all arts, needs these different gazes so that something that occurs in the dancers is felt in its own way in the audience, connecting the two locations into a place of interbeing. Barbara asks her current students to be aware of the environment and the shared atmosphere with others because they are partners in the creative process. Ann notices the ongoing interaction of body with environment, and that bodies are in a shared field, inter-affecting each other. Being around people who are comfortable in their own skin has a ripple effect, says Rae. When we up our game in terms of personal embodiment, we contribute that to the environment, making it a bit easier and more familiar for others to do the same.

Judith and Brian take the important perspective that bodies are constantly affected by the environments they inhabit. Objects like chairs, car seats, gym equipment, tables, sports equipment, and the myriad other tools and materials in our environment have a profound effect on our ability to find support and produce effective movement. We adapt to a clumsy chair by slumping, and pretty soon we get used to slumping and we make a holding pattern that reinforces it, such that we will seek out chairs that allow us to slump. We are not alone and independent in our environments. Because of this, Judith and Brian work with environmental design as a means of supporting bodies.

Our relationship to our environments, particularly to the other people we share our environments with, strongly motivates Arawana. Arawana's work emphasizes the quality of social relationships, and the relationship of our body-mind with the social body-mind. She feels that relaxing into our environment increases body-mind synchrony and coherence, and she puts great emphasis on the space we are in. Her work uses awareness-based and heart-based collective creativity to assist with social transformation. In a word, she works with and through groups. She takes a systems perspective of *collective interiority*—the interiority of a social system—as a means to access knowledge stored in social fields or social bodies. We are all cocreating social reality every moment, she states, via our interactive and interaffective bodies and their movings. Moving is not an isolated thing. Yes, it can be a private thing in certain locations, but as we get up and move about our different localities, movement threads through us all, stitching us together. And by *us*, many of the interviewees did not confine themselves to other humans or even other beings. They also saw us as embedded in landscapes, in water and air and rocks and trees. Many of these movement experts leverage this interbeing for the purposes of art, education, healing, and leading a self-reflective life.

Finding Natural Sequences

Somewhat surprisingly, all of the interviewees either hinted at or spoke directly to the notion that moving consciously can involve natural sequences of events, one emergent property in turn supporting the emergence of the next. While there was a large measure of agreement that deliberate and open attention to the body begins most sequences, the interviewees went in their own novel and complimentary directions.

Barbara's Contemplative Dance practice begins with an opening circle, followed by the first section, *sitting meditation.* This transitions into what she calls *personal awareness practice* where the mover engages in *movement research* arising from stillness practice and "using everything we already know." The third section is *open space.* Having returned to the meditation cushion, movers enter and leave the space when they wish. This adds in the element of alternating between moving and witnessing (and being moved by) others moving in the space. *Open space* is an invitation to meet the moment, the room, with others or alone. The practice ends with a closing circle. Rae, while making it clear that the sequence is nonprescriptive, begins with curiosity regarding the body and the body's stories and history. From there, movers pay attention to cultivating the enrichment of the senses, which prepares them for the next stages of liberating movement, interrogating nonverbal communication, reclaiming body image, and lastly, cultivating an *intercorporeal ethos.*

Arawana, Ann, and Edan all independently talked about the body feeling into what's next. Arawana starts her work with groups by asking for body shapes and gestures and encourages everyone to stay with the feeling of it until the shape wants to move, until the body knows what to do next. She feels that the body is always working to move toward health and only needs the right environment and conditions. Her groups end with a practice of reflecting on the experiences they have had and through witnessing the others moving. Edan states that as dancers and choreographers, we are constantly asking the body "What now?" and "What's next?" Ann feels that because humans are always on the way to the next thing for them, that the body, more than the mind, knows what's next. If in the course of human events the what's next doesn't happen, the body holds onto this, perhaps similar to Judith's idea of structural holding patterns in the body. Focusing helps us move from holding onto that uncompleted experience (called *implying* in Focusing) to completing it. The body experience knows the next step.

This sense of progressions in their work speaks to the stages of Conscious Moving. While also nonprescriptive, the stages of CM help create an atmosphere of natural flow, of a journey through time and through unfolding experiences, helping them make their own kind of sense. We could say that the body tells a story, and this story, to be understood and integrated, needs a beginning, a middle, and an end that allow a sense of wholeness and coherence to unfold.

Bodily Authority/Autonomy

Several of the interviewees saw practicing conscious sensing and moving as having social and political repercussions, particularly in the use of power, and where power is located. Movement practices that ask us to stay awake and aware, that ask us to track what wants to happen next, and that invite movements that may have been held back or suppressed have a tendency to challenge authoritarianism in all its forms. Anne talks about "the client's own change," rather than an effort to change being more in accordance with social strictures. This is what Conscious Moving calls *bodily authority* and what can also be read as *bodily autonomy*.

Rae takes it further, stating that the goal of a just, free, and liberated world is for everyone to be in their bodies just the way they are. To do this we must first recognize the body's role in change efforts, what they call *embodied activism*. Part of this activism means learning to tell the difference between feeling great and feeling virtuous, because feeling great is recognized via interoceptive awareness, while feeling virtuous exists in comparison to received rules of conduct. This all points us to the idea of being in the body to study power. And this is where empowerment can be generated and shared, through the conscious movement of our bodies, both singularly and in community.

Oscillating

Our last common theme takes us back to the beginning of the book. We find our way back to the principle of oscillating. In the interviews, oscillating took many creative directions. Ann used the term *zigzagging* to describe alternating between being in an experience and describing it with or without words. This forms an important practice in Focusing because the work does not want the client to either get lost in over-identifying with an experience or get detached from direct experience. By oscillating between experience and the description of experience, this pitfall is avoided. For instance, she might use the phrase "I can sense something within me is upset," rather than "I am upset." In this way we can stay with the upset as a casual observer. Arawana alternates self-reflecting on experiences with engagement in the experiences themselves. Edan talks about the spectrum of designed/fabricated movement all the way to authentic movement, authenticity that involves embracing everything that comes. Rae uses the term *lucid movement* (similar to lucid dreaming) as a way to describe being in the movement and aware of it at the same time. The movement is bodily directed yet we are also aware of it at the same time.

Edan and Arawana both see oscillation in the creative process, particularly via the relationship of movers and their witnesses. Edan talks about the dancer opening their senses through immersive attention (much like method acting) so that the movement onstage can be felt directly in the audience. Arawana speaks of performances with a "doer" and a "space holder," a version of which can be seen in Barbara's Contemplative Dance practice where there is an oscillation between being a mover and being a witness. Judith and Brian come at it from a perspective of the oscillation between the experiencing body and the observed body, noting that a sensitive looking at and sensing of the body by a trained practitioner can offer an important source of information to the mover. Oscillations between different locations, different roles, and different types of experiences, when done humbly and without artifice or agenda, can create embodied possibilities that were not available before.

Unique Contributions of Interviewees

Each interview possessed its own particular flavor and texture. Each type of work emphasized somewhat different interests and values. Let's take a final look at what stood out as a unique contribution to Conscious Moving.

Rae Johnson—Rae takes Conscious Moving strongly in the direction of social justice, equity, and inclusion. Their work highlights microactivisms, embodied activisms, and the body's experience and use of power. Rae spoke of the colonization of the body by consumer culture and by authoritarian systems, stating that in order to counter this, we need to cultivate the wildness that lies underneath civilization. Rae linked our body image to the social forces that surround us, noting how social strictures and ideals permeate our feelings and beliefs about our bodies.

Ann Weiser Cornell—Ann cautioned us to neither immerse too deeply in direct experience, nor go too far in thinking about it. She calls this a third path—perhaps not oscillating but an occupation of a blend of the two that allows for observing while experiencing.

Judith Aston-Linderoth and Brian Linderoth—Brian and Judith were the interviewees that took into account the physical impact of environments on the structure and function of our bodies. They ask a fundamental question: What supports movement? Their work in ergonomics and environmental design stood out as an important contribution. They work with clients in their activities of daily living, such as fitness routines, office work, and driving in cars. As well, they use physical touch—bodywork—as an intervention in their work, something that no one else mentioned.

Barbara Dilley—Barbara integrates sitting meditation practice into her creative movement work so that she looks at the enriching relationship between stillness and movement in her practice, and the impact of oscillating between sitting and moving on art-making.

Arawana Hayashi—Arawana is the specialist among us who works in boardrooms and with business leaders. She uses white boards and flow charts in her work! She tends to work through individuals and groups by using both verbal and nonverbal *generative dialogue*, which enables shared meaning to emerge between and among people. She is interested in the embodiment of an emerging (not better) future via compassionate innovation and learning for positive change.

Edan Gorlicki—Edan was the only interviewee to speak directly about the dimension of time, and time's relationship to conscious movement and art-making. He designs dedicated time (and space) to invite viewers to be attentive and present. He articulates the important function of the gaze—who is gazing and how this gaze affects experiences. He inquires into our motivations to attend consciously. He feels that creativity, like attention, can be trained through movement practices.

What an ecstatic experience it would be to get all these folks together in the same space at the same time! Throwing away the idea of a think tank, which likely strikes all of us as an absurdly imbalanced place to put people, perhaps we can create a *Conscious Moving tank*, where thinking might be seen as one of a myriad of actions, all or which possess meaning and value, that the body does. A Conscious Moving tank would support all these iterations of holding and caring for emerging experiences, trusting the wisdom embedded within them, and finding something useful and fun to do with them.

15

Conscious Moving Specifics in Healing, Art-Making, Learning, and Contemplative Practice

Even though learning, creativity, self-reflection, and healing all overlap one another so that engaging in one reverberates into the others, let's take time now to delve into some of the depths of Conscious Moving in these disciplines as they are practiced distinctly. Because none of these separate disciplines typically champion Conscious Moving as fundamental, but nevertheless use different CM practices to great effect, we will note how they use CM, and how we might position CM more centrally in these types of work. Let's begin with our radical notion that it's all about movement and that movement is everywhere. Making a deliberate transition from automatic movement processes into conscious movement processes facilitates the goals and aspirations of all these disciplines.

All these disciplines make use of both *moving with a specific purpose* (more structured forms) and *moving without an immediate purpose* (less structured forms). They can all be said to be forms of basic and applied research—all done for their own sakes as well as a way to solve something. Both basic and applied research involve searching, exploring, investigating, creating something new, describing, and controlling for sources of bias and error.

In contemplative circles, structured forms of movement, such as tai chi, yoga, and walking meditation, enjoy long histories. Barbara Dilley's Contemplative Dance work and the dance therapy form called Authentic Movement both make use of spontaneous or emergent movement processes. Art forms such as dance and music span a continuum from more prescribed forms, such as classical ballet, many folk dances, or exact replications of sheet music hundreds of years old, all the way to open improvisation. Whether Conscious Moving is more structured or less structured, it can be dedicated to learning something, to changing something, or to bringing something new into the world. Again, the best term for this might be *researching*.

Let's go back for a moment to the idea that all these disciplines mirror research processes because they all control for bias and error. In classic research, the search for information that will explain how things work or solve problems acknowledges that human inquiry is fraught with error. Typical errors involve

- ▸ Believing something is true because you want it to be true.
- ▸ Believing something is true because you have always believed it.
- ▸ Believing something is true because someone else told you it's true.
- ▸ Believing something is true because your people (however you define that) say it's true.

Conscious Moving values reining in these tendencies, just like science does, because doing so yields better results and reduces harm to ourselves and others. In science, this means taking deliberate actions all along the path of a research project. In the beginning, scientists are taught to ask open rather than loaded questions. For instance, an open question in psychotherapy might be "How are you feeling?" and a loaded question would be "Why are you so angry?" In science, when you ask a research question of a certain population, you need to make sure that this population is representative of the types of people that the answer would pertain to; otherwise you end up with a sampling error. An example of *sampling error* occurred in early theory building in human development when scientists wanting to know about moral development only studied boys. Many forays into early cancer research only studied white people. Throughout the process, the researcher needs to be on the lookout for ways in which they might be influencing the data or the results by acting in their own self-interest rather than in the interests of inquiry. And when the study is done, the results are never accepted as valid until the researcher publishes the particulars of the study (with particular attention to how they controlled for various forms of bias) in a reputable journal where other scientists can read it and critique it. Science naturally oscillates between immersive study, evaluation, and going back for further study, as is true for Conscious Moving.

Within this idea of using Conscious Moving as a tool for research, we have explored what these disciplines have in common in their use of CM. Through the lens of the four phases of CM, we can say that you need to be awake and attentive for all these disciplines to operate (Awareness). You devote time and energy to working on them deliberately (Owning). You need to stitch them into your sense of yourself and the world around you (Appreciation). And you want to make a difference with them in your and others' lives (Action). Another possibility is that they all involve altering consciousness deliberately, in the service of concentration, opening up to previously unaccessed material. They all train the ability to pay attention. As well, they all use what we have come to call phenomenological inquiry. And they all, in some way, oscillate between immersion and reflection, work and rest, structure and improvisation. In other words, they all use the Six Principles of Conscious Moving.

Conscious Moving in the Service of Creative Process and Art-Making

One could say, as the philosopher John Dewey did, that all art (verbal, visual, auditory, gustatory) is the transformation of the artist's embodied self-awareness into a sensory form that leads back to another embodied experience, that of the person appreciating the work of art.

—ALAN FOGEL, FROM *THE PSYCHOPHYSIOLOGY OF SELF-AWARENESS*

In order to understand the meaning of artistic products, we have to forget them for a time, to turn aside from them and have recourse to the ordinary forces and conditions of experience that we do not usually regard as aesthetic . . . The sources of art in human experience will be learned by him who sees how the tense grace of the ball-player infects the on-looking crowd; the zest of the spectator in poking the wood burning on the hearth and in watching the darting flames and crumbling coals.

—PHILOSOPHER AND EDUCATOR JOHN DEWEY, FROM *ART AS EXPERIENCE*

Let's turn our attention now to moving consciously in the service of creativity and art-making. As with healing and learning and contemplating, when we set out to make art, we apply our energies toward generating the conditions that make creativity possible, even likely. Conscious Moving specializes in setting up these conditions. We never know if something amazing will show up, but we can prime the pump by setting up a holding environment for it. Choreographer Edan Gorlicki spoke of this in his interview. This holding environment resides both within our body and outside of it in the space around us. In both locations, we will use the concept of *flow*.

In CM, from within our bodies, we mentally detach from the ways we usually think, and this often involves, according to creativity researchers, semiautomatic movements (walking, swimming, etc.) and what Donald Campbell calls *mental meandering,* and what Csikszentmihalyi might call *uncommitted attention.* Campbell states:

> *One of the values in walking to work is mental meandering. Now I don't think of myself as necessarily especially creative, but this creativity has to be a profoundly wasteful process. And that mental meandering, mind wandering and so on, is an essential process. (in Csikszentmihalyi 1996, 99)*

Mental meandering while the body is moving may be one of our first ways to set the stage for creativity, and it speaks to the practices embedded in the Awareness Phase. The ability of the embodied mind to noodle around without much structure or direction seems to stimulate our curiosity and focus our attention. In some forms of art, this may be the equivalent of warming up, whether it's doodling, playing scales, or limbering up tight muscles. We have also seen this meandering in free association. When we free-associate, things pop up unexpectedly, and we start to follow novel pathways with our curiosity.

> *After curiosity, this quality of concentrated attention is what creative individuals mention most often as having set them apart . . . curiosity and drive are in many ways the yin and yang that need to be combined in order to achieve something new. The first requires openness to outside stimuli, the second inner focus. The first is playful, the second serious; the first deals with objects and ideas for their own sake, the second is competitive and achievement oriented. Both are required for creativity to become actualized. (Csikszentmihalyi 1996, 60)*

So the first step toward a more creative life is cultivating curiosity and interest, which involves allocating attention to things for their own sake. In CM, however, we comingle mental free association with physical free association—mental meandering with physical meandering—because we understand the value of moving for moving's sake as being on equal footing with thinking just to think. The same novelty can then emerge and be exposed to our high-quality attention. This meandering may also help us to then find intentions for our art-making. From the book *Flow:*

> *We may call intentions the force that keeps information in consciousness ordered. Intentions arise in consciousness whenever a person is aware of desiring something or wanting to accomplish something. Intentions act*

as magnetic fields, moving attention toward some objects and away from
others, keeping our mind focused on some stimuli in preference to others.
(Csikszentmihalyi 1990, 27)

Our curiosity and attentional focus create a holding environment for flow
states via a strong concentration on the task at hand, one that slightly challenges
our ability and that helps us resist distractions. The way this shows up is in the
body's muscle tone. We are in possession (ownership) of the movements of
our bodies. Another word for it might be *control*. In Jonah Lehrer's *New Yorker*
article called "Don't! The Secret of Self-Control" (2009), psychologist Walter
Mischel is asked what determines the skill of self-control. He replied, "the strate-
gic allocation of attention." Mischel feels that what we call willpower is a matter
of controlling our attention or the ability to spotlight our attention away from
something distracting and toward something different. Mischel thinks certain
mental disorders, such as obsessive-compulsive disorder and attention deficit
disorder, may be related to the ability to control and direct attention. However,
Mischel did not mention that willpower also involves muscular action; we actually retract our arm when we are resisting reaching for the cupcake.

We want to make sure not to make the same mistakes that previous theorists
have made regarding where creativity comes from. Traditional creativity theory
holds that creativity is generated in the brain; that an inspiration comes into mind
and then is translated into a behavior. But current researchers disagree. Orth et
al., assert that action and behavior *are* the creativity. They state that creativity is
"unfolding actions that are original and functional" (Orth et al. 2017, 2), and that
creative solutions emerge in the actions themselves. They speak of *motor creativ-*
ity. And the basis of motor creativity is movement variability—they mean it in
terms of variability from social norms as well as variability from how the individual did that movement before. They assert that movement variability forms the
key ingredient in expert behavior of any kind, and that increases in movement
variability increase the likelihood of creative solutions. What brings about movement variability? They feel exploration (like curiosity in the flow work) brings
about greater movement changeability, and that this exploration predicts an
increase in motor creativity. Perhaps we can say that the Action Phase of Conscious Moving applies motor creativity to domains such as art.

So, inside us we create the holding environment for flow states by letting
go of normal attentions in preparation for a strong attentional commitment to
the creative process. This exposes hidden landscapes that we transform into art
via our concentrated efforts to keep following what wants to happen next. We

remain loyal to what emerges, and support its emergence via polishing, tweaking, stepping back to observe, and perhaps letting others see what we are doing. Regarding the idea of stepping back, John Dewey (1934) felt that art has an inherent double structure: that of immersion alternating with perspective-taking. This puts us in mind of the oscillation of attention and with Ann Weiser Cornell's work in Focusing.

Now let's look outside us, into the environment, both from the perspective of the spaces we are in while being creative, and the spaces we create when we ask witnesses or audiences to experience our art. Painters need light. Choreographers need a floor and open space. Composers need quiet in order to hear the emergent music. Graffiti artists need a wall in a public area. The space shapes the art just as much as the art shapes the space. There is an interbeing quality between self and environment, and art imbues both. This becomes particularly poignant when creativity and art-making are engaging in social commentary, calling in social contexts that can infuse the art with social meaning.

Being in the presence of art—being an audience to it—accesses our own nonverbal experiences. It moves us emotionally, and it moves us to act. While some of us make art only for ourselves, we do bear witness to what we have done, and it moves us in our world. This Action Phase always embeds into environments, and perhaps one of the important functions of these actions in art-making is not only to portray something but also to disrupt something in the environment. The mild states of discomfort that we have spoken of in the process of learning and therapy reach a new height in art-making because art brings to us a long tradition of in-your-face confrontations with social ills. Art can provide an effective, external holding environment for social action.

We can also take a look at our traditional concepts about art audiences, where people sit or stand quietly and absorb the experience somewhat passively. A Danish friend of mine once told me about some colleagues she was hosting at her place of work, two African women. She thought it would be nice to take them to a classical music concert. About an hour into the performance, the women were crying and begged to leave. It was too painful for them to be there because no one was dancing to the music. No one was calling out to the musicians as they played. No one was humming along. The audience was just sitting there, and it was horrible to be around. They thought it was extremely disrespectful to the musicians. While culture enters into this story, we can see two different models of engaging with art. In one, respect and appreciation occur by offering our silence and focused attention. In the other, respect and appreciation occur through engagement, through contributing our active responses to the art-making. In CM we want to be sensitive to cultural norms, and so we might envision the role of audience as occurring along a continuum. When we sit quietly and watch, we are still micromoving, and these tiny motions help us feel connected to the experience. When we dance and sing to the music and interact with the dancers or musicians, we contribute larger locomotor movements to the blended experience of making and celebrating art. All along this continuum, CM can provide a form of *motor creativity* that supports and shapes the art experience.

Conscious Moving in the Service of Learning

Education is not preparation for life; education is life itself.

—JOHN DEWEY

It's not that I'm so smart. But I stay with the questions longer.

—ALBERT EINSTEIN

Tell me and I forget, teach me and I may remember, involve me and I learn.

—BENJAMIN FRANKLIN

Education is the kindling of a flame, not the filling of a vessel.

—SOCRATES

We have seen before that learning quite literally involves the body. We need a certain amount of muscle tone in order to pay attention. We use reflexes and motor plans to orient toward something unknown or of interest. We can sit in classrooms more easily when we have plenty of outdoor playtime to keep our bodies fresh and active. We learn not only from what others say but also from their communicative bodies as they say it. Learning is not just a matter of listening, thinking, or memorizing. Moving with and through these processes enables the physical, mental, and emotional components of experience to braid together. As a way to ground these ideas, we might want to explore the concept of experiential learning, particularly the work of David Kolb, who is considered to be one of the fathers of experiential learning theory.

Kolb (1984) felt that learning occurs naturally through discovery and active participation and that the key to learning is involvement. He strongly critiqued most standard classrooms for their structures that put a teacher in front of students who sat quietly at their desks and having that teacher say things that a learner was supposed to just take in and remember. Involvement means giving students direct experiences of an idea or concept that direct them in active experiments. Kolb felt that knowledge is created when you have an experience and then transform it through interactions with the environment. As we have seen multiple times before, he felt that this *experiential learning* took place in four stages, and that completing a cycle of these stages resulted in the transformation of experiences into knowledge. Here are his stages:

Concrete Experience: Engaging in an activity or task. Doing something deliberately that uses attentive focus, curiosity, and exploration. We might call this "doing an experiment."

Reflective Observation: The learner steps back to reflect on the experience, ask questions about it, and discuss the experience with others.

Abstract Conceptualization: The learner then integrates this feedback and works to make sense of these events—to classify concepts and form conclusions. In research this might be called *theory building*.

Active Experimentation: Testing your conclusions in the outside world. This involves going back to the task with the goal of applying your conclusions to a new experience. You, the learner, put your knowledge into practice and show how it is relevant to your life, which ensures that knowledge is retained. In research this might involve presenting at a conference or publishing your ideas in a professional journal.

Once again, we hear echoes of Conscious Moving stages. Not only are our bodies active in learning, but we also reach toward learning. Notice how the act of learning involves a kind of oscillation between immersion and reflection, and how it oscillates between self-experience and relating to others. We might also say that Kolb sees us as oscillating between our *concrete* experiences and our *abstract* evaluation of those experiences. Philosopher John Dewey wrote a whole book about art as experience, and in a sense, David Kolb wrote a book about learning as experience.

What CM does is create a frame for using movement as the method of studying experience, such that our experiences are not just something that happens to us, but are happenings that we actively shape for our own ends. It is important here to reiterate that when we talk about movement, we do not always mean big sweeping gestures or ambling from here to there. Learning from within experiences may look like no observable motion at all, because micromovements within the body can be just as powerful learning tools as their larger relatives.

However, let's not leave the idea of larger, locomotive movements as related to learning so quickly. One way to play with locomotion and learning (as well as healing, contemplating, and art-making) is to study the peripatetics. The word *peripatetic* loosely means "given to walking about." One of the first people who was given to walking about was Aristotle, who most believe coined the term. He strongly felt that the best way to learn was to teach while walking. He is followed in the Islamic tradition by Al-Kindi and Al-Farabi, and in the American Transcendentalist tradition by Henry David Thoreau, who used walking in the wilderness as a way to "allow nature to work on you." Philosopher Jean-Jacques Rousseau felt that walking alters your sense of space and time, and though he didn't use the term *mental meandering*, he advocated for meandering (ideally in nature) as a way to examine things in your own time, at the pace that your amblings dictate. Philosopher George Santayana took the position that walking about helped us reflect on the privilege of movement, noting that locomotion is the key to intelligence. Currently, the French philosopher Frédéric Gros, who wrote *A Philosophy of Walking* (2014), took an almost contemplative tack and recommends walking in nature as a way to "hear the silence." Put this alongside all the research coming out now on the health benefits of walking, and research showing that walking boosts creativity (Oppezzo and Schwartz 2014), and we begin to see walking (or swimming, and the like) as a multifaceted boon to learning, creativity, healing, and art-making.

In this sense, learning is a kind of growing, an additive act that increases our capacity not just for knowing more things but also seeing more clearly, listening more deeply, and reflecting more carefully. Learning how to learn—how to sense and move as the means of learning—brings our whole body to the act, and as a result, we grow in wisdom. Seeing this as a life-long procedure—being a life-long learner—brings up the notion of *neotony*. Neotony is usually defined as the persistence of juvenile traits into adulthood (Montagu 1988). Rather than dismissing this as immaturity, neotony celebrates remaining youthful in our behavior as a hallmark of creativity and intelligence—being a lifelong learner. Neotony occurs largely during play. Animal species that play their whole lives (like wolves, dolphins, elephants, humans) tend to be seen as the most adaptable and the most intelligent because playing preserves and promotes life-long learning, as well as life-long belonging with your playmates. When learning and playing share an experiential focus and a valuing of conscious practice, spontaneity, and the moving body, they pack an incredible punch.

Conscious Moving in the Service of Psychotherapeutic Healing

The self is not something ready-made, but something in continuous formation through choice of action.

                                     —JOHN DEWEY, IN *ART AS EXPERIENCE*

The word *healing* implies that something is off and needs to return or be restored. To put it poetically via the song "Amazing Grace," "I once was lost, but now I'm found; was blind but now I see." Commonly, the word *healing* assumes that individuals are unwell and need therapeutic input. We now see that social systems can be off just as much as individuals, and when working with individuals, we hold this in our attention, helping a client navigate sick environmental conditions. But let's look at what the body already knows how to do in regards to restoring health and well-being.

If we look at the body through a biological lens, we can see a template for Conscious Moving phases through the study of wound healing. When an injury or pathogen enters the body, four highly programmed phases of response show up—hemostasis, inflammation, proliferation, and remodeling—and they all operate automatically and innately. *Hemostasis* refers to the activation of an emergency repair system, such as blood coagulating and clotting. First, stop the bleeding. Second, *inflammation* shows up as a means of destroying bacteria and removing debris in order to prepare for the growth of new tissue. Inflammation involves heat, swelling, redness, and pain. Thirdly, *proliferation* fills and covers the wound and forms new blood vessels to nourish the new tissue that forms. Lastly, *remodeling* occurs as the new tissue gains strength and flexibility. From a Conscious Moving perspective, this sounds a lot like waking up as a way to deal with what's bothering you (Awareness), working with what's there as a way to discard things that are hurting you or that are no longer useful (Owning), forming new structures that can be of use going forward (Appreciation), and giving your new experiences the nourishment to stick around (Action). In wound healing, some of the symptoms we feel (pain, swelling) actually signal that healing processes are operating. Much the same can be said of the Owning Phase of CM. We can get uncomfortable as we work with our wounds or stuck places, yet that uncomfortability is where we need to be to allow healing to progress.

From a psychological vantage point, a therapist working with client illness begins with open listening to the symptoms of psychological distress, then responding empathically to those symptoms, and then working together with the client on the underlying causes of those symptoms so that true healing occurs rather than just symptom relief. Root causes of psychological illness can be seen both within the individual and within that individual's social systems. As well, illness can be seen as an integrated, holistic system, because we cannot confine ourselves to thinking about what we call mental illness without including emotional illness and physical illness. They all *inter-are*, as Thich Nhat Hanh would say.

In CM, or in this case the Moving Cycle, we advocate for attentive moving as a primary medicine for supporting our innate urge to heal (Caldwell 2016). We move to wake ourselves up to our issues, to express with exquisite detail the inflaming landscape of our woundedness, and in so doing we alter it to integrate new experiences into the locations where we hurt before, and to stitch these experiences into outer locations so that the systems we are embedded in can be themselves moved and healed. All this rests on the architecture of the attentive and moving body. In a way, we can say that healing is a form of learning and a product of contemplative practice, as well as a form of creativity. Csikszentmihalyi (1990), for instance, stated that changing your personality—a common goal in psychotherapy—means learning new patterns of attention during flow states.

Attentive or deliberate moving, as we said before, keeps our paddle in the water of the innate healing skills of the body. It keeps us active in the process— we are doing this under our own power—which generates another form of psychological medicine, that of bodily authority. By *moving with it*, I generate more innate knowing of what can happen next that promotes my healing. I can be consciously involved in my therapeutic change, which enables me to resist the passivity and powerlessness that many healing systems unwittingly encourage.

Because Conscious Moving has a strong branch into psychotherapy through the Moving Cycle, I will point the reader to several of my other publications in this area (listed on www.consciousmoving.com), as a way to keep moving with this idea.

Conscious Moving in the Service of Self-Reflective Contemplative Practice

Though philosopher and educator John Dewey felt that the act of observing something was inevitably retrospective, contemplative practice champions this ability to look over or to look back into an experience from a distance as crucial for the ability to lead a self-reflective life, one that allows us to be more awake and compassionate. When we step back from an experience, we avoid getting lost in it. Ann Weiser

Cornell spoke of this in her practice of Focusing, and trauma therapists help clients do this so that they don't become overwhelmed by traumatic reenactments.

One of the most important aspects of observing experience is that it widens perspective. We not only experience something, but we are able to put that something into a context, a landscape. In psychotherapy this involves feeling the traumatic memory, but putting it into the current context—a quiet, safe space with an attuned and caring therapist—where it can gradually lose its grip on us because we can directly feel and sense that it is not happening here and now. We saw this capacity for alternating between immersion and reflection in the earlier section on art-making and creativity. Dewey (1934) talks about it by asserting that experience itself is double-structured; it is both reflective and prereflective, along with being both nondualistic and subject/object oriented. He noted that reflective experience expresses itself through what he called *narrative meanings*, and that narrative meanings exist at a distance from direct experience.

Contemplative practices train what some call *the observing self* (Deikman 1982) by strengthening the muscle of attention. By having control of where our attention goes and how it can disengage, we master our world in a fundamental way. When we can both enter and exit an experience via the muscle of attention, we are so much more at choice about how we shape our world. This forms the basis of effective self-reflection, because we can relate to *what is* over what we want something to be. We generate the capacity to minimize bias and error.

It makes sense that being in an experience, what we have variously called *inhabiting from within*, or *pre-reflective experience*, or *immersion*, can be intensely body-centered. Our bodies are literally the home of any experience. But how can the act of observing an experience also be somatic? As we saw earlier when we talked about creativity not being confined to the brain, so too observing an experience need not be pegged to cognition. This is why in contemplative traditions, one of the primary ways attention is trained is within the practice of *not thinking*. In most Buddhist-based meditation practice, you are guided to be alert to the space between your thoughts and to work to widen that space through practice so that you are aware, alert, and attentive, but not thinking. You are resting in what meditation teachers call *pure awareness*.

Pure awareness also helps us not get carried away into thought or sensation or action or emotion—the contents of experience. We see that we are feeling or thinking, and we note that and bring our attention back to the act of being aware. What this can do over time is help us know that who we are is more than what happens to us. We are a presence that both inhabits localized experiences and much more vast locations and perspectives, ones that create a holding environment for our localized experiences. The trick here is to find that inhabiting vast locations is just as embodied as the specific location of our bodily experience. It's just a matter of how we train our senses and our movements to transition from being lost to being found, from being blind to now seeing. I call this *bodyfulness* (Caldwell 2018).

The term *bodyfulness** helps us to resist the temptation of assuming that being awake is a function of the mind (aka mindfulness). Our *minding* is just one of the things that bodies do. As I noted before, this idea is controversial. We have explored some of the less controversial ways in which contemplative practice is embodied; the importance of good posture in sitting meditation (Johnson 2000), the abundance of practices such as yoga, tai chi, and walking meditation, and how they are used as spiritual practices at the same time that they are used as practices for physical health (Kabat-Zinn 1994, Ray 2016). But bodyfulness seeks to reposition our understanding toward the notion that we can experience and observe what it is like to be a body rather than dwell in one, and that this body, our body, has the capacity and the longing to be more awake.

We can also equate bodyfulness, and contemplative practice in general, with embodied research (Tantia 2020). As we awaken via our contemplative practice and return to the ongoing process of thinking and feeling and moving about, that thinking, feeling, and moving become more imbued with what Zajonc (2009) calls *contemplative inquiry*. Bias and error in our daily life can lessen because we are not so invested in our habitual trains of thought or patterns of movement. We can welcome more direct experiences, even deeply challenging ones, because we have trained our body to stay awake and present even then. From there we inquire, we engage with creative and compassionate curiosity with whatever wants to happen next. We move more deeply into life.

References

Caldwell, Christine. 2016. "The Moving Cycle: A Second Generation Dance/ Movement Therapy Form." *American Journal of Dance Therapy* 38, no. 2: 245–58. https://doi.org/10.1007/s10465-016-9220-6.

———. 2018. *Bodyfulness: Somatic Practices for Presence, Empowerment, and Waking Up in This Life.* Boulder, CO: Shambhala Publications.

Csikszentmihalyi, Mihaly. 1990. *Flow: The Psychology of Optimal Experience.* New York: Harper.

---

* I define bodyfulness as occurring when the embodied self is held in a conscious, contemplative environment.

————. 1996. *Creativity: Flow and the Psychology of Discovery and Invention.* New York: Harper.

Deikman, Arthur J. 1982. *The Observing Self: Mysticism and Psychotherapy.* Boston: Beacon Press.

Dewey, John. 1934. *Art as Experience.* New York: Penguin Books.

Fogel, Alan. 2009. *The Psychophysiology of Self-Awareness: Rediscovering the Lost Art of Body Sense.* New York: W. W. Norton.

Gros, Frédéric. 2014. *A Philosophy of Walking.* Paris: Verso.

Johnson, Will. 2000. *Aligned, Relaxed, Resilient: The Physical Foundations of Mindfulness.* Boulder, CO: Shambhala Publications.

Kabat-Zinn, J. 1994. *Wherever You Go There You Are: Mindfulness Meditation in Everyday Life.* New York: Hyperion.

Kolb, David A. 1984. *Experiential Learning: Experience as the Source of Learning and Development.* Englewood Cliffs, NJ: Prentice Hall.

Lehrer, Jonah. 2009. "Don't! The Secret of Self-Control." *New Yorker.* May 18, 26–32.

Montagu, Ashley. 1988. *Growing Young.* Westport, CT: Bergin and Garvey.

Oppezzo, Marily, and Daniel L. Schwartz. 2014. "Give Your Ideas Some Legs: The Positive Effect of Walking on Creative Thinking." *Journal of Experimental Psychology: Learning, Memory and Cognition* 40, no. 4 (July): 1142–52.

Orth, Dominic, John van der Kamp, Daniel Memmert, and Geert J. P. Savelsbergh. 2017. "Creative Motor Actions as Emerging from Movement Variability." *Perspective: Frontiers in Psychology* 8 (October 31). https://doi.org/10.3389/fpsyg.2017.01903.

Ray, Reginald. 2016. *The Awakening Body: Somatic Meditation for Discovering Our Deepest Life.* Boulder, CO: Shambhala Publications.

Tantia, Jennifer Frank. 2020. *The Art and Science of Embodied Research Design: Concepts, Methods, and Cases.* New York: Routledge.

Zajonc, Arthur. 2009. *Meditation as Contemplative Inquiry: When Knowing Becomes Love.* Great Barrington, MA: Lindisfarne Books.

16

Accompanying a Conscious Moving Session for Others

Until now we have focused the book on practicing Conscious Moving on your own or with a partner for the purposes of self-reflection and organizing toward healing, learning, contemplating, or art-making. In this chapter, we bring in the idea of being a witness, a guide, and a support for others in their CM practice. Because bodies influence each other so thoroughly, and because this nonverbal influence can be so powerful, this becomes a training in how your body can help generate a holding environment for another's work, more than what you might say to them. We invoke the principles of CM toward being of service to a mover in one-on-one accompaniment.

The CM sessions you accompany don't have to be formalized, though it can be powerful to dedicate a time and space where you can detach from ordinary life to be with these experiences. But they can also find their way into how you help your children get ready for bed, or how you navigate a conflict between family members or coworkers. Invoking CM as a practice can be either *freestanding* or *embedded* in your day-to-day experiences and is ideally practiced in both contexts.

Learning to accompany another in a CM experience follows our four phases (Awareness, Owning, Appreciation, and Action), each phase using its own specialized skills. They loosely follow the course of a CM session, but each of the four skills we look at can be used in any part of the session. To begin, here are some general guidelines for this specialized form of assisting someone.

Guidelines for Accompanying a Conscious Moving (CM) Session for Others

▶ There is no possible way that you won't influence the session by your simple presence as well as any interventions you make. There is also no way for you not to be influenced by the mover's experience, so you might as well relax and orient toward being a helpful influence and work to channel your being influenced toward the service of the mover. Another way of expressing this is that you may notice that the four phases of the cycle unfold within you as well as within the mover. These two simultaneous unfoldings intertwine with each other to form a shared experience, and that shared experience is part of the ongoing events of the session. The difference between the two of you is that the mover's CM is dedicated to their own bodily research, and your CM is dedicated to the mover's bodily research as well. You are feeling your feelings, you are noticing sensations and movements in your body, but your curiosity and open attention are oriented toward how your experiences could be linked to the mover's experiences. Contrary to classic psychotherapies, we do not believe that your experiences are somehow picking up something about the mover that they don't know yet. While this may occasionally happen, we instead orient to the notion that we cannot pick up another's inner experiences. It is more that we are both engaging in shared experiences that move us somewhat differently within our separate historical and sociocultural frameworks. Your experiences add to the mix as another source of information rather than impose a direction or a truth. This attitude of openness uses the oscillation of attention, as it is so important to pay attention to yourself and then to land your attention onto your mover.

▶ You are not the authority and the mover is not the authority during a CM session. The mover's emergent sensorimotor experiences hold the body authority needed to guide the session. Both of your jobs are to create the conditions for those sensorimotor experiences to unfold and tell their story through the breathing, moving, and sensing body of the mover. Both you and the mover have slightly different jobs.

▶ The mover's job is to literally embody energy and information that is ready to emerge and gain coherency—the telling of their body's story. Your job is to help generate and maintain a *holding environment* for this body story so that it is invited, welcomed, and held in relative safety.

▶ On a practical level, you are paying attention to the time and space. You keep track of the time and let the mover know if time constraints are showing up. This also helps frame the movers' story into a beginning, middle, and end, which assists with coherency in embodied storytelling. Spatially, you are attending to the room. Is it private enough? Is the mover about to bump into a wall because they are moving with closed eyes? If they start to organize a pushing movement, can you provide something for them to push against in order to explore that?

▶ The holding environment also supports more nuanced resources like high-quality attention, an experiential focus, a nonjudgmental orientation, and a curious and open attitude. Your ability to occupy these states yourself creates an environment for the mover that helps them do the same. You are an ally of the mover's conscious movement, taking a stand for CM even if the mover is struggling to do so themselves.

▶ In the Owning Phase, you add in your willingness to be outside your mutual comfort zones, exploring material that may come seemingly from nowhere. Emotions might arise in the mover that need you to witness, validate, and help hold. Movement impulses that show up but may not be recognized by the mover might need to be acknowledged and included by you first. In the Appreciation Phase, the mover tends to find it useful to have someone to talk to, particularly to listen via evocative languaging. The listening doesn't just involve words. You also listen to body language and emotional tones. You reflect them back without spin or evaluation.

▶ In the Action Phase you are there to help with the transition back into daily life, such that you might offer to be a practice partner for some behavior that the mover wants to experiment with. Often, you will ask open questions like "Is there anything else that wants to happen before we come to an end?"

▶ The question you will be working with is "Does the mover need any support from me in order for movement impulses and sequences to show up and express themselves?" Sometimes this support is a simple "Hmm . . ." or a few descriptive words, or a gesture that picks up and echoes something the mover has just done. Sometimes it shows up as a willingness to sit quietly and patiently, simply looking forward to what will show up next. Sometimes it can be complex and sticky and you may not know how to proceed. In these moments trust your not knowing—this can be fertile ground.

▶ Knowing what's going on or where to go during CM is overrated. Try to rest into the experience itself rather than predict what the mover might do, or find some groovy comment to make, or worry about if you are being helpful. The more you open up to the oscillation of being immersed in and then observing another's movement, the more you will find powerful and creative intuitions, and the more you will let go of old impulses to offer advice, analyze the situation, or try to make the mover feel more comfortable.

▶ We can also say that safety is relative and comfort is overrated. CM is not about feeling better (or worse), though feeling relief or joy might happen organically. But it is not a goal worth pursuing, because trying to better things will distort or suppress any experience that isn't increasingly pleasant or distractingly fun. That said, some of the most hilarious moments I have ever had professionally have been in CM sessions. You never know what will allow people to dip their toes into the waters outside their comfort zones. One other element that shouldn't be carried too far is the quest for safety. While someone recovering from trauma does need special care to the issue of safety, it is important to remember that we can never guarantee another's safety. For one, we are not that omnipotent, and for another, making safety the most important thing can give a mover a false sense of security, and create a tendency to never risk, stick with, challenge, or explore beyond their comfort zone. What feels safe to one person does not feel that way to another. Relative safety is created when you are empathic, open minded, attentive, and oriented toward bodily research. Safety is actually lessened when you work hard to control the environment and the experiences within it to prevent any unpleasantness.

▶ **The Five Intentions:** We said before that it's about how you are more than what you do when assisting a CM experience. We can say that a CM accompanier inhabits five different intentions when in a session and uses them to help shape the experience. Each intention helps create a specific atmosphere that can invite CM.

Support: Sometimes a mover cannot move something on their own, and they need a bit of help. You are a resource that does it with them until they can do it on their own. You might stand next to a mover who is feeling frightened by their anger and pick up on some of their micromovements (a fist, a growl?) and do them together. You both attend to emerging movements as a way to support the precise feeling and expression of anger.

Nurture: When something shows up in a CM experience that is new, unexpected, or very tender, that experience needs some care and holding. It might look like you putting your hand on your chest and saying, "That sweeping gesture you just made really moved me," or actually holding their hand as they grieve. Nurturing does not coddle or soothe; it simply cares for what is happening.

Provide Space: Pausing, being quiet, not saying anything, and being patient can be one of the most facilitative intentions we have at hand. Often, the "true" movement, as Arawana Hayashi might say, just needs an uncluttered environment to inhabit. Our attention still holds the environment in place, but it contributes the most by allowing spaciousness to be the resource.

Challenge: Occasionally, movers get stuck in some inherited, proscribed movement pattern that represents old habits of coping that no longer apply but that are compelling nonetheless. Our job is to mark that spot with a kind challenge. It might be that you ask, "Are you sure this movement feels right?" Or, you might be able to gently notice a micromovement going on elsewhere in the body that the mover isn't aware of doing. This intention helps people to find and explore their Zone of Proximal Development.

Reflect: This last intention helps an emerging movement be held in Awareness. Your ability to describe something rather than judge or analyze it models this crucial skill for the mover. It may be that you say, "I noticed when you said that, that your shoulders came down afterward." Or it might be a nonverbal reflection, where you let a mover know you are with them by echoing a gesture or a sound with your own. Your work is to be a mirror so that the client can see their reflection clearly.

▶ **Five Interventions:** To go alongside the Five Intentions, we also have Five Interventions. There are likely many more than five, but these offer a good start. They represent guidelines for what you might do as a deliberate intervention. Remember, just your being there is an intervention. How your body occupies the space is an intervention. The look on your face is an intervention. Your own breathing is an intervention. Your posture is an intervention. Yet on top of these often-subliminal interventions, we can make deliberate ones in the service of CM:

Repeat: As with any practice situation, you might ask the mover to repeat what they just did or said as a way to study that experience more deeply and not just move on from it. Repeating something tends to establish its importance and call up associations.

Contrast: Paradoxically, you might want to ask the mover if it might be interesting to contrast a movement with its opposite, which can give a sense of richness to the emerging associations. For instance, a mover might be deliberately studying "looking up," and they might learn something about looking up by contrasting it with looking down, and seeing what comes up. This is often effective when a mover comes in feeling opposing things, like yes and no, or right and wrong. Both are valuable body voices.

Generalize: Often a mover can deepen their bodily research by taking a movement from just one part of the body into the whole body. It could be from making their fist tense to making their whole body tense. What associations come up when they do that? Generalizing tends to make a movement more visible, and it spreads out the effort of it through the whole body.

Specify: This intervention occupies the opposite polarity. A movement that is being experienced through the whole body can be confined to one small part of it. Or, a movement that has been trapped in one part of the body can be experienced in another part. Example: I once worked with a person who experienced a lot of jaw pain. They wanted desperately to clench their jaw, but to do so would cause pain and further damage to the joint. So we found a way to clench their fist instead, and watch the clenching, and find what associations came up by transferring it to another body part that could manage the action.

Intensify: Sometimes we need to turn up the volume on a movement in order to really hear it. By making a movement more intense we allow its voice to be supported and centralized.

▶ You will make mistakes! Whether it's an intervention that falls flat, an intention that mismatches to the mover, or a comment that stereotypes something the mover is doing, we can't avoid making errors. But in most situations if we see what we are doing as an experiment and stay reflective, then errors are contextualized into the spirit of "Oh, that didn't work, did it? Perhaps something different is going on." Yes, we might want to apologize after some bone-head move, but part of the atmosphere you help create is one where the mover is empowered to find things out more than resolving or controlling things. By postponing resolution, we enable more experimentation, and in experimentation we always learn something. Mistakes are normal in relationships, and some researchers note that making errors can be crucial in any relationship because it stimulates the skill building for repairing rifts and hurts and returning to closeness (Schore 2003). Relational intelligence thrives on the ability to repair disruptions, much more than trying to avoid them.

The Four Phases and Skills of Accompaniment

As we saw before, the skills of being an effective accompanier roughly correspond to the four phases of Conscious Moving. However, the following four skills aren't necessarily in an ordered sequence—elements of each can and are practiced at any moment in the CM session, though they tend to occur alongside CM's four phases.

Being a Witness: Often highlighted in the opening minutes of a session, this skill asks you to help establish an atmosphere of nonjudgment, one where descriptive awareness supports curiosity and focus. Being a witness assumes that we are using high-quality attention and a commitment to what wants to happen next as a means of inviting and holding the mover's explorations. Our bodies are relatively quiet, and our attention is calm and focused. We take time to absorb present circumstances as well as the mover's intentions and aspirations. Some people have called the witness a facilitator of *descent*, an entering into places within ourselves that lie underneath what we normally pay attention to. In this skill, we are here to listen, both verbally and nonverbally, to the mover. We are also helping to create and maintain a holding environment. We use descriptive words sparingly and test out whether they feel in tune with the mover's experiences. The questions we might ask are for a bit more descriptive detail. The comments we might make are to notice small movements elsewhere in the body that the mover may want to include.

Being a Responder: This skill often shows up in the Owning Phase, where the mover surfaces movements that arise from their ongoing experiences. The responder likely becomes more involved, as this phase often needs active support. Here is where we might use one or more of the Five Intentions and Five Interventions as a means of helping the mover stay on track. The question usually frames itself into some version of "What will support movement impulses, and what will support body narratives to organize from the impulses?" It may be important to help the mover stay balanced on the Breathing-Moving-Sensing Self-Regulation Triangle, and it may be important to assist the mover in Entering and Relieving the intensity of their movement sequencing. We may stand in front of the mover or to the side— anywhere in the space that assists the movement processes. We may do movements with them as an act of companionship. We offer small observations about what their bodies are doing, perhaps noting micromovements that they might not be tracking. We monitor how involved or uninvolved we should be in the mover's actions.

Being a Dialoguer: In this portion of the session, we often accompany the mover through the Appreciation Phase. The main explorations are over, and we spend time together digesting the experience. This is where we tend to practice *evocative languaging*, using our own felt sensing as a contribution to the mover's integrative experiences. We may contribute our companionable reflections on what happened, and we use the relationship as a jumping-off point for the mover to begin to shape the session for use. We still listen intently, but in a way, it is the heart that listens the most, as integration occurs most powerfully when emergent experiences are cared for together.

Being a Facilitator: As the mover begins to take what they have learned into daily life, the facilitator is there to assist with the transition from inquiry, exploration, and integration into applications for daily life. The facilitator asks questions about how these experiences might move out into the world and volunteers themselves for practicing in advance of this application. The facilitator notes the end of the session, and helps the mover feel complete, for now, with the experience. The facilitator assists with planning for any further work and accompanies the mover's evaluation of the session.

Open Recipe for Accompanying a Conscious Moving Session

Whether someone is engaging in Conscious Moving for art, learning, contemplation, or healing's sake, this open recipe may provide guidance for how to lightly structure a CM accompaniment. CM sessions can take abrupt turns in unexpected directions, but it can be useful to have some sense of the natural flow of CM experiences. The following list is for the accompanier:

- ▶ The CM session starts with you oscillating your attention between yourself, the mover, the space you are in, and the time parameters you have agreed to. You see if there is anything that needs to be put into place for the CM experience to begin.

- ▶ Ask if the mover wants to begin by being with their ongoing, present moment experiences, or whether the mover has a theme or issue they want to work with.

- ▶ Whatever the mover chooses, you then assist in their making the transition from normal consciousness toward the special focus of attention that heralds a CM experience. This is accomplished by accompanying the mover as they attend to present moment events, either inside or outside their body. This bodily focus can be done on its own, or it can be threaded in with the mover talking about the theme they are interested in exploring.

▶ As the mover commits to their present-moment experiences, you might ask them for associations. Something like "Are there any sensations, words, feelings, or images that come up with this experience?" You may also offer what is called *minimal encouragers*, such as "That's it, stay with that," or " See where that wants to go," or, after you notice a micromovement in their left fingers, you might want to say, "Stay with that, and see how your left hand wants to move with it." It's important not to talk too much, as this can interrupt the conscious movement and force the mover to come out of their direct experience in order to talk to you.

▶ During the entire session, you will monitor the mover's status on the Self-Regulation Triangle—Breathing, Moving/Expressing, and Sensing/Feeling—and encourage them to add back in anything that has fallen off the triangle.

▶ This might be the best moment to offer one of the five interventions, to see what happens that might support movement impulses to become coherent sequences that tell their body story. You might say something like "Would it be OK to do that movement again, to see how it feels?" or "What happens when you do the opposite of that movement? What associations come up?" You may want to move with them during these experiments, taking your cues from what their body is doing rather than where you think it should go.

▶ If a mover begins to seem overwhelmed or unable to stay on the triangle, you can help them to deliberately exit the direct experience and take a break. The break should be deliberate; it may be the mover focusing on you and saying something, it may be attending to something else, or it may be conscious breathing. Watch for the body on its own entering back into the material, and support that, or, if it doesn't want to go back, acknowledge the ending of the Owning Phase and help them enter Appreciation.

▶ You may want to take a few moments to sit together as a way to enter Appreciation. You might want to ask something like "As you look back on what just happened, what strikes you as important or remarkable?" or "What are you noticing right now in your body, as you take stock of what happened?" You may want to speak a bit about what you saw, as a way to highlight certain moments. Make sure to avoid analyzing or making up a story about what "it" was. Carefully acknowledge and welcome the events of the experience. It can also be useful to circle back to the theme that the mover might have come in with and ask questions about how they thought the theme played out in the experience.

▸ Sometimes the mover transitions into the next phase on their own, and sometimes they may need orienting in order to move into the next process. In the case of the Action Phase, the mover might begin to naturally look toward how they will apply the session to their outside life, or you might want to observe that you have a certain amount of time left, and is there anything that wants to be said or done to feel complete? You might want to ask if there is any movement they want to go over, in the spirit of taking it home with them. Might there be anything they want to practice to feel more solid with the session?

▸ Take a few minutes to talk about the mover's theme or their daily life and allow a bridge to be built that helps the mover take CM experiences into different applications. That may involve you helping them practice this before they end the session, or it may involve designing some way to practice a movement sequence in their outside life. Ask if there is any way they might want to tweak the experience to make it more effective.

Conscious Moving morphs into different shapes depending on the individual, the setting, and the mover's intentions. We collaborate with each other and with the unknowns that show up at the door of a session. This makes for creative innovations, surprises, and possibly disorienting feelings. These are signs that the work is working! Including these moments, seeing them as the product of our fertile embodiment, goes a long way toward a richer, more nimble, and more sturdy identity, one that naturally moves toward art-making, healing, reflecting, and learning.

References

Schore, Allan. 2003. *Affect Regulation and the Repair of the Self.* New York: W. W. Norton.

Epilogue:
Our Storied Bodies

Allow yourself to be awed by life . . . you might find yourself living for a very long time and prospering.

—WILLIAM SHATNER, FROM *BOLDLY GO*

Each path we tread from place to place is a thread, each place is a knot, and the more that lifelines are entwined, the greater the density of the knot—every place is a knot of stories.

—NANCY MARIE BROWN, FROM *LOOKING FOR THE HIDDEN FOLK: HOW ICELAND'S ELVES COULD SAVE THE EARTH*

The universe is made of stories, not atoms.

—MURIEL RUKEYSER, POET

Beyond the veils of language and the noise of activity, the most profound events of our lives take place in these fleeting moments where something else shines through, something that can never be fixed in language, something given as quietly as the gift of your next breath.

—JOHN O'DONOHUE, IN *THE INVISIBLE EMBRACE OF BEAUTY*

As I look back on fifty years of being steeped in movement work, I would say that time has made me a physical storyteller. Perhaps this skill constitutes one of the pillars of aging well. I remember flying south out of Denver a few years ago, and as I watched the dry earth below, crisscrossed with seemingly random dirt roads that appeared to etch the surface of nowhere, it came to me that the earth is drenched in stories, that the land speaks its own stories with wind and water and animal tracks and even dirt roads. Who made those roads? What locations were they trying to connect? Who walked them, and what happened to those people? It saddened me that I and most people would likely never know the stories of those roads.

I also felt this sadness after my father died, after a long and storied life. My dad was part Irish, and he could tell a story, let me tell you. I realized that I would never hear him tell his stories again and that so many of his stories would be forgotten, by me as well as subsequent generations. I guess we do need some kind of mechanism for letting some stories die out while others evolve and thrive, according to some kind of literary Darwinism. But as I was looking down on the land from a distance and looking back at a life that has passed, I felt the poignancy, the sweetness, and the power of stories.

This book has championed our body's stories. J. R. R. Tolkien is reported to have said something to the effect of stories do not busy themselves with being true or untrue; they have a higher purpose than that. Now, in many places on the planet, it is being said that we live in a post-truth world, where ex-presidents can convince a substantial number of people that something happened when it didn't, and artificial intelligence can create convincing fabrications of people, words, and actions. What deliberate fabrications want to do is colonize our bodies so that we will act in an oppressor's self-interest. What stories can do is shine a light on healing, creativity, learning, and self-reflecting. Of course, some "stories" do wound, distort, and seek to do harm, but this happens when they contain unexamined bias and error and are told as a means of coercion. I would like to propose that they are not really stories at this point but are instead tools, and our bodies should not be tools. What this book champions is the power of allowing a body story to emerge, coalesce, and be told, for the purposes of healing, creativity, contemplative inquiry, and learning. This is a story's higher purpose. This is the body's higher purpose.

My left shoulder rises, and I turn my attention toward it. Hmm, shoulder, what do you want to do? My shoulder tightens and stays in place. I stay with the tension and stillness. An image of holding my breath while hiding in a corner comes up. I include that image, holding it as a support for my shoulder's experience. My torso begins to twist ever so slightly, led by the shoulder. I hear the word *Come!* as if my shoulder is leading me somewhere. I support the twist to go where it wants to go. Soon I am rising up, still twisting, and now turning around and around, slowly. I feel the impulse to open my eyes and look around me as I turn. I see the room, with its windows and floors and sparse furniture. I feel a sense of relaxation and safety. My shoulder begins to slowly drop, and I stop turning and just stand. My experience has changed, and I now work on integrating those changes. My body has roughed out a story—its own creative writing project, written with feelings, sensations, and movements. That story changes me and may change others in the retelling.

Physicist Sean Carroll, from his vantage points in the stars and in subatomic particles, weighs in on this process. He has championed an idea called *poetic naturalism*, a kind of philosophy that states there is only one world, the natural world, but there are many ways of talking about that world. In other words, there are many meaningful and moving stories, and they all speak to our world, the world we all share. There is only one body—the body of the world—and there are many ways of experiencing and communicating this body.

When you move about, you go on a journey. This book has been about journeys that transform humdrum experiences into poetic fertilities. What grows out of these journeys might land you into a classroom, a meditation hall, a mosque, a music hall, a forest trail, or at your dining room table. In these transformational journeys, the bus is our body, the road is direct experience, and the fuel is open attention, mixed in with nonjudgmentalism, curiosity, a willingness to be uncomfortable, finding the body story, and a big dose of caring.

Our *clay nature*, as theologian John O'Donohue puts it, moves us to transform within and through many different contexts, locations, and environments. We are all always embedded in the earth, and related to one another. In this way, our ongoing body stories speak not only of our individual identities but also to all our earthy kin. We can use our clay nature deliberately, as a means of sculpting new possibilities, for ourselves and each other.

To find and move our body's stories, we gravitate toward specific practices that create a holding environment that in turn invites the story to expose new information, deeper explorations of experience, and stronger ties being built with others. It is my hope that you, the reader, will find your own practices that will support you to experience your stories, integrate them into your ongoing identities, and carry them out into wider locations and relationships. Some of your practices will come from ancient wisdoms, and some will bubble up seemingly out of nowhere, a new emergence. Some of you might feel more interested in healing, and some might be more oriented toward learning or creating. Trust what moves you. Go on journeys. Let your body find the destination. Become a storyteller.

Acknowledgments

In so many ways, the text of *Conscious Moving* has been written by a village. While some have contributed directly by being interviewed or by writing a chapter, everyone who has ever studied this work has been a part of the making of this book. Thank you, thank you, thank you!

A special bow of gratitude goes out to the following folks:

To Page Zekonis, the artist who contributed the line drawings for the book—you drew conscious movement so sensitively! And you weathered the vicissitudes of publisher art departments so gracefully! Your drawings contributed much to the way this book is felt and experienced by the reader.

To Dr. Howard Branz, a physicist friend, for consulting with me about what movement is like on subatomic and quantum levels, and to his wife Dr. Carol Navsky, who helped to translate the consultation into plain English—little contributions can make big differences!

To Ursa Spaete Schummacher, whom I have been a traveler alongside for many years and in many countries; thank you deeply for your companionship and support all these years! You inspired parts of this book just with your presence, as well as with your actions.

To Ute Lang, who very much wanted to contribute a chapter but due to family matters had to bow out of the project. Ute, you have been such a contribution to this work, both through your ongoing study and practice of it and in your gracious efforts to organize trainings. A deep bow of gratitude to you!

To Norbert Heckelei, who graduated from Naropa, went back to Germany, and invited me to teach in Cologne. You got it all started in Europe!

To Elmar Kruitoff, who took over for Norbert and brought the work to Hamburg. You have been so generous, so kind, so funny, and so contributive to this work!

To the core "Hamburg Group"—Ute, Ursa, Thomas, Amelia, Barbara SR, Barbara B, Gretl, Marion, Elmar, and others. You all formed the laboratory where our research of the work took root. So much of this book traces back to our times together.

To Barbara Schmidt-Rohr, Kira Cords, and Rachelle Janssen, who together keep the light on in Europe and help me to stay organized, which is challenging for me! You are all so graceful and patient and kind, as well as being amazing teachers and advanced practitioners.

Appendices

Appendix A:
The Movement Continuum
(or Mobility Gradient)

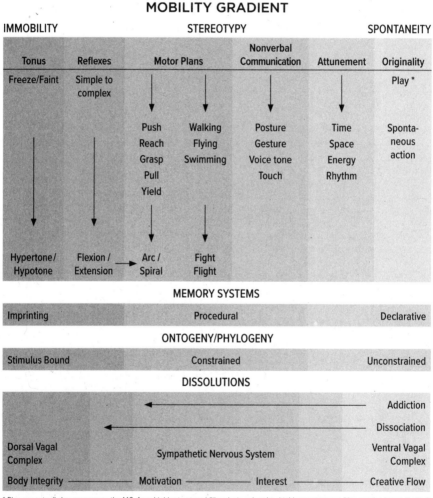

MOBILITY GRADIENT

| IMMOBILITY | | | STEREOTYPY | | | SPONTANEITY |

Tonus	Reflexes	Motor Plans		Nonverbal Communication	Attunement	Originality
Freeze/Faint	Simple to complex					Play *
		Push	Walking	Posture	Time	Sponta-neous action
		Reach	Flying	Gesture	Space	
		Grasp	Swimming	Voice tone	Energy	
		Pull		Touch	Rhythm	
		Yield				
Hypertone/ Hypotone	Flexion / Extension	Arc / Spiral	Fight Flight			

MEMORY SYSTEMS

| Imprinting | Procedural | Declarative |

ONTOGENY/PHYLOGENY

| Stimulus Bound | Constrained | Unconstrained |

DISSOLUTIONS

		Addiction
		Dissociation
Dorsal Vagal Complex	Sympathetic Nervous System	Ventral Vagal Complex
Body Integrity ———	Motivation ——— Interest	——— Creative Flow

* Play can actually be seen across the MG, from highly structured (like playing chess) to highly spontaneous (like creative improvisation)

Figure 3: An Expanded View of the Mobility Gradient

Appendix B:
Resources for
Conscious Moving

BLOGS AND GENERAL WEBSITES:

Diana Thielen: www.movementactivism.com

The Moving Child: www.themovingchild.com. Good resource for working with children and parenting. Has books and films on children's movement.

CONTACT INFORMATION FOR THE BOOK'S INTERVIEWEES AND CHAPTER CONTRIBUTORS:

Arawana Hayashi: www.u-school.org and https://arawanahayashi.com/

Barbara Dilley: www.barbaradilley.com

Rae Johnson: https://raejohnsonsomatic.com

Edan Gorlicki: https://edangorlicki.com

Judith Aston-Linderoth and Brian Linderoth: www.astonkinetics.com

Ann Weiser Cornell and Focusing: https://focusingresources.com/

Melissa Walker: www.embodiedrelationshipscenter.com

Thomas von Stuckrad: www.seeleundsingen.de

Christine Caldwell:

    www.themovingcycle.com, www.consciousmoving.com

    Facebook: www.facebook.com/Moving-Cycle-Institute-103661712221488

    You Tube Channel: https://youtube.com/@christinecaldwell.MovingCycle

Joana Debelt: www.linkedin.com/in/joana-debelt-606545134

Amber Gray: https://ambergray.com

Gretl Bauer: gretl.bauer@ewe.net

Antje Scherholz: antjescherholz@gmx.de

Rachelle Janssen: www.rachellejanssen.com

Laia Jorba Galdos: www.wholeconnection.org and www.jorbacounseling.com

Index

A

Action Phase
  accompanying sessions for others, 267, 274
  on continuum from personal to political,
    101–108
  evaluation and, 107–108, 111
  examples of, 228, 231
  identity exploration and, 146–147
  learning and, 166
  microactivisms and, 101–103
  practice examples for, 109–112
  Restorative Movement Psychotherapy and,
    129–131
  scaffolding and, 110, 112
  sense of completion from, 107, 111
  social nature of, 99–101, 104
  standalone practices for, 108–109
  transitions and, 108
  witnessing and, 102
activism
  embodied, 248
  micro-, 101–103
adaptation, 24
ADD (attention deficit disorder), 18
addiction
  bodylessness as root of, 153–155
  etymology of, 35
  snoozing through life and, 152–153
  therapeutic relationship and, 155–157
ADHD (attention deficit and hyperactive
    disorder), 18
Albom, Mitch, 155
Alexander Technique, 7
Al-Farabi, 259
Al-Kindi, 259
appraisal, 22
Appreciation Phase
  accompanying sessions for others, 267,
    272, 273
  coherency and, 85–87, 92
  evocative languaging and, 88–89
  examples of, 228, 229–230, 231
  grace and, 86–88
  identity exploration and, 146
  learning and, 166
  meaning-making and, 85, 90
  musical, 89, 90–91
  open recipe for, 95–96
  practice examples for, 92–95
  as process of integration, 84–85
  Restorative Movement Psychotherapy and,
    128–129
  standalone practices for, 90–91
Aristotle, 259
art-making
  Action Phase and, 101, 105, 107, 255, 256
  attention and, 18
  audiences and, 256–257
  change and, 14–15
  Conscious Moving and, 185–186, 189–190,
    203–205, 253–257
  figure/ground relationship and, 34
  as grief work, 186–191, 198–199,
    202–205
  sense of completion and, 107
  sharing, with family and friends, 200–202
associations
  free, 19, 20, 254
  generation of, 22–23
  movement impulses and, 23
  welcoming, 44–46
Aston Kinetics, 4, 14, 69, 237
Aston-Linderoth, Judith, 4, 14, 69, 103,
    237–240, 243, 244, 246, 249, 250, 281
Aston-Patterning, 4, 238
attachment, 59
attention
  bare, 34
  definition of, 16–17
  figure/ground relationship and, 33–34
  focusing, 33
  importance of, 17, 154–155
  learning and, 17–18, 20
  oscillating, 20, 37–39, 179
  on present-moment experiences, 44–46
  as root of direct experiences, 244
  structuring and determining experiences,
    16–21, 36
  uncommitted, 254
attentional athleticism, 33, 244
attunements, 58–59, 72–73
Authentic Movement, 7, 102, 169, 251
autonomy, myth of, 135–137
awareness. *See also* Awareness Phase
  changing, through psychotherapy, 35
  conceptual, 119
  embodied, 119

pure, 262
somatic, 119
Awareness Phase
   breathing and, 33
   examples of, 227–228, 229
   focusing and, 33
   identity exploration and, 140–143
   learning and, 166
   micromovements and, 36–37
   open recipe for, 48–51, 78–79, 95–96
   practice examples for, 46–48
   practices for, 37–46
   Restorative Movement Psychotherapy and,
      122–126

B

Bainbridge Cohen, Bonnie, 6
bare attention, 34
Bauer, Gretl, 15, 18, 89, 185–191, 197–205,
   206, 281
Behnke, Elizabeth, 7, 22, 36, 69
belonging, sense of, 118, 138
Berger, John, 31
Blaumeier, 223
bodily authority (bodily autonomy), 24–27,
   103–104, 248
bodyfulness, 178, 263. *See also* Erotic
   Bodyfulness
bodylessness, as root of addiction, 153–155
Body-Mind Centering, 6, 32, 122
body narratives, 25, 59–64, 73–74
body oscillations, 13, 57–59
body schema, 19
brain
   development of, 83
   left and right hemispheres of, 62–63
breathing
   awareness of, 32–33
   -moving-sensing triangle, 67–68, 219,
      271, 273
Brown, Brené, 152, 159
Brown, Nancy Marie, 275
Brown, Rita Mae, 34
Butler, Kelly, 99

C

Campbell, Donald, 254
Carroll, Sean, 276–277
challenging, as one of the Five Intentions, 269
change
   art and, 14–15
   of awareness, 35

learning and, 14–15
therapy and, 14–15, 35
co-committed relationships, 156–157
Cognitive Behavioral Therapy (CBT), 35
coherency, 85–87, 92
collective interiority, 246
comfort zone
   moving outside of, 158–160, 245
   snoozing and, 152
completion, sense of, 107, 111
conceptual awareness, 119
connection, 126–128
Conrad, Emilie, 127
Conscious Moving (CM). *See also* Action
   Phase; Appreciation Phase; Awareness
   Phase; Moving Cycle; Owning Phase
   accompanying sessions for others, 265–274
   addiction and, 150–160
   art-making and, 185–186, 189–190,
      203–205, 253–257
   definition of, 3
   desire differences and, 178–183
   in educational contexts, 161–170, 257–259
   fundamental principles of, 12–27
   in group settings, 207–221
   integrating, into the work of others, 235–250
   open recipe for entire cycle, 112–114
   as process, 12
   psychotherapeutic healing and, 224–225,
      260–261
   as research tool, 251–253
   resources for, 281
   starting sessions, 49–51
   tank, 250
   training, 118
consent, embodied, 181
contact, 126–128
Contemplative Dance, 7, 102, 247, 249, 251
contemplative inquiry, 263
contemplative practice. *See also* meditation
   Conscious Moving in service of, 261–263
   grace and, 86–87
Continuum (movement practice), 127, 129
contrast
   embracing, 159
   as one of the Five Interventions, 198,
      269–270
control, concept of, 255
Cornell, Ann Weiser, 88, 111, 238, 240, 242–
   245, 247–249, 256, 261–262, 281
COVID pandemic, 134, 186, 188–191, 202, 241
creativity, 32, 165–168, 253–257
Csikszentmihalyi, Mihaly, 17, 31, 32, 39–40,
   254, 261

culture
   components of, 119
   neuroception and, 119
curiosity, 162–165, 219
cycles. *See also* Moving Cycle
   definition and, 13
   movement and, 13
   spirals and, 13

D

Dalai Lama, 103
Dance Movement Therapy (DMT) groups,
   207–208
Debelt, Joana, 20, 32, 66, 161–170, 281
descent, 271
description, staying in, 22
desire differences
   body-centered approach to, 175–177
   definition of, 172
   desire styles and, 173
   effects of, 173
   Erotic Bodyfulness and, 178–182
   Erotic Mapping process and, 181–183
   reasons for, 172–173
   reframing, as challenge, 174–175, 177–178
   as source of conflict, 173–175
detail, original, 41–42
Dewey, John, 253, 256, 257, 258, 260, 261, 262
Dialectical Behavioral Therapy (DBT), 35
dialoguer, being a, 272
Dilley, Barbara, 7, 102, 236, 239, 240, 243, 245,
   247, 249, 250, 251, 281
direct experiencing, 242–244
discomfort
   learning and, 45, 245
   tolerating, 245
Disney, Walt, 196
displacement, 118
dissociation, 39
dissolutions, 6

E

Einstein, Albert, 35, 257
Ekman, Paul, 36
embodied activism, 248
embodied awareness, 119
embodied consent, 181
embodied somatic resonance, 57, 178
engaged pedagogy, 167–168
entering and relieving, 65–66, 74, 110
environment, influence of, 245–246
Erikson, Eric, 136

Erotic Bodyfulness, 178–182
Erotic Mapping process, 181–183
errors
   sampling, 252
   types of, 252
evaluation, 11, 107–108
evocative languaging, 88–89, 272
experiential learning, 32, 165–168, 257–258
exteroception, 120, 219
eye opening and closing, 220

F

facilitator, being a, 272
Feder, Tyler, 169
Feldenkrais Method, 7
felt sense, 126, 242, 244
fight, flight, freeze, or faint defense
   strategies, 158
figure/ground relationship, 33–34
Five Intentions, 268–269
Five Interventions, 198, 269–270
flow states, 40, 253, 255
Focusing technique, 43, 88, 238–239, 242, 244,
   247, 248, 256, 262
Fogel, Alan, 19, 31, 88, 253
Frabotta, Richelle, 174
Franklin, Benjamin, 257
free association, 19, 20, 254
Freud, Anna, 22, 36
Freud, Sigmund, 19, 23
functional holding, 69

G

Galileo, 33
Gardner, Howard, 32
gender identity, 162–163
Gendlin, Eugene, 88, 238, 239, 242
generalizing, as one of the Five Interventions,
   198, 270
generative dialogue, 250
Gestalt therapy, 4, 32, 224
The Goofy Practice, 196
Gorlicki, Edan, 237, 239, 240–242, 244–247,
   249, 250, 253, 281
grace, 86–88
Graham, Martha, 99
gravity, relationship with, 14
Gray, Amber, 117–132, 281
grief work
   art-making as, 186–191, 198–199, 202–205
   definition of, 186
   history of, 186

group therapy, 207–221
    interventions for, 219–220
    levels of consciousness and perception of
        the Moving Cycle in, 212–217
    motivations for adapting Conscious
        Moving to, 209–211
    multiple circulating processes of Conscious
        Moving in, 217–219
    therapeutic attitude for, 208–209

H

Hakomi, 31–32, 43, 224
Hawkins, Alma, 4
Hayashi, Arawana, 236, 239, 240, 242, 243,
    245–250, 281
H'Doubler, Margaret, 99
healing
    connotations of, 260
    Conscious Moving in the service of,
        260–261
    as spiral, 131
heart mind, 120
hemostasis, 260
Hendricks, Gay and Kathlyn, 156, 157
HERE & NOW practice, 49–50
holding environment, generating and
    maintaining, 266–267
homeostasis, 13
hooks, bell, 161, 167
human experience, continuum of,
    120–121

I

identity. See also identity exploration; self
    concept of, 134–135
    discernment and, 145
    fluidity and multiplicity of, 244–245
    gender, 162–163
    as process, 135, 139
    self vs., 135
identity exploration
    Action Phase and, 146–147
    Appreciation Phase and, 84, 146
    Awareness Phase and, 140–143
    Moving Cycle and, 139–140,
        147–148
    Owning Phase and, 143–145
improvisation, 5, 7, 18, 56, 90–91, 188
individualism, 135–137, 147
inflammation, 260
inquiry. See Pressure, Pleasure, Inquiry
    practice

intensifying, as one of the Five Interventions,
    198, 270
Intentions, Five, 268–269
interbeing, 136–137, 245, 256
inter-bodily resonance, 218
interdependence, 136–137
interoception, 119, 120, 219
interventions
    The Five Interventions, 198, 269–270
    for group therapy, 219–220

J

Jacobson, Edmund, 19, 69
James, LeBron, 86–87
Janssen, Rachelle, 35, 150–160, 281
Johnson, Rae, 101, 105–106, 236–237, 240–244,
    247–249, 281
Jorba Galdos, Laia, 84, 133–148, 281
Jordan, Brigitte, 26

K

Kolb, David, 32, 257–258
Kübler-Ross, Elisabeth, 186

L

languaging
    evocative, 88–89, 272
    trans-, 164–165
learning
    attention and, 17–18, 20
    bodies, caring for, 168–169
    change and, 14–15
    Conscious Moving in the service of,
        161–170, 257–259
    creativity and, 165–168
    curiosity and, 162–165
    discomfort and, 45, 245
    experiential, 32, 165–168,
        257–258
    movement and, 161–162, 170
    play and, 259
Lee, Tony, 129
Lehrer, Jonah, 255
Levine, S. K., 203
Lindemann, Erich, 186
Linderoth, Brian, 238, 239, 240, 243, 244, 246,
    249, 250, 281
locomotion, 13, 259
loving-kindness practice, 92–93
lucid movement, 249
Lunar Breath, 127

M

Macy, Joanna, 203
Maitri, 92–93
matching, 69, 73
McGavin, Barbara, 238
meandering, 190, 254, 259
meaning-making
    Appreciation Phase and, 85, 90
    effects of, 243
    postponing, 22, 232, 241, 243
    Restorative Movement Psychotherapy and,
        128–129
meditation, 17–19, 22, 34, 35, 40, 41, 66, 92,
    110–111, 195, 201. See also contemplative
    practice
memories
    caring and, 88
    as reconstruction, 59–60
    traumatic, 129
mental meandering, 254, 259
Merton, Thomas, 78
microactivisms, 101–103
microaggressions, 101
micromovements
    attunement and, 59
    awareness of, 36–37
    examples of, 36
minimal encouragers, 273
mirroring, 122
Mischel, Walter, 255
mistakes, 270
mobility gradient. See movement continuums
motor creativity, 255, 257
motor plans, 5–6
movement. See also Conscious Moving
    of attention, 154
    bodily authority and, 24–27
    cycles and, 13
    gravity and, 14
    impulses, 23, 63, 73–74, 180, 240–241
    learning and, 161–162
    life and, 2–3
    for movement's sake, 240–242
    oscillation of, 12–13
    phenomenological nature of, 21–24,
        153–154
    as primary language, 120
    restriction of, 15–16, 163
    sensation as type of, 24
    spirals and, 13–14
    as unifying principle, 1–3, 7,
        9–10, 139

movement continuums
    biological movement, 4–6
    deliberate investigation of, 16
    energy and, 16
    expanded view of, 280
    health and, 15
    interdependence of, 56–57
    movement practices, 5, 6–7
Moving Cycle (MC). See also Conscious
    Moving
    development of, 4
    end of, as beginning of the next, 230, 232
    group therapy and, 207–221
    identity exploration and, 139–140,
        147–148
    levels of consciousness and perception of,
        212–217
    on the movement continuum, 7
    Restorative Movement Psychotherapy and,
        118, 131
    as therapeutic specialization of Conscious
        Moving, 3–4, 225, 261
    video demonstrations of, 225–232

N

neotony, 259
neural integration, 83
neuroception
    ANS and, 120
    culture and, 119
Nhat Hanh, Thich, 1, 18, 66, 103, 245, 261
Nietzsche, Friedrich, 1
novelty, introducing, 196–197
nurturing, as one of the Five Intentions, 268

O

O'Donohue, John, 275, 277
Oliver, Mary, 31
oppression
    definition of, 117
    effects of, 118, 131
    felt in the body, 106
    power and, 117
original detail, 41–42
oscillations
    of attention, 20, 37–39, 179
    body, 13, 57–59
    definition of, 12–13
    examples of, 13, 248–249
    experiential learning and, 166
    of gas and brake, 68–71

between left and right hemisphere
dominance, 63
of movement, 12–13
between work, play, and rest, 14, 66,
74–75, 168
Otis, Sophie, 238
overwhelming experiences, working with, 64–68
Owning Phase
accompanying sessions for others, 267,
271, 273
body narratives and, 59–64
control of gas and brake in, 68–71
examples of, 227–228, 229, 232
identity exploration and, 143–145
learning and, 166
movement continuums and, 56–57
open recipe for, 78–79, 95–96
overwhelming experiences and, 64–68
practice examples for, 75–78
practices for, 71–75
Restorative Movement Psychotherapy and,
126–128
whitewater canoeing analogy for, 55–56, 64
Owsjannikowa, Marianna, 202

P

paraverbal qualities, 177
pendulation, 66
peripatetics, 259
peristalsis, 14
Perls, Fritz, 32
Plato, 136
play, 14, 66–67, 161, 168, 259
pleasure. See Pressure, Pleasure, Inquiry
practice
poetic naturalism, 276–277
Polyvagal Theory, 118, 119, 121
Porges, Stephen, 119
power, concept of, 24–27
praxis, 83
pre-effort, 176
Pressure, Pleasure, Inquiry (PPI) practice, 15,
186, 188, 190, 191–198, 203, 215, 233
Progressive Relaxation, 69
proliferation, 260
proprioception, 20, 120, 219
pruning, 83
psychotherapy. See also group therapy; Moving
Cycle; individual therapies
change and, 14–15, 35
Conscious Moving in the service of,
224–225, 260–261

group, 207–221
as whole-body experience, 233
PTSD (posttraumatic stress disorder), 23,
118–119. See also trauma

R

reflecting, as one of the Five Intentions, 269
refractory period, 14
remodeling, 260
repeating, as one of the Five Interventions,
198, 269
research
basic vs. applied, 241
characteristics of, 251
Conscious Moving as tool for, 251–253
errors and, 252
resource bridge, 183
responder, being a, 271
restorative justice, 93
Restorative Movement Psychotherapy (RMP)
Action Phase and, 129–131
Appreciation Phase and, 128–129
Awareness Phase and, 122–126
benefits of, 131–132
development of, 118, 121–122
Moving Cycle and, 118, 131
Owning Phase and, 126–128
phasic approach of, 122
Rhiannon, 187, 188
rhythmic movement. See oscillations
Rilke, Rainer Marie, 117
Rousseau, Jean-Jacques, 259
Rubinstein, S. Leonard, 83
Rukeyser, Muriel, 275

S

safety, relative, 122–126, 268
sampling error, 252
Santayana, George, 259
Satisfaction Cycle, 32
scaffolding, 110, 112
Scharmer, Otto, 236
Scherholz, Antje, 87, 207–221, 281
Schore, Allan, 19
science. See research
self. See also identity
autonomy and, 135–137
continuity of, 138–139, 141–143
identity vs., 135
observing, 41, 262
searching for, in therapy, 139–140

self-actualization, 143, 168
self-awareness, embodied, 19
self-control, 255
self-efficacy, 211
self-regulation
    balancing, 67–68
    definition of, 122
sensation, as type of movement, 24
Sensitivity Cycle, 31–32
sensorimotor loop, 24, 71–72
Sensorimotor Psychotherapy, 43, 66
Sensory Awareness, 7
sequences
    concept of, 27
    finding natural, 247–248
Shatner, William, 275
Siegel, Dan, 83
Simons, Matt, 159
snoozing through life, 152–153
Snyder, Allegra Fuller, 4
social engagement system (SES), 174
social inhibition system (SIS), 174
Socrates, 108, 257
somatic architecture, 175
somatic awareness, 119
Somatic Experiencing, 43, 66
somatic resonance, embodied, 57, 178
space, providing, as one of the Five
    Intentions, 269
spacing out, 39
special education, 162
specifying, as one of the Five Interventions,
    198, 270
spirals
    cycles and, 13
    healing as, 131
    movement and, 13
stories
    of the body, 227–232
    power of, 275–277
stream of consciousness, 23, 91
structural holding, 69
support, as one of the Five Intentions, 268

T

tai chi, 5, 7, 251, 263
therapeutic relationship, importance of, 64,
    103, 155–157

THERE & THEN practice, 49,
    50–51
Thielen, Diana, 281
third space, 129
Thoreau, Henry David, 259
titration, 66
Tolkien, J. R. R., 276
touch agreements, 226
touch and go, 65
transitions, 108
translanguaging, 164–165
trauma. See also Restorative Movement
    Psychotherapy
    as defining life experience,
        117–118
    dissolutions and, 6
    processing of memories, 129
    PTSD vs., 118–119
    putting it in the past, 130
    working with, 118–121

V

von Stuckrad, Thomas, 20, 223–233, 281
Vygotsky, Lev, 45, 65, 68, 110, 112, 245

W

Walker, Melissa, 57, 172–183, 281
Whitman, Walt, 133
window of tolerance, 216
witness
    being a, 271
    consciousness, 41
    power of, 102
Woolf, Virginia, 23
work-play-rest triangle, 14, 66,
    74–75, 168

Y

yoga, 5, 7, 244, 251, 263

Z

Zaporah, Ruth, 185
Zone of Proximal Development,
    45, 65
zoning out, 39

About the Author

Christine Caldwell, PhD, BC-DMT, LPC, is the founder of and professor emeritus in the Somatic Counseling Program at Naropa University in Boulder, Colorado, where she has taught coursework in somatic counseling theory and skills, clinical neuroscience, and diversity issues. Caldwell's Moving Cycle involves body-centered psychotherapy, and is called Conscious Moving when applied to other disciplines, such as artmaking, contemplative practice, and education. Caldwell has taught at the University of Maryland, George Washington University, Concordia, Seoul Women's University, Southwestern College, Pacifica, Santa Barbara Graduate Institute, and SRH University in Heidelberg. She trains, teaches, and lectures internationally, and has published more than thirty articles and book chapters. Her previous books include *Getting Our Bodies Back, Getting in Touch, The Body and Oppression*, and *Bodyfulness*. She is also an editor for the *Journal of Dance, Movement and Psychotherapy*, the *International Journal of Body Psychotherapy*, and the *American Journal of Dance Therapy*.

About North Atlantic Books

North Atlantic Books (NAB) is an independent, nonprofit publisher committed to a bold exploration of the relationships between mind, body, spirit, and nature. Founded in 1974, NAB aims to nurture a holistic view of the arts, sciences, humanities, and healing. To make a donation or to learn more about our books, authors, events, and newsletter, please visit www.northatlanticbooks.com.